Anthony King initially trained as a musician at Leeds College of Music. After many years working as an entertainer, King became a counsellor, gaining qualifications from Rusland College, Manchester College of Arts & Technology, University of Central Lancashire, and The University of Manchester where he gained a Master of Arts degree in counselling. He is currently working towards a doctoral degree in Manchester.

King is an integrative psychotherapist, using cognitive behavioural therapy (CBT), person-centred counselling, and eye movement desensitization reprocessing (EMDR). He works as resident counsellor at Blackpool College and has a thriving private practice. He is an accredited member of the British Association for Counselling & Psychotherapy, a member of the British Association for cognitive and behavioural psychotherapies, and lives between Blackpool and Salou with his beloved family.

Please see www.worryguru.com for more Anthony King information.

BROKEN BRITAIN?

Acknowledgements

To Leona – the elixir of life.

Thanks and love to Fiona for her indefatigable belief and support, Tim for setting me on the journey of a lifetime, Dr McNeil for giving me a chance and keeping me away from antidepressants when I needed CBT, and to Donald Gartside for igniting my interest in words … every school should have English teachers like you. Thanks are also due to Dr Terry Hanley, Dr Clare Lennie, and Dr Henry Hollanders of the University of Manchester who make things seem possible and teach things I never knew. Big thanks to my sister-in-law, Anita Bird, for proofreading into the night and all the team at Pegasus.

Anthony King

BROKEN BRITAIN?

Vanguard Press

VANGUARD PAPERBACK

© Copyright 2010
Anthony King

The right of Anthony King to be identified as author of
this work has been asserted by him in accordance with the
Copyright, Designs and Patents Act 1988.

A CIP catalogue record for this title is
available from the British Library.

ISBN 9781 8438 659 1 9

*Vanguard Press is an imprint of
Pegasus Elliot Mackenzie Publishers Ltd.*
www.pegasuspublishers.com

First Published in 2010

**Vanguard Press
Sheraton House Castle Park
Cambridge England**

Printed & Bound in Great Britain

Preface

The clients and participants I have spoken about herein have given me their permission to do so on the condition and promise that they were disguised. I have done this in many ways ... changing names, places and some details, but the theme of the story remains accurate. Any other similarities to friends and family are purely coincidental.

I have used he/she interchangeably in the hope that nobody will be seriously offended by those labels after reading this book. A series of exercises appear for you to do throughout the book and you might enjoy doing them. It is not essential for you to do these but you might get more out of the book if you engage in the exercises and buy yourself a nice journal.

It is suggested that readers consult a medical or general practitioner for individual advice on health issues. This book should not be used as an alternative to appropriate medical care. The author and publishers cannot be held liable for any errors and omissions, or actions that may be taken as a result of using it.

Contents

Introduction 17

Parts in the following sections pertain to Life Tree sections – roots, core, branches etc., as per the Life Tree drawing.

Part 1 – Exploration..24
    Life Tree 25
    Exercise..26
Part 2 – Your Roots...27
    Circle of Truth 27
    Exercise..29
    Scroatism 30
    Your family background 37
    A note on attachment 45
    Bad Role Modelling....................................48
    Common British put-downs.........................57
    Living on your knees 62
    Exercise..68
    Your genes and DNA..................................68
    Love 71
    Exercise..75
    Your school...76
    Exercise..79
    Religion & Spirituality...............................80
    Exercise..89
Part 3 – Your Branches 90
    Your spouse/his or her family/your ex-partners 90
    Love 92
    Maslow's triangle.......................................94
    Exercise..103

Your job 104
Ambition 105
On transference 110
I'll try anything once..118
The industry of a prime minister.........................118
Action makes dreams come true 120
Life is unfair...121
Rules 124
The Sting..131
Who wants to be a millionaire? 133
Exercise..139
Addictions..139
Wartime attitude to food 143
"Be a good boy and eat it all up." 145
"Eat up your chips then you can have an ice cream." 145
"It's me genes."...152
Sugar 156
Anchors...162
Hypoglycaemia 163
Exercise...177
Your hobbies & interests/fun, holidays...................178
Exercise..179
Your offspring: sons & daughters...........................180
Exercise...184
Religion & Spirituality...184
Exercise..186
Part 4 – Your Trunk/Core...187
The winds of change 188
What is anxiety?...189
The importance of sleep...207
Learn to Observe...208
Exercise..211
Society & Advertising...212
Immorality and the media 220
Exercise..226

Part 5 – What you can do to make things better.............227
   Highs & Lows..229
   Cognitive Behavioural Therapy (CBT) in a nutshell.231
   De-stressors...237
   The Gap...238
   A Poison Tree 242
   Exercise:..245
   The Rain that falls – nourishment.......................247
   Anthony's Karma Life Diet 249
   Exercise..251
   The sun that shines – the light.........................253
   Desiderata 259
   Exercise..260
   Selected Reading List & reference points................261
   Afterword...265

Introduction

Reader, lo! A well-meaning Booke. (Montaigne's salutation to his readers)

It came to me in a dream. Lewis Carroll reported such dreams in his nocturnal meanderings, as do many writers. George Michael, in an early *Wham!* song, enthuses: 'Sometimes, you wake up in the morning with a bass line, a ray of sunshine'. So this was how it happened. The aforementioned writers have undoubtedly brought much joy to a great many people and it is my hope that within these pages, you find illuminations and even answers … or whatever you're looking for. Even joy. *Broken Britain?* offers some solutions for living in a fractured society. The stencil that overlays *Broken Britain?* is Life Tree, which as you will discover, is a metaphor for existence.

Before falling asleep one night, I asked for answers. I was already fifty thousand words into this book but I had no skeleton on which to hang the contents, no focus. Then I awoke with a start, and the answer.

This book has noble aims. However, it is written largely for the lay reader and therefore, wherever possible, I have tried to avoid highfalutin language. This has not always been entirely possible as some language can only state its meaning through the specificity of a large or medical word.

As a writer who came from relative poverty I have the good fortune of retaining the so called common touch that I think prevails throughout the book. Many books like this are written by people who have had highly privileged backgrounds (although they tend to deny it) and they are a joy to read for others who have had similarly privileged backgrounds. However, as I argue in subsequent pages, this privilege, whilst unavoidable, means that those writers can never know what poverty or being without is really like. Many were privately educated and reared to be leaders so writing and becoming an author are second nature to them. As with retired MPs, it seems entirely plausible for them to knock a book out as a matter of course. Just because I came from a working-class background doesn't mean that my book is any better; far from it ... it wouldn't be would it, since my schooling was low grade and gritty, where not much was expected. My education revolved around woodwork and metalwork, and secondary school kids like me were supposed to be content with stumbling through *The Sun*, enjoying page-three and the odd cartoon. There was no privilege for me so this book shoots from the hip as I *know* council estates, low culture, hunger and even about being without a bed for a few nights. Just as I could not know what awaiting execution on death row is like, a writer from wealth cannot really know what it's like to be poor. How can they then write about a society that they have never known? I know that their quest is about *creative* writing but that, by definition, is creative rather than *experienced* writing. Authors in the creative category think that all things are possible; they are doers, optimists, and believe that getting on your bike is the solution. So, for example, anyone who enjoyed Nigella Lawson's early life (and later life), could hardly fail to become successful. Read about her on Wikipedia.

There was no Eton, Westminster or Oxbridge for me; I'm just someone who came from a terraced house with an outside toilet and got a bit clever by reading a lot and pushing myself to attend anxiety-provoking courses. I got on my bike as Norman Tebbit once encouraged us all to do. I now want to write about life and share my insights with those whom they might help.

My stance as a counsellor and writer is from the point of view of a wounded healer. Counselling is my main job and a (sort of) way of life. In my opinion, only those who have experienced a broad spectrum of life can be truly effective as counsellors. In other words, it can help if you've had a chequered past or been plagued by troubles. Again this isn't the fault of those born to great things – that's just the way the mop flops, but I think it's a bit rich for them to advise others on how to get out of poverty when they themselves have never been in it.

So this book is written by a member of the proletariat for the proletariat. Most mental health professionals such as psychiatrists and the like are most likely to have come from a middle-class background and would therefore be stretched to fully appreciate or empathise with the life challenges of their patients; they simply do not know hunger or chaotic parenting. I do acknowledge my own experience of poverty and this has added a dimension that is impossible for the lucky to write about.

Life Tree is supposed to provide food for thought on rainy days. Meant for more than just a toilet read, it might grace coffee tables in the hope that it inspires debate. The age-old question, 'what's it all about?' seems to be even further from our consciousness as we submerge deeper and deeper into the quicksand of consumerism whilst being hoodwinked by successive governments and the controllers of industry. I don't mean to suggest that we are all doomed but simply to raise some questions, some rhetorical, and, in doing so, crystallise some current ideologies about where we're 'at' now we have our collective teeth into the new century.

I'm not the one who has all the answers, nor am I a mystic who hears voices or receives divine messages. I'm glad about that! I propose to examine current Western culture and try to find some meaning – if there is any. I believe that this meaning, or what defines us, has become so eroded that it is almost invisible except perhaps to the chattering classes. As Sting once sang, 'There is no political solution', and, 'I believe I've lost my faith in politicians' – and that seems to be right. Politicians seem only to pretend that there are answers to social unrest, but, as everyone knows, their spin has become so obvious, it's detestable. More on spin later.

My favourite author of fiction is the recently departed Sidney Sheldon. I think I've read everything he's ever written and most of his novels are fast-moving page turners; some would call them trashy holiday reading but I think they're great. Recently, Sheldon published his autobiography after a glittering, hugely successful career as a writer, spanning six decades. His life story reveals very humble beginnings but culminates in his being the toast of Hollywood and one of the most translated authors who ever lived. This book is not a tribute to the great man. I became fascinated by the way some people like Sheldon seem to 'make it big' whilst others loll around in the doldrums. Others have dreams that will never come true, and still others never dream at all, seemingly content to live their lives in the shadows, fearing what the light may reveal and the anxiety it may arouse.

Notably, most people fall into the last two categories and this is perhaps the way things *should* be since we cannot all become Sidney Sheldon. If all our dreams and goals came true, just imagine how different the world would be. Everyone who auditions for TV talent shows would go on to become a world famous recording artiste; everyone who flew a plane would become an ace fighter pilot; everyone who cooked a tasty omelette would become a master chef; all writers of children's fiction would become as wealthy as JK Rowling: the list is endless. There is only so much room for the Elton Johns or Stevie Wonders of this world, and whilst these people are undeniably very gifted, the West is full of also-rans who are literally kept alive by dreams that may never materialize. Sadly, most of us do not aspire to becoming a toilet cleaner yet there are more toilet cleaners than superstars.

This book is based on the metaphor of a tree: your tree of life. Along with other things, I shall look at the human condition and how it is goal-directed, pooling together a plethora of sources that I have accumulated and summarized over the years: self-help books, spiritual 'guru' books, business strategy books, and other similar props. Perhaps as importantly, I'll also be looking at the things that hinder our lives and prevent us living life to the full.

In my work as a counsellor, I have found that most people are basically afraid of doing what they want for the following reasons:

1. They haven't got the money to fund a dream.
2. They think people will laugh at them.
3. They may be found out to be a phoney or a fraud.
4. By not doing something they keep their hope alive … if they don't do it they can't fail.
5. They may have no talent but don't realise it.
6. They may not believe themselves worthy of any great accolade, excessively boastful perhaps, but lacking in talent or substance.

I'll be having a look at the keys to success and failure and what it takes to make a difference to *your* life. Naturally, success is a relative thing, meaning different things to different people. Success is also nebulous in that it's hard to define. From a counselling point of view, the anxious person may define success by leaving the house one day, free from agoraphobia and feelings of impending doom. Success might mean money. There are lots of books available to help 'normal' people become millionaires … I don't know whether they work or not as the results are hard to research. Most people just read the first chapter then fall asleep; this applies to many books. There are also lots of autobiographical books in circulation, written by those who have found wealth, but because wealth is so subjective and depends heavily on your background, I argue that it is almost impossible to follow a set recipe. What works for Duncan Bannatyne or Felix Dennis or Richard Branson might not work for you. More often than not, success depends upon being born to the 'right' family and whether or not they support you. This need not mean financial support … it can be a word of encouragement or a pat on the back. How you are raised undoubtedly affects your future prospects; this is part of my 'roots' section of your tree. If you were raised in challenging circumstances it will be harder for you to extricate yourself from the mire, if indeed you ever do; sadly, most do not.

Success is so individual, subjective, and personal, that following a plan is almost impossible as we are all so very different. Sure, there are some things you can do and some things you shouldn't do if you want to be successful, but most books written by entrepreneurs are just a means of making *them* richer as you can no more copy their formula than you could their eye print. How could you? You're different. Obviously an MBA degree won't do you any harm if you want to become a top business person or captain of industry.

This is not a book that tells you what or what not to do. You can buy other books for that and fall asleep after the first chapter when you realise that your millionaire barrister father won't bail you out. If you have a doting, millionaire barrister father then you won't need this or any book so you might as well enjoy your life and buy a dog for your Prada handbag.

This book aims to help normal people, perhaps those who are anxious, frightened or wary – in the hope that they might lead a fuller or better-adjusted life: to free them from self- or other-imposed shackles. We are all shackled to some degree and I propose that once our wings have been anointed with unconditional love, we will be free to become whoever or whatever we wish to be. We may even find that when our needs for love have been met, we no longer strive to define ourselves with a designer bag.

I will look at the façades we hide behind, our denials, addictions, and how we set ourselves up in quagmires that prevent us from tasting the elixirs of life. In this respect, the book is about reality and 'truth'.

Life Tree is also quite unusual. I didn't intend it to be but I have written from the heart and that's the way it has turned out. Some of the writings are based on research, some are observational and therefore ethnographic, and some of it is autobiographical. So, in this sense, it's polemic. I acknowledge the fact that it's quite unusual to be heavily autobiographical in a self-help book but hopefully this adds colour to the writing and enables readers to relate to a real person, living in the real world, trying to cope with real problems. I have tried to cover various aspects of life and I hope you will have an enjoyable read … perhaps, like me, you will have a life-changing experience. Maybe this book will be catalytic in your process of *becoming*. Although arguably, and intentionally, depressing at times, this book is not intended as some sort of Ballardian or apocalyptic tome, nor does it have the brimstone zeal of Revelations.

I have tried to avoid being patronizing. Life Tree is about life, adopting a philosophy of life in the 21st century, fulfilling one's goals and one's destiny, whatever they might be. *Broken Britain?* is intended to be a crossover book; part self-help, part philosophy, part motivational, so you can take from it what you will, in the hope that you will find it inspiring and applicable to your own existence. It has been formed from observations and my many interactions with clients and the world in general, at many different levels. My main hypothesis revolves around *the tree* and the next chapter explains why.

Finally, you might not want to read this book for it reveals 'truths'. Obviously, there are very few 'truths' but I have attempted to uncover some lies that infiltrate the heart of our existence, with a view to making things better. Life Tree is for anyone and everyone. I've personally been looking for a book like this for twenty years and I couldn't find one. So I decided to write it.

Part 1 – Exploration

As humans, we are all members of one universal society yet we are also individuals within that cosmos. The things that affect you might not affect me and vice-versa; some things will affect both of us. Whilst we stand together we also stand apart; this is the nature of living, the essence of being. In the grand scheme of things we are insignificant but to ourselves and the people who know us, we are important.

The following drawing shows a tree, proud and strong, with a good trunk, roots and branches. It is balanced. This tree is a metaphor of you as a living being within this planet Earth. You are rooted to the ground and you are affected by a vast array of influences. The drawing in itself is fairly self-explanatory and herein lies its simplicity, the key to this whole idea. What unfolds however, is not so simple.

The Life Tree

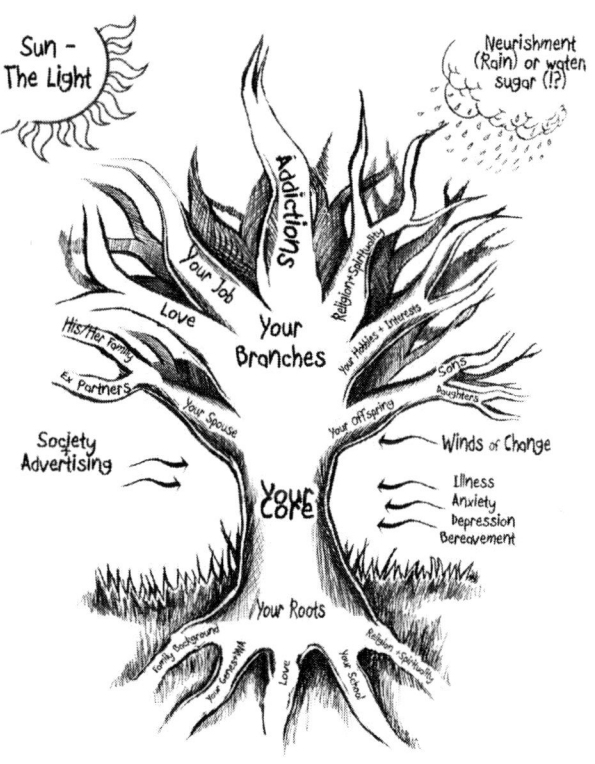

Exercise

Go now and get yourself a nice notebook or fancy journal and on page 1, draw yourself a tree like the one shown above. Make your journal a large one so that your tree fits onto the page and you can add things as we go along, not only to the tree, but to subsequent pages. I'm not going to tell you what to write on those subsequent pages but you will know as the book unfolds. This will be your personal journal on your travel throughout this book. Start by drawing your tree. Throughout all your exercises and your writing, compose in an unbridled way, letting your pen flow. This work is for your eyes only. Spelling and grammar doesn't matter for these purposes: all that matters is what you draw and write and only what it means to you and you alone.

Part 2 – Your Roots

Some of your roots can be hidden, buried away within your subconscious mind. Not the unknown knowns that Donald Rumsfeldt once famously referred to, but unknown unknowns. This can be nicely illustrated using the Circle of Truth you will see illustrated below. I created this circle in order to extrapolate personal shadows and unknowns that we all carry within our psyches.

Circle of Truth

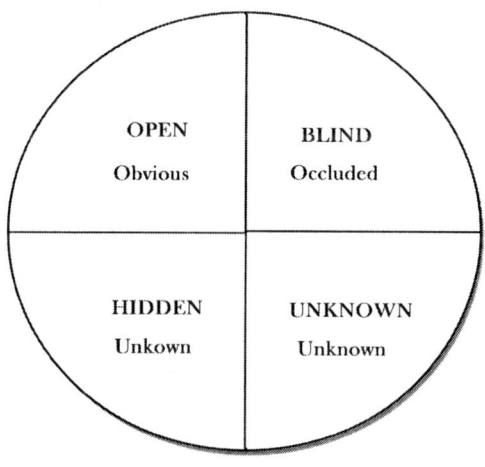

Draw the circle in your journal and fill it in according to the knowledge of yourself.

Obvious:
The obvious area of the circle, obvious to the rest of the world; it's the part you are aware of, and happy to show the rest of the world 'out there'. There are your attitudes, behaviour, motivation and values that you are aware of, and which are known to others.

Occluded:
This segment of the circle is that part of you that you *don't* want others to know about unless you reveal it by choice. Likewise, it's what you don't know about *others.* It covers beliefs, feelings and impulses that you control – maybe because you think they may be anti-social or are fearful of people's reactions. So you erect a barrier. The degree to which you share yourself with others is the degree to which you can be 'known'.

Unknown:
There are things about you that you don't know, but that others can see – mannerisms and unconscious behaviours. There are things you may imagine about yourself that others do not see at all! The only way you can know about them is by getting other people to tell you – that can be difficult for those close to you as they probably don't want to hurt you. But when others say what they see (feedback), in a supportive, responsible way, and you listen, you can test the reality of who you are and are able to grow.

Unknown unknowns:
The last segment is that part that is closed to both yourself and others. You can only presume this by looking at what you have done, in retrospect. It is your true depth – what motivates you what influences you, your deepest beliefs and feelings. Maybe this is the source of your 'uniqueness' – what makes you different from those around you. From time to time something happens – is felt, read, heard, dreamed – something from your unconscious is revealed. Then you 'know' what you have never 'known' before.

The Circle of Truth is particularly relevant to Your Roots as it exposes several possible blind spots that lie within each of us. These blind spots may be childhood issues that you may have chosen to forget or even forgive, in your quest for a quiet life. However, if you are going to cleanse the inner you, these hidden events and memories need to be addressed. Only you personally will know what happened to you and it is up to you whether to share this with anyone. You might prefer to keep this in your private journal.

The circle seeks to question the following areas ...

a) Known knowns – this is what you know about yourself and what everyone else knows about you.
b) Known unknowns – this is what you know about yourself but other people don't know.
c) Unknown knowns – this is what you don't know about yourself but others know about you.
d) Unknown unknowns – this is what you don't know about yourself and others don't know either. This is unconscious or preconscious stuff.

Exercise

Go to your journal and start four fresh pages as per a, b, c, d, above and list the first things that come into your mind. Write freely and without inhibition. You will need to ask your intimates about (c) and you will not be able to fill in (d) at all ... yet.

We now look at a random interviewee who, like all my participants, has been anonymized ...

Scroatism

Mark works for a well known service in a challenging neighbourhood, not too far from where I live. He kindly agreed to this short interview with me. I have condensed some of it and extracted the salient points. Mark is 40 years old, married with two young children.

Mark: The job wouldn't be so bad if it wasn't for the scroats.

Me: Scroats?

Mark: Y'know, the feral kids that they talked about a few years ago. That's what they are, like animals when they get together.

Me: And what do they do that's so bad?

Mark: Just generally terrorising anyone and everyone. It doesn't matter; young or old, they'll have a go at anyone, effing and blinding in their faces, just taking the piss.

Me: Where do you think they came from? What caused 'scroatism' if I can call it that?

Mark: Yeah, scroatism's a good word for it. I don't know. You can see what a scroat is in a woman by looking at some reality programmes. They are feral children grown up. No manners, showing their tits and arses and getting pissed every chance they get.

Me: In another time then a scroat would have been a low life or just someone disadvantaged, low on life's chances?

Mark: Yeah, I suppose so, but they've always been around but not as bad as it is today. My Dad was a cop and I've heard all his awful stories but at least then kids had a bit of respect for the uniform. Now I think they'd stab you if they thought they could get away with it. It's just people like you – with the greatest respect – who call them disadvantaged. And the girl scroats are even worse than some of the lads.

Me: Do you think that girl power and the Spice Girls helped or hindered all this new female anger and do you think it's about feminism and being equal?

Mark: Well I think the Spice Girls probably influenced girls to believe in themselves and become more powerful but I think the girls who are scroats took the message the wrong way. Girls

30

and teenagers today want to drink as much as blokes and act as disgusting. They're not ladies any more and they want sex and openly ask for it. That's why there's so many underage pregnancies.

Me: So it's not really about female liberation but women becoming as bad as men?

Mark: Yes I think so.

Me: I don't think this scroatism is caused by the scroat him or herself though do you? That's why I say disadvantaged, because most of these sub-prime folk have come from highly dysfunctional homes and all that.

Mark: Yeah, I think it perpetuates itself: single mothers having kids too young and then their kids having a kid too young, et cetera et cetera …

Me: So in a way, they are to be pitied.

Mark: Yes if you're at a distance like you are, but not when they're spitting at you. One lad last week called me a cunt and threw a brick at my head. I don't feel much pity when that happens.

Me: That must have been terrible. How does that make you feel about how society is going?

Mark: Well it's probably already gone to the dogs. It's like that Richard Littlejohn used to say in *The Sun*: to hell in a handcart. It's just gone worse and worse since Thatcher was in. She said something about society …

Me: Yes, she said there was no such thing as society I think.

Mark: Huh, well she should walk round with me one night shift.

Me: So when you speak to these scroats what do they say, y'know, if you have a conversation with any of them?

Mark: Well some of them are all right actually. It's just when they get together in their gangs, and they'll be listening to that American gangster music about guns and bitches. What really amazes me is that the girls seem to like the music that is slagging them off.

Me: Yes it's misogynistic isn't it? All about hating women and all that. So what do they say to you?

Mark: They just say they're bored and there's nowt to do. They all want to be pop stars or models but they'll all end up like Vicky Pollard or that Catherine Tate one.

Me: Lauren.

Mark: Yeah it would be wouldn't it?

Me: So models or Lauren?

Mark: Yeah and I think they're bad role models anyway especially the new breed of celebrity that can't actually do anything; can't sing or actually do anything.

Me: Why celebrities though?

Mark: It's all about the money and not doing anything. I've got MTV and that's what all the videos are about. Women are there as sex objects writhing about and there's nothing wrong with that but young girls aspire to it and want to become like it.

Me: So it's money for nothing?

Mark: Yeah, all that lot who are in the media; they've infected the minds of young British girls. They're all just tarts aren't they?

Me: I think it's the way our permissive society has gone. I think we show more and more flesh, have lap dancing bars, have celebrities in *Hello* Magazine and *OK* who are famous for being famous. Y'know, people like WAGS who are there in the shadow of others. I think in this way we get a distorted picture of reality and younger people might think that all you have to do is be a model or a bit of a singer or marry a footballer to be rich, and, this seems to be partially true anyway. That is one thing, but then younger people see this as a way out of poverty.

Mark: Yeah, what would these WAGS be doing if they hadn't married into money? Probably serving in Greggs.

Me: Well, you've got to have good looks for being a WAG or a model I guess.

Mark: Yeah, so the young just think it's easy to get in to the big time and have a perfume out and bang, you're sorted.

I liked Mark's unbridled honesty and I really like the word scroat and its derivatives: scroat, scroatess, scroatistic, scroatism. The scroat is marginalised, ruthless, and unpredictable. It's easy to think of Mark as some kind of Alf Garnett bigot. But is he bigoted or does he simply speak the truth as he knows it? Behind the anonymity of an interview it's easy to be honest. I don't think he has any particular hatred for anyone and no -isms or -ists affect his vocabulary. He's just an average man doing a tough job in the face of adversity in a declining, broken Britain. Once parents abrogate their responsibilities or defer them to the state, a scroat is born.

Mark and I talked for a lot longer as I found him entertaining and interesting. An old counsellor once said that she thought she was the sum of all her clients and I guess there's a bit of Mark in all of us, even though it's not politically correct to admit it. Mark challenged my own political correctitude and wrongly assumed that I came from a white bread world of books and croquet on the lawn. I also discovered that Mark embodied a typical reaction to many of those I spoke to about where Britain is going and why so many Brits are seeking to leave this country as soon as they can. The following observations are conclusions from the time Mark and I spent together ...

If she (the scroatess) is lucky enough to be pretty, she will perhaps become a lap dancer ... if she can't sing. Her thong will overflow with grubby Franklyns. Morality matters little: only money. Individually, the scroat is a vacuous entity of low morals and low education. The scroat only finds strength within a gang and it is in this emporium he wields the greatest threat to other members of society. He will usually have come from a broken home and have suffered an abhorrent mixture of bad parenting, chaotic family life and abuse. Both sexes will have tattoos and body piercing. Vicky Pollard from *Little Britain* and Catherine Tate's *Lauren* are prime examples of what Mark means. The scroat will aspire to becoming a 'gangsta rapper', and having a plethora of *bitches* on his arm. The scroatess longs for fame and adulation that she so lacked as a child.

Things haven't always been this way. Female singers and stars used to be able to act or sing, and of course some still do, but there are a minority of so-called celebrities who seem to get by just by doing nothing. It seems as if our role models are the ones with the least to offer if they exist due to celebrity in itself.

However, the scroat is created and he very rarely chooses his way of life so my words about him are not meant to be insulting or comedic at all. Herein lies a paradox. Whilst it is popular to poke fun and parody scroats, as in the shows I have just mentioned, it is a cruel thing to do almost akin to mocking a *cripple* or a dyslexic. Whilst the aforementioned popular shows swathe themselves in irony (because if they didn't they'd be politically incorrect), they still mock the ones who cannot defend themselves: those who did not create their life style. At first glance, it appears that I am using a naughtily sourced word (taken from scrotum) and that I want to pour scorn on *low life* people for the sake of comedy, self-aggrandisement, or snobbery, but this is absolutely not the case. Unlike the cited TV programmes, I have not chosen to clothe my scroat in an obnoxious character, and whilst this is plainly against the current thinking in entertainment (i.e. you have to use a character in order to make politically incorrect comedy), I have decided to be real instead, rather than making this a thinly disguised attempt at humour. I can think of nothing worse than being privately educated with a lovely life of milk and honey and then ridiculing lower class people, albeit within the guise of a comedy character. This does not mean to say that I have no sense of humour. I can laugh at *Vicky Pollard* and *Lauren*, but my laughter evaporates when I acknowledge that these *funny* characters are very sad and they exist in reality and the characters have been created by white, middle class, privileged people who get rich at the expense of poking fun at the deprived. My laughter turns to revulsion and the irony becomes a vapid ruse. The scroat is arguably a pejorative word but, to me, it is also a term of endearment.

It seems that irony must be maintained, as if we have to be someone else or become a character in order to protect ourselves, and lest we show our true colours. This goes some way to explaining retro fashions and the need to appear to be somebody else, or an actor acting in the guise of another. Why can't we just be ourselves ... are we too embarrassed? Similar things have happened to theme parties and the commodification of events. It is now popular to see that grooms-to-be are not content to go marauding around Amsterdam and looking for a prostitute with whom to have a last fling (and give herpes to his blushing bride); now stag parties have become commodified and groups are invited to participate in mountaineering in order to facilitate bonding. Why can't they just meet up and discuss the terrifying experience of losing one's singleton status?

More depressingly, I discovered that the girls who are so keen to display their wares to all and sundry are not really showing girl power; the derivation of the word could hardly have gone more awry. Where is the power in behaving like a male lout? It seems that girl loutishness has become a mark of sexual liberation and so the feminist message has been distorted from its initial intent. The idea was to create equality but not equally bad behaviour. The debauchery one sees in any drinking town centre of a weekend is testament to the fact that everyone now seems liberated and gross. These fleshy displays are not spiritually satisfying; they are just a way of escaping a humdrum life for a short time. Behold the current trend in sexualized pop videos whose graphic and lurid elements contain little more than the objectification of young women as they willingly accept their roles as *hos* and *bitches* at the behest of some gangsta rapper. Our broken Britain has become more to do with promoting soft porn than morality.

In order to create meaning in life it is fortunate if we find ourselves surrounded by people who support and love us ... even need us. We also need to be stretched mentally by academic endeavours. This need not mean taking a PhD (unless you're up to it) ... it can mean learning about something new in whichever way you choose. We also need some sort of philosophical morality by which to live: a set of norms and values that keep us on the straight and narrow.

Growing up in this quagmire of sexualisation and the glorification of (usually but not only) the perfect female form, it is no wonder that female teens are obsessed with their appearances and become plagued with eating problems and the like. The teenage years need not be so angst ridden for they are over all too soon. Your fourteen-year-old boy or girl is soon to go out into the harsh, unfair, cruel world and they still need all the love from you that you have to give. They are still your babies and perhaps one day they will be looking after you. Try not to see them as a threat to your masculinity or femininity; as you approach middle age, go gracefully and let them flourish. They are not your mates to compete with ... they are your children whom you should love unconditionally. Oscar Wilde said that youth was wasted on the young and how many times have we heard people say, 'If I knew then what I know now …'. Well, you didn't know did you, and neither did I. That's what being young is all about. Try not to project all your own failed dreams onto your offspring … it causes resentment. The idea is that they find their own way and live a life that is true to themselves. The transience of youth is all too short and should be cherished if possible.

You may notice in your own area that the scroat or yob or teenage tearaway or feral child congregates in groups. Since we are all pack animals, they, like us, like to be with their peers and equals … birds of a feather and all that. Observe too how young teenagers huddle together anywhere outdoors where they might find some warmth; near a kebab shop or a cheap alcohol outlet. In my own area, these unwanted children gather on a wall near my local leisure centre where there is a warm air-conditioning output pipe, so they can be cosy as they snog each other. This is not a *hug a hoodie* paragraph but I cannot help but feel pity as they have become society's outcasts, the great unwashed. Their friends are other unwanted children so they find solace in the company of each other and a can of strong lager, maybe some drugs or a sniff of glue. As much research shows, these are the rejected children of broken homes and they clearly have nowhere to go. They are bored and rebuffed by society and they get into mischief. They become rebellious, obnoxious, and anti-social. The other night I saw four teenagers running into oncoming traffic for the thrill of it. Unwanted by their incompetent, dullard parents, unwanted by society, it's little wonder that the teenage pregnancy rate soars … they do it for love … to feel the love they have never known. Sadly, they just attract more trouble to themselves. Pregnancy aside, I think that what these unwanted rebels need is simply somewhere warm to go that sells drinks at cost price. Somewhere like a shelter that's a bit grungy, with non-alcoholic drinks and soup galore, a shelter that contains street furniture that is indestructible. Somewhere they could wreck or draw graffiti if they chose to; somewhere that they could play hideous music at a volume of their choice. The shelters would have to be open 24/7/365 as I notice a greater proliferation of unwanted children on the streets during festive times. These shelters wouldn't look like a *Sandals* resort but at least they'd provide a much needed haven. But who would fund these shelters?

The parents of these unwanted teenagers will be on their second or third marriage – if they are married at all – so the cast-off teen desperately needs somewhere to go; there is often no room for older children in families whose parents have moved on to pastures new. Parents deceive themselves if they think that children from their first relationships no longer need them … they need them for life, but unfortunately, many parents are found to be completely lacking in ideas and love. This is gross neglect. If your child is on the street tonight drinking cider and waiting to mug someone, YOU have failed as a parent. Youth should be a magical time, a time of change and development. All I see around me in most town centres is discarded human debris and it is a tragic sight.

Your family background

1967

It was a hot summer. It was 1967, the summer of love. In the news were The Beatles, the Rolling Stones, Eric Clapton, Pattie Boyd, Lionel Bart, and Twiggy. The UK ached with new possibilities and the recent proliferation of the birth control pill meant that morals could drop to a lower level than ever before. Some would have called this freedom, which it undoubtedly was, but it inevitably bred irresponsibility. Teenage girls and young women could experiment with sexuality like never before in the name of flower power and hippyism. It was a time for free love and sex with anyone without regard for the consequences… or the babies that resulted in forgetting to take the pill.

Janice was nowhere near swinging London but caught a flavour of the times through the psychedelic music and popular magazines of the time. Janice lived near Manchester in a poor suburb overspill of Manchester called Hattersley, a town to be made notorious by Myra Hindley and Ian Brady, the Moors murderers, Harold Shipman, and Ricky Hatton (undoubtedly Hattersley's finest export). Janice was twenty years old and had not been a big achiever at school. She had an offer of a job in a local shop which was turgidly boring. However, Janice lived for the weekends when she would attend the local dancehalls and let her hair down. If it had only been her hair she'd been letting down she might not have got *into trouble*. Having little knowledge about contraception, and being very pretty, Janice was a natural target for all the local lads. She also craved love and attention as her own father had left her and her mother (herself a war-baby) when she was only three years old. Janice became promiscuous yet tried to keep her good name, giving just enough of herself so as not to be labelled a tart. It was only a matter of time until Janice became pregnant and the baby could have been sired by any number of men. She really didn't know who the father was and this was a big taboo in 1967. As soon as she discovered her plight, she considered having the baby adopted, then she considered getting a back-street abortion (the local butcher used to do them to supplement his income), then she considered keeping the baby and trying to make ends meet. Whatever she did, she would have to do it in conjunction with her Mum, so that night, she told the news and all hell broke loose. There was another twist in this tale for Janice had also sampled a few local African men who were all too happy to accept her favours. This meant that the baby may have been born a half-caste as well as being a bastard. This news almost killed Janice's pious mother and, whilst this doesn't seem so shocking in 2010, it was dynamite in the sixties when keeping up appearances meant everything to everybody. With her mother's collusion, Janice decided to have the baby with a view to having it adopted if it turned out to be the *wrong* colour. Fortunately (or unfortunately) the babe was born a passable shade of white and Janice connived and manipulated a local lad into marrying her, pretending that the baby was his. He was from a *better* family and so at least he could bring some much needed respectability to the sorry mess. It wasn't even as if she wanted the title of scarlet woman; she just craved attention and relied on her looks to get her by. Unfortunately, her intellect was no match for her looks and this is how Janice found herself at the end of 1967.

Like most marriages that are based on a lie, Janice's marriage to Phil lasted about 9 months and the *chap-by-chance* baby was given permanently to Janice's mother to bring up. This grandmother had been with the baby almost since birth anyway, and found the child quite a gap-filler in her own life since she had no partner and very little to do except worry about Janice.

The baby Jack grew fond of his Grandma and she adopted his mother's role. Phil also stayed around on and off and the baby was pleased to see familiar faces whenever he could, as long as his Gran remained a constant fixture.

1987

Jack sits in a bed-sit wondering where it all went wrong. He had good intentions all his young life and he has good intentions now. Today is his twentieth birthday and he has treated himself to a few lines of coke. The flat is quite squalid and as well as being twenty today, he has just become a Dad for the first time. This should have been a pleasing time but it was tarnished by memories of the past, current debts to loan-sharks and drug dealers … not at all like a soap-powder advert. Last week he bought some Persil to make his whites even whiter but nothing would wash away the deep scars in Jack's tumultuous past. His Gran had died a few years ago leaving him with an inconsistent mother and almost unknown father, who wasn't his real father anyway.

"What the fuck have you been up to while I've been out?" demands Jack's partner Kim as she enters the grim flat. Hello would have been superfluous.

Kim is carrying a 6-month-old baby sort of by the arm, as she scowls at Jack.

"What the fuck 'as it got to do with you, you cunt?" replies an embittered Jack, the fuel of his first line making the last sentence sound braver than he intended.

"You fuckin' make me sick, you lazy twat. Have you been snorting that shit again?" asked Kim, ignoring the smell of Callum's dirty nappy.

"Yeah babe, come over here and you can 'ave some. I know you want a bit."

"Yeah, but Jack, we're supposed to be making a fresh start innit?"

"Well, it's me birthday and I thought we'd have a last bit of Charlie and then that's it – right?"

It wasn't all right but it was the only thing they knew; the only thing that made life a bit more palatable. This was the case for so many eighties' youths who were born as a result of the free love sixties. They never had proper parenting, no good role models, and amorality and irresponsibility was rife. Perhaps this explains the rise of off-your-face dance music and the rave culture that emanated around Ibiza and Cyprus at that time. It became a place to escape.

<u>2007</u>

Callum is now nineteen and his Dad left him when he was 3 years old. From that time he saw him spasmodically but at least his Mum stayed with him. His Mum had and still has a lot of boyfriends and makes no secret of her promiscuity. Gone are the days when having lots of lovers was something to be ashamed of. Callum's Mum is anything but demure.

Callum himself had tried a few drugs – most of them in fact – but his favourite was E. Nothing seemed to excite him more and everyone else was doing it so why not. His mother couldn't say anything to stop him because she was always stoned or pissed, so who was she to cast aspersions?

Callum had his first E tab around the age of 14 given to him by a kid on the estate where they all lived in Barnsley. He'd also had a few local girlfriends who were very keen on him because he could give them drugs and because he looked like *Slim Shady*.

As well has drugs, Callum was also no stranger to the local police, who had visited and arrested him many times for drugs, joy-riding, theft, criminal damage …

Janice, Jack, and Callum are products of the last sixty or so years. Their behaviour now permeates our society and they are all around us. They are the types that always seem to be around anti-social behaviour and it is no surprise to read about their untimely, early deaths in our local newspapers. These people are not bad, they have just lost their way.

Teenage children sometimes disappear, trying to make a better life for themselves, usually in London or at a holiday town. They find cheap, casual work and sometimes fall into temptations too old for their ages. I would assert that the only similarity between most of them is that they are the grandchildren of baby-boomers. Children like Jack and Callum have been well researched and written about endlessly. They are the chaff that was created on whimsical sexual irresponsibility and the chaff that falls out of the bottom of our late-stage capitalist society. One can read Dickens' books and take gallows comfort in the fact that things have always been bad and that there have always been *low-life's* around. However, this does not diminish its importance and we no longer send them to Australia for their petty crimes. It seems that the Thatcherite belief that the Market would sort out society – was wrong. It doesn't. Even if you love your child unconditionally, there is no saying that the drug dealers won't get to them and tempt them with a sample. Even in the 17th century, the philosopher Thomas Hobbes (1588-1679) noted that human beings were innately selfish and hedonistic; scroatism has always been with us.

Callum is considering going to college to become a plumber. His current girlfriend is expecting their second child.

He cried and he cried
To the mother and maid
Left stuck in position
In which he was laid
And they to just pass
Would be something far better
Ignored as his tears
Got wetter and wetter
As the people they passed
And he stared at their riches
Jealous of wealth
But yet they had stitches
So gone was his patience
And so was the time

> So trying to balance
> Upon a straight line
> To hear their sweet voices
> To make his life rhyme
> (Leona HS, 2009)

And the beat goes on …

> I was walking with my daughter near our local park in Blackpool when I heard the screams of a child and the soft thud of a trainer being kicked into his face. But this was no random mugging … if it had been we wouldn't have been so shocked. The child was on the floor and it was his elder sister who was kicking him in the head and face.
>
> "I told you to get 'ome now, you fucker," she screamed, bending down to him.
>
> We stood stock still watching the scene unfold. As she kicked him one last time, he rolled over, his nose covered in blood. He had stopped screaming, wiped his nose on his sleeve, and he got onto his bike and rode off presumably towards home, slightly in front of his caring sister. Tragically, he looked as if this event was the norm in his sad little life.
>
> I wondered whether to say something or intervene but the scene was over very quickly and in this boy's life, it was just another day. You could see that the way he rode off, an air of acceptance came over him as if he had to appear tough and take his beating. It reminded me of *The Bacons* comic strip in *Viz* magazine, but this was no joke. What sort of messages will this older bully be laying down towards the younger sibling and what sort of life can he expect when reared by people like this?

The questions a scene like this raises are almost too numerous to mention.

And again …

> Again with my daughter, we were just leaving Blackpool Pleasure Beach and witnessed another scene of abuse. A boy of about 5 years old was walking nearby with his father and

mother, both late teenagers. For no apparent reason, the father bent down to the child and shouted at the top of his voice directly into the child's ear. It was so loud that a few people turned round and the child dropped his crisps. The father then hit him for dropping the crisps! As if this wasn't upsetting enough, the small child then rubbed his ear and lost his balance because of the severe volume of the abusive yell. Again, I would have said something but I have no doubt that I would have been met with a violent response. It is difficult to be a floaty counsellor when I see this all around me.

These kind of scenes are commonplace in 21st century Britain and if anyone intervenes or evokes the ire of the abuser, they too are met with abuse. Who can put a stop to this behaviour, and has our society declined so much that we become desensitised to scenes such as these?

In the picture below, we see the babyfaced thug who killed a father who dared to intervene when the attacker and his gang were interfering with the man's car. The dead man was brave and leaves behind a distraught family. Bravery has been rewarded by death as is so often the case. It is little wonder that people would rather shut their curtains and ignore any fracas lest they themselves become victims. It is beyond doubt that many teenagers are out of control. I still do not believe they are intrinsically bad, but their behaviour certainly is. Without moral guidelines and boundaries, and with the influence of certain aspects of society, it is no wonder that children have gone to seed. More than anything, I believe that parents have an awful lot to answer for. These parents are parents only by biology, not by their skills in rearing the next generation.

Unlike Dickensian times, Governments pay lip service to the problem but I don't really think they created the problem anyway. The problem of scroatism is created by bad parenting. Latter day Governments do little to help when they encourage crèches and working mothers as this leads inevitably and obviously to the child being without his mother. I know that these are incendiary words and many readers will rail against them, but a child simply should be with his mother during his early years. The evidence points this way and it is that simple. This is assuming that the child's mother has adequate parenting skills and does not believe that, by being born, the child has ruined her liberty.

But who is to teach us how to raise our children? The Government? The National Institute of Health and Clinical Excellence? The Bible? Our friends and families? If any of these do the teaching, it assumes that you think that they know what they're talking about. I personally don't believe that any advice on child-rearing should be given by those without children, with the exception of medical advice. It would be akin to teaching someone to drive having never driven yourself. That's why I'm always suspicious of Government Ministers who have no children ... how can they know the full picture of life? What gives childless MPs the right to encourage women to work? They themselves can work all the hours they like as they have never had children to run home for, so that's okay, but why encourage anyone else to work? These proselytising, unspeak, newspeak, self-aggrandising, demi-gods sicken me as they brazenly duck and weave questions on TV about issues around society. How can they know about children in society having never raised a child? It's truly unfortunate if these spouts wanted children and were unable to conceive, but more often than not, it is my view that their precious careers and egos are more important than child-rearing. I'm not saying 'It's the nanny state gone mad', because there are undoubtedly some good bipartisan government incentives. I simply think that only those who have had children should be advising others how to bring them up, and even then, only if it is invited.

"There's no manual", people cry, when it comes to bringing up children. Well this myth is simply not true. Bookstores and libraries are full of advice and books on child rearing if only people could be bothered to read them. Having not enjoyed the best upbringing in the world, my wife and I attended parenting classes hosted by our local council where we learnt quite a bit. Also, television shows like *Supernanny* and the like are full of good advice about what to do and not to do with children. So, there really is a manual. There are a lot of manuals. Attachment guru John Bowlby, claimed that good mental health was based on good early attachment with a carer in the first three years of life. A secure base is vital if a child is to develop and grow and become curious (and so to learn) in future years. The first three years of life are also a time when our brains see most neural growth, activity, and where synaptic connections are formed. This is a time when we become wired up. The more something happens to us at this point, the more likely the brain will learn and be used in this way. This is known as use-dependent-development. Needless to say, if bad things are happening, a child will come to expect the worst for the rest of their lives. Counselling rooms and psychiatry practices throughout the world are peopled with patients who have been harmed (wittingly and unwittingly) in this way. With too many negative experiences, the ability to learn and to love is compromised. The brain develops as a kind of mirror of the experiences we have had as toddlers – good and bad. Ideally if she is to go on to experience a good life, the child needs to be away from continual flight/fight experiences and needs reliable care for her synapses to develop. If you are an unfortunate, it means that your resting state will be anxious as you were bombarded with negativity since birth. I paint a grim picture and it's no wonder consumerism can thrive in view of the fact that most of us are living in a sense of fear, tinged with deprivation. This is exacerbated by working patterns of modern parents; hard to provide evidence for this statement but take a look around our broken and immoral teenagers who are never far from the headlines. It's all anecdotal but it exists.

A note on attachment

The way we were raised is of paramount importance in shaping our future lives and emotions, our trials and tribulations, and our general outlook and demeanour.

Based on Bowlby's work, and in a nutshell, attachment theory suggests:

Personality Types

<u>Type A: Insecure</u>

The child is avoidant of proximity to Mother & Father and happy to be left alone. Carer is predictable but insensitive. The child is punished or ignored for showing feelings. They suppress emotions and hide them even from themselves. Self becomes unlovable, worthless, learning that others are unreliable. They don't listen to how they feel as they've learnt that it doesn't matter. They avoid intimacy but cognitive (thinking) development is good. All feelings are dismissed.

Predominantly: thinking only, not feeling.

<u>Type B: Secure</u>

Child seeks and maintains contact and trust. Has positive response to reunion with Mother or Father. Carer is predictably sensitive. Predictable response to stress. 'It's okay to show my feelings as I know I'm loved'. Empathic, trusting, moral, understands and is in contact with own emotions. Self is lovable and worthy. Others seem caring and responsive. It's okay out there in the wider world.

Predominantly: Integrates both cognitions (thinking) and affect (feeling) and becomes a fully functioning adult.

<u>Type C: Insecure</u>

Ambivalent … resists proximity then a love/hate flip towards the care-giver. Carer is unpredictably sensitive. Rewarded intermittently (like gambling) so child tends to amplify emotions, sometimes acting out. Self is unlovable and ineffective. The world is crazy and <u>only</u> feelings matter, so these children rely on how they feel rather than what they think.

Predominantly: Affect only; often become tearful mystics or, in an earlier age, sages.

<u>Type D: Disorganised</u>

These unfortunates are children of abuse or trauma. They are contradictory, severely upset and appear peculiar with inappropriate affect. Carer is unpredictably insensitive. These children receive unpredictable or dangerous care. Multiple-, or part-strategies are used; regressive behaviours as if in an emotional no-man's land. Self is unworthy and 'bad'. Self has been severely damaged; no trust, dislike touch, confused and hopeless. Poor empathy, violence and anger are their currency. Overwhelmed by emotions of rage that need to be quashed.

> Predominantly: Cognitions and affect are chaotic.
>
> Parallels can be drawn between what Jung originally termed introvert and extrovert behaviour which also has its roots in childhood, the introvert depending more on inner life and feelings, the extrovert on outward life and cognitions.

Although there is no magic wand to repair all the damage (unless you are one of the few lucky ones with no damage at all) … stability, integration, counselling, reprocessing, and even re-parenting, can do some remedial work and help one recover. The idea is that you try not to damage your kids in the first place. Consistency is the key, but being consistently evil won't help, no more than a smack in the mouth will help silence a crying child whose message to you is a cry for love.

One of the main themes in Life Tree is that faulty attachment leads to a gap that leads to a miserable life that advertisers promise to fill with the lie that a certain product will make us feel happier. If you're not buying products, you might be using substances to ameliorate your inner turmoil (which might be housed in your unconscious [or pre-conscious] mind and therefore outside your awareness). Advertising at its best will make you do things that are completely outside your awareness, preying on your unconscious and unexpressed desires.

If life is all about beliefs, this means that some parents actually believe they are doing the right thing … really believe it, others are doing the right thing and worry that they're not, and others are doing the wrong thing, know it, and don't care! Still others want to do the right thing but don't know what the right thing is … they are clueless and so take their lead from washing powder advertisements in order to replicate what they think a happy family should look like; in buying their consumer goods, they unconsciously believe they will become a happy family. Naturally, advertisers know this and naturally, the purchases don't work, but at least it keeps the economy alive – just as it keeps the economy alive to encourage mothers to go back into work as soon as they have given birth. This in turn leads to more disenfranchisement, unhappiness and a deepened chasm that can never be filled by the purchase of an advertiser's product.

It also leads to a sense of unreality. Because 'new' people have had no role models, they have to make something up, so they adopt lifestyles of others and become addicted to reality TV shows ... the family they might never have had. They become intrigued about what might happen to soap opera characters, so impoverished are their own real lives. This leads in turn to pseudo people who are acting in certain manners and adopting characteristics that they have picked up through the media. People acting within their scripts and introjections is interesting; particularly pseudo-caring and how people think they must behave because they feel they ought to, rather than because they feel it is genuinely right so to do. To care or be a carer you must actually care. To be anything you must live it or you are a mercenary. This amounts to becoming more real, the *proper* you and not just a contrived version.

Bad Role Modelling

Some parents or spouses supply the *right* conditions in order for anxiety to thrive and, like a growing mushroom, they provide a dark, grim comfort zone. There is an unmistakable correlation between our upbringing and the lives we go on to lead; this is obvious and well researched. Due to wonky rearing procedures, we might clothe ourselves in hostility or become too trusting and therefore make ourselves available for others to exploit. As parents, we should be as careful as possible not to visit our own anxieties upon our children. However, this is incredibly difficult to avoid. We may even think we are great parents, and that we're right about everything we do ... therein lies the key to repeating problems of the past. It is weirdly surprising that most instances of child sexual abuse and rapes (child or adult) are perpetrated by people known to the victim, often their own family members. I could fill another book with instances of such abuse in the lives of my own clients ... it is rife and commonplace. It is all handed down through the generations as in Philip Larkin's 'This be the verse' and can take a very strong and informed victim to break this cycle. Tragically, a lot of abuse victims go on to repeat their own sufferings and do what was done unto them. This need not only apply to sexual abuse as it also includes physical abuse and other emotional tortures that commonly exist within families. This is the 'It never did me any harm' brigade. In reality, it is not character building to be smacked or beaten by an adult; it is demoralising and ruins self-esteem and teaches us that violence is an option for the answer. If in doubt, smack it.

In 1961 psychologist Albert Bandura set up an experiment at Stanford University to learn about the effects of adult behaviour upon children. A selection of twenty-four children were placed in a room and subsequently watched an adult treat a large doll to a series of brutal behaviours, treating it badly and pummelling the doll! The children were at the impressionable ages of three to six. When the adult left the room, the children mimicked him, and attacked the doll verbally and physically.

A control group of children witnessed another adult behave kindly towards the doll and, when he had left the room, they too were gentle. This kind of copying is called modelling and makes one wonder of the impact an abusive home can have on a child. Bandura's experiment gives us some answers. If a child sees abuse, he copies abuse; he becomes what he has known.

Reflect to think about what your children might be watching on television or violent, destructive computer games; or, even worse, consider the child who sees his father hitting his mother. In this modelling, the child learns that it is permissible to beat women and will take this into his adult life. No amount of tears and flowers will make up for this. If you are a person who feels that uncontrollable urge to use violence – male or female – leave the situation then go and get some appropriate counselling.

It should be fairly obvious that an abusive upbringing often leads to a troubled life; this has to be an irrefutable correlation. It seems that psychologist Eric Berne was right to suggest that we are all born princes and princesses and that subsequent life events (usually bad parenting) serve to turn us into frogs. This fits nicely with Philip Larkin's wry comment from the poem

This be the verse: "They fuck you up" and Oliver James's creative extrapolation of Larkin's poem in his eponymous book.

Unfortunately, you can create a psychopath by simply providing the wrong care for your baby. Don't worry too much about that last sentence because if you are worried about the wrong care, you won't be the one who would be creating a psychopath ... in fact you wouldn't be reading this or any book. Sadly, children that are not properly reared, seem to develop unusual circuitry as if their caring sides are somehow neutered. Because they were not cared for, they learn how not to care. This is the psychopath. They suffered angry and abusive childhoods featuring chaotic parenting, often resulting in random, violent outbursts and other damaging behaviours. This teaches the psychopath to expect trouble or create trouble where none might have existed, simply in order to feel ... it was his childhood currency.

After childhood, on the rampage, the psychopath visits his early disturbances upon our own streets and to people he may or may not know. Observe the killers Mark Dixie, Levi Bellfield, and Steve Wright; notorious in 2007's Britain. I wonder what sort of childhood these people had. Read almost any book about killers to discover the recipe for disaster that is contained in too many childhoods.

In the 1950s a psychologist named Harry Harlow performed some iconic experiments with small rhesus monkeys showing how different experiences affect them. Shortly after being born, the monkeys were taken from their mothers and placed in cages with fake mothers: both these fakes had light bulbs inside them to emit warmth and one was wrapped in a soft towel. The other fake was surrounded by a wire gauze so as not to be cuddly. Both the wire monkey and the soft one were able to administer milk. It was found that the suckling young monkeys preferred the cuddly monkey over the wire one and even if the cuddly one ran out of milk, the youngsters would go to the wire one for milk, have their fill, then return to the softer one for comfort and 'love'. It was also recorded that if the monkeys were in fear, they would go to the soft model for reassurance and comfort.

It is plain to see that the monkeys needed a live, cuddly carer in order to thrive as the monkeys who had been reared by the fake mothers found it difficult to interact with their peers. The same has been found in austere orphanages of yesteryear. Harlow also raised some monkeys to be isolated from the others. These tragic creatures became withdrawn in later life, scowling, rocking backwards and forwards, and some even self-harming by biting themselves. Even when a real surrogate monkey mum was introduced to the socially damaged young, they never recovered or became 'normal'. Transactional Analysis tells us that 'folks need strokes' and this is true for any creature. Observe how the cat purrs as you stroke her gently. We also need to be stroked in some way or another or we metaphorically shrivel.

Coupled with dodgy imprinting, modelling, and parental conditioning, many people these days seem to want to attach to and emulate role models from the world of celebrity. Your early life may have been couched within the confines of a bad family; perhaps nobody rescued you from your horrors. Perhaps nobody stroked you. A client of mine recently reeled in shock when I told him about the concept of unconditional love; he had never heard of the notion and did not even know it could exist. Many of us never experience unconditional love or know of its existence unless we are very lucky.

Following a famous prison experiment where some students had to pretend to be gaolers and some prisoners, Philip Zimbardo in 1971 found that, although the students were only playing a role, the gaolers actually turned bad and began torturing their peers in various ways! Zimbardo concluded that 'bad barrels' were the breeding ground for 'bad apples'. It might be that your family barrel was bad and you've since turned your back on it. If so, good for you. Life Tree is about trying to right past wrongs where possible, shed some light, and take responsibility for your future. This is why the fantasy of celebrity culture is so seductive. We look at our own grey lives and see the glitzy life of an A-lister and want a slice of it. If your breeding ground was bad, it's no wonder that you would like to find an escape. Celebrity offers this escape to a lucky few who are prepared to bare, and even lose, their souls.

Sometimes, society is no better than the bad barrel of a bad family. Our role models of celebrity play a huge influence upon us, especially if we are young and gullible. In my initial drafts of *Broken Britain?* I was going to list a host of celebrities who I think are partly responsible for the demise of Britain today. Then I was reminded of libel and slander and concluded that it is almost impossible to cite anyone at all without evidence or concrete proof. Many of those I was going to mention are very rich and very famous and probably very litigious. Although misbehaving stars and celebrities should take notice that Britain is a very forgiving place and the judgements of the fifties and sixties are long gone. So if I did cite you in this insignificant little page, it wouldn't matter anyway because you are adored by everyone and have lots of besotted fans and enough money to gag people who might damage your reputation – even though no words would damage your reputation because most of Britain doesn't actually care what you do! (The only exception to this is child abuse.)

So, if you are a 'naughty' celebrity, you will probably be forgiven. You wouldn't have been fifty years ago, and you might not be now by certain sections of society, but mainstream Britain aspires to be you. If you are an avid drug abuser you will be forgiven if you make all the right noises about rehabilitation. If you have children to a variety of different men, so what? Nobody cares that much anyway. If you are a sex worker, it won't matter that much if you are earning money as most of Britain only cares about money. Morality and religion have almost disappeared now and if one starts to judge others – God forbid – then the judgement becomes worse than the act one is judging. As far as examples of bad role modelling is concerned – the actual people – talk or hear about them at your local bar or next family gathering, then you can judge for yourself.

Something has changed. Society has become very tolerant of drug users. Can we name a big star who doesn't or hasn't used drugs? I suppose there will be a few. Consider the folly of sacking every entertainer or presenter who had taken drugs … there would probably be very few people left in the industry. So perhaps we have to tolerate them. This is one thing, but why then pretend that no-one takes drugs at all? This is hypocrisy in the purest form. If we do not want our children to be drug users, then we should not tolerate our celebrities using drugs. If we do tolerate it, we give out a message of acceptance and therein lies the paradox. If celebrities can get away with it and still be famous and rich, then why shouldn't everyone else? One can even have a sex video out on the internet and get away with that too. It's a shame the Romans didn't have videophones. Scandal has always existed but perhaps nowadays it's more apparent. I maintain that it is irresponsible to be an obviously proud drug user in the face of the fact that drugs ruin people's lives.

Rap music – I need not cite a particular rapper as most of it is misogynistic, homophobic, and violent. Rap celebrates *gangsta* culture, drug use, and pornography. Much has been said and written about rap music and its effect on the young who listen to it. If you are religious, rap is evil. If you are a disenfranchised young teen who wants a receptacle for his inner turmoil, rap is perfect. *Mein Kampf* infiltrated the psyches of a whole nation and led to horrific consequences. In my opinion, rap plays the same role and oftentimes the lyrics are almost as appalling as Hitler's book. What harm can you do with a pen? A lot. Couple those lyrics to the pornographic videos that usually accompany them and you have a recipe for badness.

Without wanting to sound like a beard or look like a Dad dancing at a wedding, I like Eminem for the wrong reasons; the lyrics on his first three albums are witty and funny and very engaging. Marshall Mathers's passion is almost peerless. Sadly, the message can so easily be taken the wrong way.

In the sixties and seventies, having children to different fathers meant that you were a whore or a fool. Nowadays it doesn't seem to matter at all. Many young women want a carefree life with a variety of partners. How startlingly things have changed. My concern is that many women who have many children by different fathers put themselves in financial jeopardy and often rely on benefits in order to feed their children.

At this point I was going to make a list of antics carried out by footballers but the list would be too long. Dogging, spit-roasting, swinging, and all that. It warms your heart. None of this would surprise the Romans though who were doing it all before the premier league existed and, in the spirit of tolerance, perhaps the attitude should be get on with it if you can get away with it? It has not escaped my notice that many who moan about hedonism unconsciously envy the hedonists! They moan because they're jealous. After the fall of Rome and the rise of Christianity, Western society has become entrenched in hypocrisy. Half of us want to be hedonists, enjoying each day regardless of the consequences, and the other half of us want to resist everything and wait for a better life after death. The latter are the ones who write to newspapers bleating about celebrities and broken Britain. This might sound like a contradictory argument but if the celebrities are really enjoying themselves, what has it got to do with anyone else? So the question one should ask is: are you a Roman or a Christian!

Reality show contestants – intriguingly, many of them become famous for doing nothing. They are not musicians or artistes or great thinkers … merely contenders on an intrusive TV programme. Some of these people portray a belief that one can become rich just for having appeared on a show for a few weeks. I wonder if they're ever prepared for the ensuing media scrum once they leave the show? Jade Goody's recent, sad demise was another telling indictment of how society invades the normal lives of others, even in death. We seem to be curious about the sometimes boring lives of others instead of looking into our own existences.

Of course, no one is all bad and many of the stars I haven't mentioned probably do a lot for charity and all that. I wonder if it is so reprehensible that some stars reveal to us their genitals as they leave their cars? Many stars these days are known for their sex video scandals … it's as if the celebrity life style has such an effect upon them they find it impossible to control themselves. As these stars deliberately flout laws and flaunt their naughty ways, alongside them goes society's morals which are Christian/Jewish/Islamic codes. There is nothing you can do about this and moaning won't help or change anything. If you are infuriated by any of the stars' antics, I'm afraid you'll just have to get used to it because there's nothing you can do. It's as if everyone has vices, but they claim to be squeaky clean. If anyone claims to be squeaky clean, don't believe them; that's a good place to start, and that way, you won't be disappointed.

You can only ever change your own behaviour and become squeaky yourself – if that's what you want.

But there is more to it than flashing your bits to the press. There has also been a marked decline in respect ... respect for one's self and others. The popular business shows on TV show the dreams of entrepreneurs being analysed and often massacred. Big business cheeses rant and rip into people's ideas without any humility on their own part, confirming that the UK needs to be put even further down in terms of ego and confirming the 'fact' that if you're not successful, you're a loser and an idiot.

These so called business gurus often display no humility and are filled with hubris, confirming their own perceived genius; Richard Branson always seems a bit humble to me, as does Bill Gates ... thank God there are at least two left. There are a lot of millionaires who claim that the first million is the hardest part – after that, the money makes more money (unless you are a cretin who stuffs it up his nose); so it's a bit rich to sit on a business programme if you've inherited it all ... perhaps the best advice the lucky could give is "Hey, be born into wealth" – for what do they know about making money or poverty or shopping for cheaper food?

With celebrities, their money gives them the freedom to do whatever they please and they flaunt their hedonism wherever they please as well. This is all very well for them but has a deleterious influence on the young minds that so admire them. If you are a really rich person reading this, and you are invited to go on a business programme, why not simply say ... well, I was born rich and I became richer and, to be honest, there is little chance for *you*. Not much social mobility takes place anyway – just the notion that it exists. Look at most people you know and where they were born and what they do now ... most of them will be in about the same position or a little bit better off.

Naturally, I've got to be careful what I write as I may evoke narcissistic rage in some of these people who believe they have created their own wealth. Having been brought up being told that they are going to be great one day, it may come as a shock to them that they haven't created anything, but simply been given the right tools to maintain it. The lucky and the ones who have lived lives anathema to the lives of the scroat ... they couldn't be more different. Anyway, I hope not to upset anyone. *Broken Britain?* is about observations, not judgements. The intention is to highlight reality. Others who have done this were simply laughed at or ignored: Marx, Beethoven, Mozart, Da Vinci, Newton, etc.

Politicians are no better at providing a good example. Most of us can recall affairs of the heart that have toppled political careers. We could easily judge those sagas and cast aspersions, but who can say when Cupid's arrow will strike. I don't fully despair as troubles such as these have always been covered up and one only has to read Dickens to know how bleak times were back then. It's not much better now in actual fact but at least consumerism, bling and shopping malls make it all appear more palatable by placing a veneer of gloss over the steaming bile that is life in the 21st century.

People in Britain like to mock each other and put each other down. This can protect them against their own insecurities as they project their nastiness onto others in the guise of humour. When they see they have upset someone they will say they're only joking. More often than not, the person being ridiculed just laughs it off so as not to upset the tormentor. In my view, this creates a sense of insecurity and uncertainty that feeds upon itself.

Common British put-downs

Subtle, 'well-meaning' put-downs include:
"Don't get too big for your boots."
Why not? So I can end up in a dead end job and be a loser like you? Sometimes people talk about being encouraged *not* to build their hopes up. Some parents want their children to remain humble. Perhaps because their child's success could threaten the parents' sense of insecurity. Comments such as these are fuelled by jealousy.
"Keep your feet in the ground."
Why?
"You're getting too clever you are ..."
Too clever for what exactly?
I say subtle and well-meaning comments because they appear to be well-meaning but they are delivered usually by someone who is jealous of the success you *might* achieve. These comments are a way of undermining your confidence and should be treated with a polite contempt.
Someone once said to me: "You don't suit a posh car", after I'd bought a posh car. Why not exactly? Because yours is a shit one? My response here is not driven by arrogance but the person was subtly saying that I was not worthy of a posh car. How rude. In the same week someone else *joked* that my new car looked like the car of a drug dealer! Another insipid comment but very telling about the one who delivered it. Still another said they preferred the 'Kompressor' model. Of course, these comments are fuelled by jealousy and one has to insulate oneself against the put-down comments of others. Try not to be dragged down by them. Your real friends will genuinely admire your car and be pleased for you. Tell ten people that you've just bought a 500SE Mercedes-Benz and observe their reactions: their comments will reveal how they feel about you and how they feel about themselves in relation to you. Their responses will be manifold: "Oh dear, you'll get it scratched"; "Oh I bet that costs a lot on petrol"; "Oh, how did *you* ever afford that?"; "Oh, you'll look like a drug dealer"; "Oh a posh car won't suit you" ... and many others will give many other responses that don't begin with 'Oh'. If I chose to be pulled around in a rickshaw all day, what

right it is for anyone else to comment? I ignore these despicable dullards as much as possible and their words really don't bother me. There are some, however, who would become very upset by such comments. To these poor souls, their confidence would really be shattered.

Your detractors are the people who will undermine you and drag you down to their level <u>if you let them</u>. In not allowing their comments to take effect you are rising above them; don't be phased by their thin-humour and don't let them cast doubt in your mind. By ignoring them, your Mercedes will become even more annoying to them. I have observed many clients becoming extremely upset by an offhanded joke or comment told at their expense.

People will always be around to have a go at us and, depending how sensitive we are, they can hurt and scald our inner selves. It's the British way to be self- and other-effacing and no-one seems to like a big head. However, if the put-downs are too crippling, this can have a detrimental effect upon our psyches that can be with us for the rest of our lives. Much of how we 'turn out to be' comes from childhood 'givens' and the families in which we were raised.

Child rearing is a fine balance between too much discipline, the wrong kind of discipline, and setting the right boundaries so that young ones eventually learn to construct their own parameters for existence. Without boundaries of any kind, we go on to live lives of laxity, resenting those who apply societal boundaries such as the police or teachers. If we are not taught right from wrong, how will we know what not to do? I think this perfectly highlights the binge drinking problems in Britain today where we see hoards of young men and women who are plainly out of control because they were never taught to control themselves … never given boundaries or limitations. Perhaps they were never shown what was right or wrong because their parents themselves had no knowledge, having been brought up by careless free-love exponents. We now see streets littered with careless miscreants, drunk, on drugs, and having sex in alleys. Those who argue in favour of liberal alcohol laws suggest that countries such as Spain, Italy, and France suffer no binge drinking; but our louts are quite different to our European neighbours. Most importantly, those countries often cited as paragons of responsible drinking are predominantly Catholic and I believe that this has instilled a set of virtuous and noble values into its populace. Additionally, older European countries are more family orientated and their offspring are more likely to have been nurtured properly by their mothers; this is not the case in Britain – a fractured, fragmented country that has little hope of recovery whilst politicians encourage mothers to work and some advertisers keenly push their poisons down our throats at every opportunity. So we see the results of this debauchery every weekend on our town and city streets. The problem is amorality brought about from the sixties and the results of a late industrialized nation at the end of its life which has nothing to offer to ameliorate an alienated and disengaged youth.

In order for parents to make good future citizens out of their children, they need to teach wrong from right and be good role models themselves; subsequently the children then learn responsibility and independence. If a child regularly sees his father or mother binge drinking or smoking pot, she is likely to copy and normalize this experience. Even though they are drinking poison, the French don't seem to teach binge drinking because alcohol forms part of their mealtimes (together as a family) and therefore alcohol plays a different role. I think the wine-loving British middle-class has strived for this continental experience but I'm not sure if it has worked. And since it is cool to be bad, there is almost a shame about being middle-class now, so middle-class university students will happily get *shit-faced* with their blue collar counterparts if only to prove that they are not as middle-class as their peers believe. They want to be seen as renegades, rebels.

It is in teaching good boundaries and behaviours that the next generation comes to hold responsibility within society. The child becomes independent and leaves the nest. For this development, certain parameters need to have been installed. From their first steps when learning to walk, to their first flat or leaving home for university, each move towards independence will involve some degree of discomfort ... out of this will come growth and personal development. Parents have to bestow this independence upon their offspring and allow them to grow in confidence. That is – if the parents get it right. Obviously many parents get it wrong, so ingrained is the bad model and fragmented family that now exists in the UK. It appears that most people want to get rat-arsed just to escape their humdrum routines and they show this model to their children who go on to copy it.

If the family doesn't welcome certain emotions – and many families don't, emotions will become suppressed and perhaps return to bite us in later life. Instead of being helped to express negative emotions, they are denied. It would take a strong child to say 'I'm not going to be like my parents because they drink too much and talk shit and embarrass themselves'. In this quest for independence, children will simply copy bad examples because most children believe that their parents' way is the right way.

Eventually, all the genuine feelings become buried and suppressed within the unconscious mind. Intoxicating substances become an attractive way to escape from bad feelings and unexpressed emotions. The lure of drugs and alcohol becomes so appealing, so that the damaged person can hide within their offerings. Naturally, we have defence mechanisms behind which to hide but there is always a chance of leakage when the person is perhaps stressed: then the hidden emotions leak out and can cause havoc. In this sense, the child will become swamped by family patterns and normalize the seemingly normal behaviour, whether it's binge drinking, throwing up after a big meal, or even sexual abuse. Wrong things become 'right' and abnormal behaviours appear normal in the family. This normalizing tendency can lead to us thinking we're in the right when we are actually wrong or in error ... projecting blame perhaps onto everyone else. So they go on drinking or snorting in order to cover up anxieties that were never addressed ... to compensate for a bad upbringing.

Some parents may not even be able to relate to their own children, at some level denying their existence. The reason for this is usually found in the parents' own childhood. Those who have had odd upbringings are often odd around children, finding it difficult to relate to them. Often, these are the people who have cats instead of children! It is no wonder that those with unhappy childhoods (though they often deny this to be the case) choose not to repeat the experience. If you were not loved as a child, how can you now give love? The child in this family will never experience congruent love; perhaps he will become a token baby, something to dress up in designer clothes: an extension of the mother's own insecurities.

A scientist called Konrad Lorenz discovered that goslings became *imprinted* by the first living thing they saw. The young geese followed and copied any animal who could have been their mother. Imprinting of a kind also goes on in later childhood too when children copy their role models. They habituate patterns of behaviour and take up these patterns as their own. It is too easy a cop-out to blame schools for the state of today's youth when any blame can be laid squarely on the shoulders of faulty parenting. This all happens before school age anyway, so why blame bad teachers or the education system?

If the family used a certain chemical substance to alleviate certain feelings, we can easily and logically see how addictions can arise and become ingrained. It becomes the way a family functions and a way to suppress its skeletons.

Many families project inner turmoil onto others, subconsciously allowing another agency to carry their own bad feelings. It can easily be seen that supporting extremist groups like the BNP (and many others) is a way of projecting our inwardly bad feelings onto other groups. One can use extremist political organizations to carry one's own hatred. Additionally, if something is going wrong in your life, a soft target will always be easy to find onto which to vent your venom. What we should do of course is look within ourselves and make changes from there, from within. People who are happy on the inside don't go around racially abusing others or blaming others for "taking our jobs"; instead, they retrain and work on their own personal angst in order to enrich their own lives … in this way, they become consequently happier and less likely to project their hatred onto other (probably innocent) groups. It is easy to find scapegoats for one's anger. English people used to hate the Irish and/or the Scots, then it was the Afro-Caribbeans, then the Asians; now it's the Eastern Europeans. All immigrants are trying to make a better life for themselves and wouldn't you do the same in their position? Brits (like me) who hate the weather are leaving this country in droves to go to Australia and Spain, where they go on to colonize and make ex-pat communities, just as the Asians have done here. As a people we like to be in familiar groups with those who share our norms and values. If you would do the same as the Polish or the Romanians, why blame them? Why not improve your own life instead? Here, a variety of psychological phenomena take place such as splitting (seeing *them* as all bad), paranoia (*they* come over here, get benefits and take *our* jobs), projection (projecting your vitriol onto others and ignoring your own inner state, instead of looking at why you're so angry) … All these defence mechanisms are fuelled by anxiety and fear of the unknown.

Living on your knees

There are people of my acquaintance who still live with their parents at the age of forty. In current culture they would be labelled as 'sad' as they have plainly not made their own way in life and are content to allow their parents to go on looking after them. The people I'm thinking about don't have any physical ailments preventing them from becoming independent, but they must be socially crippled mustn't they? These forty-year-old children have full-time employment and some qualifications but have never had regular partners and they have never flown the parental nest. I think these kinds of situations were more common two-hundred-plus years ago in pre-industrialized Britain when we were more rural, but there is no real or obvious reason why two forty-year-old siblings should still be ensconced with their parents in a small house. There is a sweet sit-com like feeling about all this but there is also the spectre of having lived a wasted life. They make excuses like not being able to afford mortgages but all their peers have managed it. So what keeps them bound to Mummy and Daddy's apron strings? Perhaps it's fear? Eric Berne suggested that we get mortgages in our twenties, when we are most potent, yet by the time we pay them off, we are in our middle to late forties when all our zest has been squeezed from us by the travails of life. Perhaps these siblings have cleverly avoided being sucked into this impotent state by hiding behind their parents forever. But is this really living?

Do you want to make your children so dependent on you that they will never grow fully formed adult wings, never feel separate enough from you that they ever have the courage to break away? If you want this to happen, you can do this by putting them down (thinly disguised as humour but laced with sarcasm) and in doing so eroding their confidence to the degree that they never feel worthy or self-assured enough to get a partner or a home of their own.

Little Billy was the apple of his Nan's eye. She took over his care because his mother didn't want him shortly after he was born. His mother was a good time girl and didn't need a baby in tow ... he would have spoiled her fun. She resented his being born without acknowledging her own vital role in the process. Fortunately, Billy was more than rescued by his Nan and her friends who brought him up as a good Christian, took him on holidays and generally adored him. It could have been very different for Billy. Had his mother or unknown father been responsible for his upbringing, he would have probably ended up like most unwanted baby-boomers ... unloved, on the streets, bitter and angry. Billy's story could be a book in its own right but, most importantly, he recalls being grateful that those older carers rescued him and showed him 'the right way'. We can see that Billy's life and the lives of many others in similar situations can be blighted by ruinous upbringings. Billy was lucky to have been rescued. Many are not.

It is interesting that Billy was almost completely without a male role model throughout his entire childhood. This is increasingly common with the ever-growing rate of single-motherhood. We all know and agree how hard single-motherhood must be, whilst we wonder who created this aloneness. It is controversial and (nowadays) politically incorrect to even mention males who are brought up without male role models and how they often turn out to be gay. Like the overweight, homosexuals are keen to make genetic interpretations of their state; however, it can still be observed that most gay males have distant (perhaps alcoholic or useless) fathers, come from mother-dominated households, and have not 'learnt' how to become a heterosexual man. Freudians would probably argue that gay males are seeking their father in the form of phallic representation and relationships with other men and the more promiscuous they are, the greater is their need for a father. This is a weighty statement and one likely to cause anger in modern Britain, but it is an explanation I can quite buy since my own gay clients are commonly without one or the other sex parent. Readers unfamiliar with psychoanalytic ideas may find this a bit rich, or even shocking, or insulting – to others it will make perfect sense. I do not speak for the psychoanalytic community by any means and it has become very fashionable to embrace gay culture; therefore my comments are not homophobic (because I do not fear or resent homosexuals) but merely observations. We always seek to find what we believe is missing and this is done on an unconscious level, although it is fashionable to put it down to genes. In many ways, the explanation of homosexuality doesn't matter that much but rather that we, as a permissive society, acknowledge *they* exist and do not torture them. For more on this, see the work of Nicolosi.

An iconic figure in the writings and research of child rearing was the very eminent John Bowlby, and he is in no doubt about single parentage. Again, I know how modern Britons say they don't like to judge anyone and being a single parent has now become normalized, but Bowlby (2005) seemed very clear in his argument that it was best that two people raised a child ... its father and mother ... and it takes a lot of energy and commitment. This seems to make a lot of sense yet hedonists seem all too keen to walk away from their responsibilities so keen are they to pursue their own happiness and get another partner if their current one doesn't *make them* happy. A friend of mine, who has just deserted his two young children and wife told me that he still loved his wife but he was not *in love* with her. I had to stifle my contempt upon hearing such a well-worn cliché. This friend has decided to leave his family because he's not in love any more. So what? His two children adored him and now he's gone. Is not the adoration of your children enough for you to stay married, or at least try to work things out with someone whom you once loved?

Often, people raised in chaotic families are more likely to have illegitimate children, to become teenage mothers, to make unhappy marriages, and get divorced. Again, this makes sense. This is not to say that if my friend had stayed married his offspring would have gone berserk … on the contrary. But there is another modern myth that if you don't represent the smiling family pictured in TV advertisements then you should seek a more happy life. Again, this is where advertising sets its claws into our collective unconsciousness. I think we've all heard, "well, me and the wife weren't happy and the kids could feel it, so we had to split up", or variations thereof. Of course, if you and your wife are throwing knives at each other then perhaps you should be parted, but if you have children, surely you should have altruistic aims rather than me, me, me. I know as a fact that my friend's children will be devastated by his disappearance. My self serving friend is involved in fulfilling his own goals. Many people are so wrapped up in themselves and fulfilling their own egos that they neglect their responsibilities completely. Maintenance payments do not compensate for your presence.

Conversely, there is no need to tolerate abuse and if you are being *domestically* (physically or sexually) abused, then it's probably best to get away and take your children with you. If someone is hitting you and you stay around, you are giving them the message that their behaviour is acceptable. Also, I have found with numerous clients that if partners hit you once they will hit you again, and again, and again. Each outburst of violence gives way to tears and apologies and flowers, and promises never to do it again, but it inevitably happens again. It almost always does and in my experience as a counsellor, I have never met an abused client who has been abused only once … this is also reflected in the experience of my colleagues. Some people, because of their pasts, have a tendency to stay with their abusers; perhaps they have low self-esteem and feel they don't deserve a better partner. Others always seem to end up in the same destructive relationships, seemingly attaching themselves to harmful partnerships and coming out battered and bruised all the time. This is often known as co-dependency, where you feel that you can't be without your abuser (perhaps on an unconscious level) and you don't really want to free yourself.

Undoubtedly, these sorts of relationships can have profound effects upon your health. Continued stress upon the nervous system; and especially stress in one's home-life or love-life; can be a precursor to many illnesses as well as auto-immune disorders. It is regrettable that many of us feel unable to leave harmful relationships when they have run their course. Disease often becomes a manifestation for a sad life and a sign that something is amiss. Much research points the way to healthy states once again being reinstated after toxic relationships have been left behind.

This kind of toxic-relationship co-dependency is not helped by the proliferation of love songs that permeate our unconscious minds and serve as an accompaniment to our daily lives: they constantly churn out the notion that one cannot exist without another. The list of titles is endless: "I can't smile without you" (why not?), "Stand by your man" (why? Because he's 'doing things you don't understand?'), "You are my destiny" … you can find your own love songs and identify why the lyrics are never usually based on rational thinking. They perpetuate the myth that we are nothing without our significant other. Logically this is nonsense and it is another way our subconscious minds become polluted, making us dependent on others. Unnecessarily so. This can lead to a state of co-dependency where one partner has low self-esteem, believes love songs, and ends up becoming abused. Obviously, the songs in themselves don't make one co-dependent, but they don't help. More on co-dependency later.

Unfortunately, the Bible, and books like it, can encourage us to suffer abuse or stay with unsuitable partners. We can even be encouraged to tolerate beatings and the like just because we are told we are sinners. Are we sinners just for being born or for being human or for what reason? Proverbs 23:13 says: "Withhold not correction from the child for if thou beatest him with the rod, he shall not die". Proverbs 23:14 says: "Thou shall beat him with the rod and shalt deliver his soul from death". And what should we be beaten for? Adultery? Lying? Envy?

Obviously the way we interpret the scriptures has great bearing on how we live our lives through them (if we do) but I would question their relevance in today's society. Without them, what are we? Human – that's about it.

The Bible, and similar books have a lot to answer for. I think the Bible is a bit like Eminem … you take from it what you will and interpret it in a way that suits you. Whilst this sounds odd, that's what most religious groups do anyway, and that's why there are so many denominations – because no one can agree on the word of God, if indeed there is a word. I can almost imagine a convention on how best to beat a child. As I type this sentence someone under-16 is getting smacked 'for their own good'. Although Proverbs says that if we beat the child, he will not die, some parents, following this advice, don't know when to stop and go on torturing their offspring until we have notorious cases like Victoria Columbie or Kimberly Harte or Baby P, and so many others, who actually suffer excruciating and indescribable cruelty at the hands of their evil *care* givers. When you hit a child, something inside them dies; you will see that a light has been extinguished in their eyes. You will have added to their future bank of unhappiness and despair. Consider the effects of writings such as Proverbs on witless or scroat parents; it's little wonder that so many children become ruined by their upbringings. I wish I could say that they meant well. How much well would I mean if I smacked *you* in the face for your own good?

Exercise

In the spirit of Alcoholics Anonymous' *Big Book*, and other 12-step programmes, you need to make amends for any past actions that may have caused you shame.

Start by making a list. The list could include money you have borrowed (or stolen), children you have hit, people you have hurt, things you said you would do but did not. It is now time to make amends. Pay-back time.

If you have suffered at the hands of others, make a similar list.

Eventually you will have two lists that you can examine and decide how you are going to make amends and how you are going to heal yourself. Can you approach people whom you have hurt or the people who have hurt you?

Is there any means for reconciliation?

Your genes and DNA

Here is a typical (abridged) segment from a client session I recently engaged in:

Zandra: It's me genes and they've found a fat gene. Well I don't know really and maybe it's just wishful thinking but it must be something to do with my genes as I just can't stop eating.

AK: You can't stop?

Z: Well I stop eventually but sometimes I even get up in the night for a midnight feast, y'know like that old R.Whites lemonade advert? But with me it's not lemonade, it's biscuits and cakes and crisps and ice cream … anything tasty.

AK: And you do this when everyone else is asleep?

Z: Yeah, because I'd feel so guilty otherwise. Stuffing my moon at three in the morning. Then my daughter wonders where all her school snacks have gone. But I think she knows.

AK: And how do you feel when you eventually stop?

Z: Sick … sad … guilty. That's why I think it must be genes because I can't seem to help it.

AK: Well as far as I know genes have little to do with it. We spoke in our last session about sugar and how it's metabolized and the insulin response didn't we?

Z: I know but it's just so fuckin' sad innit?

AK: Well, you're just human and too much sugar is addictive and you mention all the foods that are laden with sugar and fat.

Z: Well thanks for that. You've made me feel worse now.

AK: I didn't mean to make you feel bad, Zandra ... I just want to bring home the sugar response and ...

Z: Yeah I know all about it. I even read that Jangoly book and it all makes sense.

AK: So ...

Z: Well I don't really know why I binge and I suppose I want something to blame it on. What do you say?

AK: Well what if there was a fat gene? Even if there was, it wouldn't necessarily compel you to over eat. I think that what we put into our mouths is vastly more important than any genetic connection. I also think that scientists are desperate to discover some kind of blame for obesity so we can all go on munching sugar and processed foods and blame it on something beyond our control, i.e. genes.

Z: Mmm, so should I have an apple?

AK: Only if you want to. It's all about choices. You choose sugary, processed foods but you could equally choose fruit couldn't you? Fruit can be sweet too.

Z: Yeah I suppose so, but it's not like a chocolate orange is it (laughing)?

AK: No, but at least you don't have to unwrap an apple.

Zandra is desperate to lose weight and has tried every diet I've ever heard of. There is a hugely prosperous diet industry that thrives off people who are looking for answers. Zandra is human and she lives in this Western world where processed foods are mercilessly pushed at us at every opportunity. I recently stopped at a motorway services on the M1 and was shocked to find a VAST array of confectionery on my way to paying for some items. I capitalise the word vast because I think of myself as a particularly savvy consumer when it comes to being sold to, but this really was the most extravagant array of sweets I have ever seen in my life, anywhere. The merchandising displays had crossed that line between subtle and garish and, to use a metaphor, I was looking at a Thai lady-boy with her bits hanging out, so ludicrous was the display. No one else seemed as moved as I was with the spectacle, as they loaded their arms with big crisp packets and large chocolate bars lest they got hungry between this service station and the one twenty miles down the road. Literally everywhere you looked was a bar of temptation, a brown lump of sugar and fat. It's no wonder that people like Zandra (and myself in past years) are tempted to throw something down their necks as they wait in the queue. Make no mistake, queues are good for profits at these selling points and that's what it's all about ... profit. Once you can see you are encouraged to be a hamster on the capitalist's treadmill, perhaps you can check out of it and vote with your tempted fingers. This has nothing to do with genes or DNA. Obesity rarely does.

Medics will be scrambling frantically in science laboratories to find this elusive fat gene so that massive drug conglomerates can medicate and sell drugs to us. At the time of writing I am unaware of any fat gene or anything like it, but I am very aware of aggressive retailing, awesome advertising and manipulative sales techniques. If readers want to know why Britain is getting fatter, call at a motorway services shop and see for yourself. More importantly, if genes make our eye colour, and scientists are to isolate a fat gene (a gene which encourages us to put on weight or means that we have a slow metabolism) this would still mean that you would have to eat a load of sugar and fat to remain obese. Herein lies a paradox. Most people are looking for a fat gene to blame for their own lack of control. It's as if we like to blame anything and anyone but ourselves. But I ask you ... who puts the food in your mouth? The increasingly popular gastric band and stomach stapling operations also highlight how some people seem so unable to refrain from *bad* foods, that they go to these extreme lengths.

This chapter is necessarily short because I am not a genetic scientist. For sure, your genes made you who you are, but I believe that, in the nurture/nature debate, life and our outcomes are more about nurture, so it's no use blaming genes for every ailment.

Love

If you had a lovely early life, great. If you had parents who supported you in your dreams and didn't apply pressure on you and loved you unconditionally, that's great too. However, most of us don't fall into this category. Our parents should support us and encourage us and should know about 'theory of mind' … most parents don't. You can read about theory of mind in most child psychology books or look on Google. If you are to grow into a rounded adult, you need unconditional love. This means that you will be loved no matter what you do and no matter who you marry, and no matter what career you choose. Because parents are keen to project their own failed dreams onto their children, they get caught up in making their offspring live their lives for them like 'mini-me' in the Austin Powers' films. This is a tragedy.

In many ways, early sufferings are like the Newton's cradle. You may know the Isaac Newton law that states that to every action there is an equal but opposite reaction. If you suffered bad early care, it is likely that you will have a more challenging later life, unless you repress all your memories. The reaction to your early life comes out eventually in your behaviour and emotions (or you might just be slightly odd or a loner and not care).

If you are to fulfil your dreams as a growing teenager or even an older person, it is beneficial if you have a support system in place. You should have had one as a child but the evidence is all around us on the streets that many teenagers are the result of an emotionally crippled, destitute childhood that was devoid of love, permanence and often entailed physical and sexual abuse. Sadly, these people have not been loved and you can see this on their pained, gnarled faces as they huddle in shop doorways and caress their tins of cider and spliffs. They neck their equally impoverished teen sex partners in the subconscious hope that the love they lacked will be found in the arms of someone who has no love to give. Then they go on to have illegitimate (politically incorrect word these days) babies whom they cannot love. If you were never loved how can you give love to anyone else?

The importance of what I shall call 'The Boiler Room' is most essential to the making of most successful people and to the ethos presented in Life Tree. Many 'winners' have had support from others during their quest for fame and fortune. This is not to denigrate these achievers, it's just that they have been given lots of assistance to get there; it is just the way that life has transpired for them. The people who offer their support (boiler-folk) usually love the trainee millionaire (or they wouldn't do it) or they at least tolerate them. The boiler-folk are quite happy to feed, finance, and encourage their protégés until their dreams are met.

This essential support from a boiler room can be emotional – very important for encouraging success – or it can be financial; perhaps even more important if you're hungry. If you have both, you simply cannot fail if you have one iota of ambition and you're not a dullard.

The world is full of successful people who had a boiler room and have been, often unwittingly, groomed for success. Writing this, I realise I might not even be able to get it published as most publishing companies seem to be run by nepotists or beneficiaries of boiler rooms, so these words might evoke their ire. As you now look on the inside cover, you will perhaps notice that this book is self-published via Lulu.com and, if it's not, it will have been a very lucky stroke on my part if a mainstream publisher ever takes it on. I can't afford to bribe anyone, I haven't been on a reality TV show, and I don't know anyone who has a flicker of influence in any sphere whatsoever, so my chances are slim! The same thing happened to David Icke. Although he is not everyone's cup of tea, he is an indisputably successful writer with a point to make – yet he had to self-publish for the same reasons as I will have done. For some, the truth is an irksome bed partner. Perhaps this is why Karl Marx died a pauper and the irony is not wasted on the fact that he who bleated about the means of production had no capital success when approaching capitalistic publishers; and consider the double irony of being buried in Highgate ... one of the poshest areas of London! Even Marx had a benefactor and it wasn't unknown for his comrade Engels to give him money for beer and food. So I've set up a beautiful paradox ... I write a self-help book which rants about society and the need to know someone influential in order to fulfil your goals ... and then the book doesn't get published. There's bitter irony for you.

David writes:

"Because they never wanted me as a kid, I always felt like I was in the way. I went to university eventually – which was a miracle – but I dropped out because I simply didn't have the support that my peers enjoyed. Their parents would buy them things and bail them out. The student grant was a grant at the time but how can the state make up for a friend of yours who had a Dad who pays all her bills and accommodation and a Mum who sends her a shopping cheque every month? I was just out of it. My parents split up when I was young and my mother had a lot of boyfriends; I think she stopped just short of charging them. I think that when your parents separate, they just become interested in their new lives and want you to just fade away. I had no assistance whatsoever and it made me sad and angry. I even slept on a police bench one night, claiming that my hotel was closed ... in actual fact I had nowhere else to go. I could have ended up a tramp but I eventually got a wee job that alleviated my immediate problems. It was hard, and it still is. I will never forget the fact that I was unwanted, deserted ... the great unwashed. I still see my Mother today but it's a shallow, superficial relationship with small talk. I will never forgive her for abandoning me."

The relationship between boiler-folk and dreamers must be symbiotic. That is to say, each participant in the game must give and take something. I have seen many fledgling careers shatter upon the rocks simply through lack of finance at the last hurdle. In the early days of my counselling training I had a colleague who could not complete her training because she simply could not afford to carry on. She had no support from anywhere and could, I felt, have achieved great things had finances permitted this.

The boiler stoker must get something out of this symbiotic relationship unless he loves and supports you unconditionally and is quite happy to be your benefactor; perhaps he is waiting for an assumed or promised pay-off when your dreams come true? Perhaps the boiler stoker's muse is well hung and gorgeous? This will help as there appear to be many well-heeled, rich women (whose husbands have died creating that wealth) who are willing to fund a young man's dreams in order to get a dose of rampant attention. Tragically, six-pack young men are often not that bright: more gym, less reading time.

This explains the golf-club-wife syndrome. Notice at your local private school how many women swan around in posh cars appearing to have nothing to do all day but arrange luncheons and have colonic irrigations. Some of these women will plan to invest in property which will go awry until their rich husband or boyfriend rescues them. These women usually *belong* to rich men who have highly paid jobs or, more likely, will have inherited their money and pretend they have worked hard for it, never acknowledging their luck. In exchange for being financed, the wife will have to look good and take to wearing lots of make-up as she ages or even going for surgical enhancements. In exchange for her gold card, the wife usually has to relinquish some of her personal power, perhaps by becoming an accomplished fellatrice. However, one doesn't see evidence of her oral adroitness as she infers she's a self-made winner, driving by in her Porsche, a manicured finger in the air. I'm sorry if this sounds like sexism and sometimes it works the other way round, in which case the man should be hung (not hanged).

Boiler room workers should support your ambitions and the bigger your boiler room, the more chance of your success. Most self-help books write on the premise that it is possible to achieve anything you dream about if you engage in positive thinking, or change your state (NLP), or adopt an endless array of book-selling gimmicks. This is a fallacy largely created to sell books and inveigle another sucker into believing in the American dream. Very often, the dream is but a nightmare. Nothing beats having someone who will bet on you when your chips are down. So you must be a genuinely good seller of dreams, or have lots of sexual techniques up your sleeve. Your chips may always be down and you might end up a loser.

If you're not interested in having someone else stoke your boiler, you might have to stoke your own, which will distract you from your goals if you have to earn a living to support yourself ... far better to have someone else to do this for you, unless you want to become a shelf-stacker for a global conglomerate who is hell bent on taking over the world, exploiting developing nations, whilst paying you a minimum wage. Or, if you are without morals, you might become a sex worker or a drugs' mule ... although not recommended as your colon will inevitably suffer with both these vocations.

Marx had Engels to bail him out of hardship so he could be free to analyse capitalism. Freud married into money. I once knew a very green socialist who would harp on about green issues then borrow someone's car.

It all sounds a bit manipulative and Machiavellian to try to find someone who will love you and support your dreams, but I am merely referring to a balance in your relationships. A ying-yang if you like. If you can sell your dreams and someone will buy them and support you unconditionally, you're laughing.

Exercise

Were you loved? Are you loved now? Who supports you?

Would they be there for you if you had nothing?

Here, I would like you to write two stories in the form of a fairy tale.

Story One – will be a story of your real life. Make sure that the outcome is one that you would like.

You will choose your own character in both stories.

Story Two – Write the tragic story of how your life may transpire if all goes awry.

How do the stories compare?

What can you learn from them?

Your school

Stephen Fry waxes lyrically about everything, including his time in public school. Paradoxically, and arguably, his schooling helped make him the success he is today, but watching Stephen on TV always gives me the impression that he is upset. I didn't think this in his halcyon days of 1980s Fry & Laurie when he shone like a comic genuis. Despite this, he is *the* veritable word-meister. He doesn't hide the brutality and general wickedness he suffered at school.

Perhaps you suffered at school, or maybe you hid in the shadows. It never seems to matter much what school you went to when it comes to suffering as suffering, like success, is a relative thing. So, if you went to a posh school and got bullied, this will have tortured you just as much as it would if you had gone to a dreadful school and got bullied. Bullying has no social class and it happens in most schools and sometimes on into adult life. Some argue that bullying is functional and prepares one to face life, as life is unfair and school bullying is an early mirror of this unfairness. You won't be thinking this whilst you are getting your head shoved down a dirty toilet or being anally raped. The "it never did me any harm" brigade will have repressed their pain deep within their minds and may not consciously know the harm it did them. There is obviously a strong connection between the person we become and the schooling we experienced. These experiences are never forgotten; they are recorded in the subconscious mind and stay with us forever. Teachers and parents who torture children are storing up a legacy for the future. This can be psychological bullying as well as physical abuse.

Mandy had painfully low self-esteem when she came to see me for counselling. She also had a hand-washing compulsion and was assailed with obsessive thoughts of harming others. Ironically, Mandy was a very attractive blonde woman in her early twenties who one would not normally associate with low self-esteem. On the outside she seemed to have it all, but, after two superficial sessions, floods of tears arrived as she revealed her past …

"I grew up in a poor Northern town and we never knew where the next meal was coming from. My Dad was a local drug dealer and user and my Mum was an alcoholic who also used uppers, downers ... anything to get off her face. This was bad enough but from the age of about ten, my uncle and a next door neighbour would interfere with me. They started it off as a joke at first because I developed early so they used to make comments about my boobs and stuff. About a year later they would take turns in having sex with me and would buy me sweets and stuff as a payment. I knew it was wrong and I felt guilty but they said they'd kill me and bury me on the moors if I told anyone. I even thought my parents knew but they wouldn't have cared anyway. I remember the agony of going to school whilst all this was happening; my school work just slipped away and I became ignored and ignorant. Those two perverts would do anything to me, too crude to mention and they were disgusting. It really hurt but I knew I couldn't tell anyone. The day after my sixteenth birthday I ran away from home to London. I bet no one even missed me except the paedophiles. I haven't even been in touch since with anyone up North. In London, I just couldn't survive and got involved in prostitution. I had my looks and I knew I'd get by. I never did drugs because I'd seen enough of them as a kid. Because I was so young, a pimp would sell me out for high prices to businessmen. I can't count the number of men I've had, all kinds of sex, groups, couples and weirdoes of all kinds. One of the clients I met was actually into adult films and asked me if I wanted to star in one. This seemed like a better arrangement than the one I had with my pimp and I just went for it. This way I got to keep all my earnings and it couldn't be any worse than the life I already had. I was now nineteen years old and desperate to quit sleazy prostitution anyway. So that's how I got where I am today. I've starred in countless films and I've made a lot of money but I just feel so empty. Recently, I've been having really aggressive thoughts that just come into my head, that I might kill someone in the street or steal a baby or something. I also can't stop washing my hands [they were red raw]. That's what brings me to counselling today."

This was Mandy's early life; a life which provided her schooling in the evil way some people can treat children. It is not as uncommon as one would hope. Mandy's OCD (handwashing and obtrusive thoughts) is a manifestation of the anxiety that has arisen from living a life she didn't really choose. Needless to say, Mandy has a host of skeletons in her cupboard and will have repressed many of her horrific childhood memories. In every prostitute there lies a victim. Usually a victim of abuse. Everyone failed Mandy. Should the school system have detected Mandy's abuse? Even if they had, would she have admitted it for fear of being killed? Undoubtedly she was bullied and abused by those who should have known better, but this is no uncommon experience. I have known clients report that they were traded sexually in exchange for drugs – by their own parents! Mandy's harsh school was the school of hard knocks and unforgivable sexual abuse. No wonder she ran away; who can blame her? However, there is hope for Mandy and others who had similar early lives. To her credit she is a survivor and I feel that when she acknowledges the depth of her exploitation (which still exists today) she will work on freeing herself from its grips. The money is good for her but they will get rid of her when she loses her looks, so it's all transient.

We should all look within to see what upset us in our own 'schooling'. Whether you've had Mandy's awful experiences, as I said earlier, it's all relative and I believe that early pain should be addressed if only to ameliorate the inner angst that can permeate our consciousness. This angst now arises in Mandy when she is more settled than ever before; her anxiety arises. She's not going mad, she's 'just' anxious and there is much hope for her. I don't believe in forgiving these tyrants who infested her early life but I believe in working through these experiences with a suitably qualified counsellor or psychotherapist in order to process them in her mind. This processing usually leads to a decrease in anxiety. Events that are not processed come back to haunt us. Tillich thought of anxiety as being our reaction to the fear of non-being ... that in some way we disappear or become annihilated. Whilst this concept would not necessarily be within Mandy's awareness, we can see that in her anxiety, the threat of submergence exists. Kierkegaard adds to this when he writes about a fear of nothingness. In many ways, once we have solved the 'riddle' of anxiety, our answers become clearer; in this respect Freud suggested that this solution must therefore cast light onto our whole mental existence.

Of course, not everyone suffers at school. Schools probably have noble aims. Faith schools even brainwash young minds with what they believe to be honourable, religious beliefs … if this is a noble aim? On the whole, school is a preparation for future life and its lessons are both social as well as academic. Other schools prepare us for military action: Onward Christian soldiers, marching as to war … albeit Christian recruitment. With the recent rise in faith academies, there is little hope of taking religion off the agenda in the foreseeable future. In my view, this is a shame since I don't believe it is wise to brainwash anyone; brainwashing is not really the right term; it's more a case of persuading young and fertile minds to believe certain things that are without evidence. The faithful would see nothing wrong with this; the realists would think it was all a theatrical farce. Having said that, religion may be an easy and convenient way of keeping us in check … being good because of religious decrees might be no bad thing.

Exercise

Were you brainwashed by your school into believing certain things?
Were you tortured or bullied at school?
Have you gone on to torture or brainwash others as a result of your school experiences?
Did you get what you expected out of school and leave with the right qualifications?
Would you consider returning to education?

I know someone who is a bigot: he hates most people and every other culture, religion, colour, and creed, and is happy to project all his negativity onto the shoulders of others. He proudly exclaims: "They should all be sent back and everyone thinks like me." This poor man really believes that all foreigners should be expatriated and England should return to being a totally white nation. And I mean *really* believes it. When I probe a little further (whilst walking on glass) to gauge the extent of his hatred, I suggest: "Well, not everyone thinks like you actually (as they really don't!) and England is a nation of mixed people and always has been." He replies with a multitude of weak racist retorts that are statistically unsound and are the rantings of a very bitter, lonely man. It is senseless for me to go on. I make this point because England is full of people like this: people who don't celebrate difference but fear it. People who project all their bad inner feelings onto others. I don't think they know they're projecting but immigrants become a soft target for these embittered people. The bigots even have a point to some degree about the strain immigration makes on our infrastructure, but their projectile bitterness is so venomous that it becomes simply appalling. Many people project their inner anxieties and bad feelings onto others, perhaps onto a family scapegoat who becomes the black sheep, instead of looking inside themselves and asking themselves why they are so angry. Sadly, this very man has two children of mixed race. I wonder how those children felt growing up knowing that their father hated their origins.

Hitler thought it was an abominable sin to mix one race with another and that it was against the will of the eternal creator! Could it be that *normal* English people identify with this diatribe?

When I was younger, in the seventies, I attended a nice church primary school, St. Peter's Church of England in Lancashire. I remember singing a hymn-type song called 'Family of Man' and this is always the way I've thought about it. We are all born more or less equal but subsequent events go on to either make us prosper or damage us. Founder of the

Transactional Analysis movement, Eric Berne, claimed that we are all born princes or princesses and then turned into frogs by others and life in general: I agree with this. Aren't we all brothers with different mothers? Could it be that our racist and bigoted friends feel ignored by politicians, think that their country is being taken over, most of them having been without nice things, feel that others are getting more than them? Is it simply a matter of jealousy coupled with inner torments that find desperate immigrants a lovely soft target on which to vent their bile?

Religion means not only having your own set of beliefs and practices but sometimes blithely believing that everyone else is flawed. They're not. Most countries in the Western world are mixed racially, cosmopolitan and highly flavoured. There is a plethora of religions and most people are indoctrinated into the religion of their parents. White Britons seem to be increasingly secular whereas Muslim Britons are the opposite of this. Ideally, religion should teach us how to live, preferably in a way that hurts nobody else and that is tolerant. So often this is not the case and one only has to look around the world to see huge unrest fuelled by religious intolerance and clashes of ideologies. I have often looked at these situations in a very simplistic way and suggested that if I lived in a political hot-spot, I would simply go home and cease fighting. Isn't peace the thing that everyone wants? If everyone else went home, the wars would be solved in one stroke. John Lennon's songs amply describe the options for peace and his famous bed stuff had the right intentions. Of course, people seem unwilling to simply go home such is the hatred, injustice, greed, bad government, totalitarianisms etc around the world. It is a tragedy and beyond the scope of this book. Tony Blair can sort all that out: at the time of writing he is something to do with Middle East peace. Isn't that ironic?

It seems that, in my bigot box above, everyone has a beef with someone else instead of acknowledging that we all belong to a human race. Everyone is so obsessed with territory and this happens on a local level as well. I have a friend who is incensed if his neighbour parks an inch over his border. The continual movement of people around the globe seems to have caused great unrest for those who have been invaded: the Africans, the Maoris, the Aborigines, the Native Americans, the Irish, The Palestinians ... and anywhere else where history and governments have reallocated land, renamed nations, and generally had a field day at the expense of others. It happens even today on a much more subtle level and Noam Chomsky's books are testament to the spread of democracy and the detritus it leaves in its wake, as is *Colossus* by Niall Ferguson.

I've had too many clients as a counsellor to maintain hatred or bigotry towards anyone; it's just not plausible or practical. Surprisingly enough, it's hard to dislike clients when you meet them in the emporium of counselling. I've met all creeds, colours, and sexual persuasions and they've all been thoroughly decent people. I've always found that people are okay on the whole – once you get to know them. This means that if you want to enjoy people, you have to be able to look past their behaviours and defences; if you can, overcome your fear, go out there and mix.

Fear means that people are keener than ever to cling onto their religions in spite of what is going on around them. Fear also means that people stay isolated in their homogenous groups. I often feel that very religious people wear their religions on their sleeves as a defence against invasion and other ideas. Although many great thinkers have been thoroughly against religion, it is not great thinkers who are religious. Marx believed that religion was like a drug for people (opium), comforting them in times of upset, and perhaps he was right. But would Karl happily travel to the Gaza Strip and put this theory to those terrorists/freedom fighters who absolutely believe in dichotomous ideologies? I don't think he'd last long.

Whether religion is drug-like or not, I believe it gives joy, comfort and hope to a great many people, myself included. I read Richard Dawkins' outstanding *The God Delusion* and it evoked some anxiety within me. Although his reasoned argument against a deity may well be right, I don't want to face that yet and perhaps I never will. As a *member* of the Church of England, I have a relatively dilute faith in comparison with Islam or Buddhism. However, I wouldn't go out spitting at Catholic children on their way to school no more than I would strap a bomb to myself on a plane. There is certainly a deep passion in these people that I cannot even comprehend. But I don't think this is about religion, I think it's more about hatred. It's like the War of the Roses or the Saxons or the Vikings and such deep scars go on forever, so whilst I would simply go home, most people would not … or so it seems.

I think that religion should be about tolerance and loving thy neighbour, despite their beliefs. Why would anyone be so upset by seeing someone wearing a burka? What has it got to do with anyone else what you might choose to wear? A burka is like the mini-skirt but opposite; it attracts a lot of attention for all the wrong reasons. A woman should be able to express her sexuality and show off her legs just as a woman should be able to express her religion.

The religion I am referring to in this section is the religion that you have grown up with. Were you indoctrinated by beliefs that you thought were weird or pointless at the time? Religion means way of life and I am not decrying anyone's way of life. As far as I'm concerned you do what you want unless it harms someone else.

We often use religion to guard us against the fear of death. This is nothing unusual since many people who are not religious, have been known to offer a silent prayer when they are facing an operation or worried about a loved one. This calls to mind Marx's comment about religion being an opiate. It does indeed seem a strange thing to believe in something that nobody can prove exists or has seen with their own eyes. Perhaps we do it out of habit. Some would say that if god existed, he would have never given us religion at all. Certainly, religion has a lot to answer for in terms of war and killings.

Richard Dawkins writes with great wit, aplomb, and humour about the impact of religion. I found his tome *The God Delusion* very entertaining and thought-provoking. As a 'believer', I find his points hard to swallow without summoning a kind of depression in me. However, he makes very important points about indoctrination and the labelling of children into a particular religion. Why should we indoctrinate children? Perhaps it keeps them off the streets and gives them a moral code. I would suggest that this is better than allowing everyone to run amok, as do those mentioned earlier, who have no religion whatsoever. "Religion is excellent stuff for keeping common people quiet", said the Emperor Napoleon. The philosopher Seneca said that: "Religion is regarded by the common people as true, by the wise as false, and by the rulers as useful". So with this in mind, perhaps it's better to let people go on believing, if only to keep them on the straight and narrow.

And that's the key phrase: the straight and narrow … that's what religion gives you, a compass with which to navigate life. If you look at different parts of the world – particularly the religious hot spots – they are bad enough *with* religion so what would those angry folk do *without* it? This will sound patronising, but if you're occupied in prayer, at least you're not stealing my car!

It is fairly obvious that if people with strong but different beliefs are to be forced to share each other's space, there will be an inevitable clash of some kind. It seems hard for politicians to realise this. In my opinion the reason politicians cannot accept this is because they have themselves come through debating societies at Oxbridge where they can argue points then go away as friends, rather like lawyers often do. 'Normal' people are not like this … they take points personally and seriously, especially when it comes to religion. They don't want to agree to differ; they want to change and convince. There is a great deal of splitting in religious communities: we're right and everyone else is wrong. With this kind of juvenile ethos there will be continued trouble around the world until the end of humankind, and religion is usually at the heart of it.

Whilst this is very incisive, I still wonder what lost souls would do without God. Perhaps it's better to leave things as they are. It would be okay to be brought up as a child in an enlightened household, with books and inspirational teachings, and scholarly visitors dropping in to attend cheese and wine parties and quote Derrida; but most people don't live this life and I would suggest that a bit of religion does nobody any harm if it prevents them sleeping with their sisters and scratching my car. These things are happening in the real world. Better they be blinkered than go berserk. Monty Python's *Life of Brian* amply shows how people seem to need something to believe in. Most of us seem to need this belief in something or other and if it's not religion it's football or music. Without belief it seems we're doomed to face the question of meaninglessness and most of us want to avoid the probable fact that we are all rather futile!

We go on to install drivers into our children, ensuring that they carry on our often wonky beliefs. Why should children be *anything*? Why should he be a follower of anything? He is just a child, a *tabula rasa*, which again, is all very well if your parents are wise and existential, but not if your parents don't have a clue and they worship a football team or a reality TV show. You might then be better off as a believer.

Why do we feel compelled to indoctrinate our children with a set of beliefs? Are we not setting them up for a life of anxiety, based on some ancient writings? In 2007, two medical doctors were discovered to be driving a car full of bombs into Glasgow airport. What sort of doctors were these? And what kind of beliefs must they hold? Do their actions not contravene the Hippocratic Oath?

Obviously, there's a line to be drawn between total obedience to a cause and complete amorality. Is either right and who says what right is? I believe that if any faith can become more moderate and dispel the need to kill others, then there is perhaps a place for it.

So steeped and ingrained are these beliefs that I suggest it is wrong to argue with the religious – one must simply accept the difference. If you are secular and you argue with someone who is very religious you will never win because they firmly believe in their own convictions, so what's the point? If you know you're right, be content with that. I remember a young Muslim child who attended my daughter's school until she came of age to go away to be taught at a Muslim school. I often wonder how she will have changed in the subsequent seven years. I can say no more but I would ask even the most religious reader; is this treatment fair, and where is your proof? More to the point, what exactly is the point?

I personally believe that it is the extremists and fundamentalists we have to watch out for – no news there. But if you believe that your *brothers and sisters* are being bombed in Iraq, does it not make sense to take up arms and fight on their behalf? Anyone can see why they do it; anyone can see why anyone does it, but it relies on very strong beliefs that feed in the first instance upon indoctrination. I do believe in God, but I wouldn't kill anyone about it – even if they scratched my car.

People with strong beliefs inevitably cause trouble if someone disagrees with them or infringes their divine right. If they believe that God really exists, beyond a shadow of a doubt, then they might well defend it to the death if this is their notion. This comes down to one's relationship with God and often one's relationship with authority figures. It also has something to do with child rearing. Most experts would agree that boundaries need to be in place in order to raise a self-disciplined child who will become a functional member of society. These boundaries can be other-imposed as in a belief in God or by instilling a fear of hell and the devil, as per Catholicism. We learn that Blair is a devout Catholic and this makes me shudder a bit. However, to take us back to the problem on Britain's streets, or what I refer to as scroatism, it is plain that the Godless sometimes have difficulty in taking orders or doing what is right.

> The paraphrased rant of client John: I'm no Richard Dawkins, and I wouldn't want to be, I don't know how he gets away with it. It's a wonder there's not a fatwa on his head like Salman Rushdie. Anyway, I can't understand all this God stuff; whether they're Muslims or Jews or whatever. The thing is, when you're dead you're dead. I can't understand why anyone doesn't seem to get it. It was sad when my Dad died but I never for one minute thought that he was off to heaven or he'd come back as a bird or go to hell. I think that people don't want to see reality and religion has caused most of the wars of the world ... and for what? What is solved by it? It seems to me that people need to believe in something, anything, instead of looking at reality and enjoying what life they have now, free from believing in ghosts and fairies. I mean, it's all very nice for kids and Christmas, but it's meaningless really. There is no

hereafter. The thing is, why can't people see that their lives are just a short blip and totally without any reason. They're not part of some big plan; they're just a collection of cells, waiting to die. It's even worse when you see religions that completely take over your life – I don't wanna mention them but we know what they are. I won't mention them in case I get shot by a fanatic. I mean, are these people for real? Why do they need to do all that shit? What a total, meaningless waste of time. Of course, governments and leaders would never have the balls to say it in case they lose votes and it's certainly not pc, but I ask you … what a waste of time. But then I wonder what else these people would do if they weren't praying five times a day or swinging incense around? They've probably got nothing else in their lives anyway and they've been indoctrinated from birth to believe in something that doesn't exist. If you look at the countries with the strongest beliefs, they're all feudal, despotic nations so I suppose they need something to believe in to soothe the misery of their existence. Trouble is, if these people see that there's nothing to their lives but squalor and disturbance, what have they got left? Nothing. That doesn't explain why Muslim Asian doctors in this country even believe in Allah. Surely they're bright enough to see through it? I know one thing though, if you take away their religion, even if you could, nothing would fill the gap.

Then you've got clowns like Bush and Blair, acting as if spoken to by God himself. I suppose it gives them a free hand to do whatever they want if they're acting in the name of God. In this way, they've got similarities with the suicide bombers because they're also acting in the name of God. If it wasn't for the fact that people are getting killed every day, it would be a joke. Have you seen that episode of *Blackadder* called 'beer' where the auntie turns up with crucifixes on her head and shoulders? Well, I think religion is like that: purely ridiculous. I think Monty Python had the right idea in *The Life of Brian* and I remember the Christians

> being up in arms about trying to ban it, and, more recently, the Jerry Springer opera. That's the trouble ... everyone is up in arms and offended. Well, I am offended that most of the population on this earth believe in something that doesn't exist and they can't see it. I wonder if they know how stupid they look in their religious garb and all that nonsense they spout. I despair.

In February 2008, the Archbishop of Canterbury suggested that Sharia law might be used in conjunction with the existing legal system in the UK. Again, everyone got up in arms, some even asking for his resignation. Why were these people so very upset? They obviously have strong beliefs and I wonder why? Perhaps it's all a sign of emotional immaturity. So what if this is what the Archbishop believes or suggests; nothing will happen anyway. Two years later, nothing has.

Over recent years, those disenchanted with organised religion have been embracing their spirituality. Bookstores abound with alternative belief books and, since there is an obvious demand, I see topics such as paganism, wicka, magic, crystal healing, cosmic ordering, astrology ... the list is endless. It's as if people really want something strange to believe in. I say strange for all this pertains to the supernatural. Spiritualism has been going strong since Victorian times and you can even go to spiritualist churches and hear messages from your beloved dead, or visit a medium for some news.

Perhaps people are looking for an escape from the obvious mundanities of life or perhaps this new flowering of weird belief cultures mirror the fact that our nation is on the change and people are looking for something to hold on to. These days, one cannot rely on jobs for life, nobody is really secure, and so examining possible spiritual allegiances can give the lost a sense of inner peace that seems so lacking in 21st century Britain.

Exercise

I would like to ask you to look deeply at your own beliefs, not just because they were handed down to you, but to see if they are relevant to your life. Do you really believe that God exists or are you just going through the motions? Has your religion made you bigoted? Do you think that you are right and everyone else is wrong? Perhaps you will reflect on these questions and add the answers to your journal.

Part 3 – Your Branches

Your spouse/his or her family/your ex-partners

Paul married too young; he was 'all at sea' after the death of his grandmother who had brought him up. He needed someone to cling to and subsequently transferred all his love onto his new bride. This was all very well to begin with for his bride gave him pleasures he never knew existed. However, as the years went by, he realised that he had missed something ... being young, being foolish. Still married, and fifteen years down the line, Paul was mid-thirties, searching and looking. Paul and Amanda now had three children whom he adored and he would never have wanted to leave them. He also had a well-paid job as an assistant bank manager.

Paul had gone from being a child in his upbringing to being a child as a man. For all intents and purposes, his wife had become his gran. They had both looked after him, ironed and cooked for him, even told him what to wear.

However, a dark cloud lurked on Paul's horizon. He was gay.

He knew he liked boys from the early days at school in the 1980s but being gay was such a taboo for his family at the time, he had never discussed it and chose instead to repress his feelings and live a lie.

Now, at thirty-four years old, Paul knew that he had to make some kind of move but he didn't want to hurt anyone. Instead, he created a secret life, eventually plucking up enough courage to meet men from a gay internet site. This offered excitement and casual sex, often in 'cottages', but Paul found it meaningless and it provoked extreme anxiety within him.

Paul was also the treasurer in his local Catholic church and this added another stress to his already very stressed life. He thought that his gay liaisons were a complete secret and then he met Luke ... a man with whom he would want to spend the rest of his life.

He came to see me for counselling about this quagmire.

Paul is striving for independence as he's never really had any. He now finds solace in the arms of Luke and wonders how to tell his family. It will mean a total change in his whole existence. Paul would do well to become independent and free.

One of the ways to become happier in a relationship is to become financially independent ... or as much as you can. If you are co-habiting or married to someone, you must contribute in order to maintain your self-esteem. Otherwise, someone will be keeping you and you will be on a weak wicket because of this. One caveat ... if your husband is a millionaire and you have five children to look after, you may prefer to stay at home and ensure that they are well cared for. However, even if you earn pin money, you will feel better about yourself compared with earning nothing at all. In some ways, we can see in Rod Stewart's marriage to Penny Lancaster a sign of equality in that she works as a model and photographer although she need not work at all. This will undoubtedly strengthen their relationship; the marriage may even last.

Being financially independent means that you will not be subservient or answerable to anyone. I appreciate that this is all very well if you can earn a lot like the WAGS, but you have to use what you can, the tools you've got, so even if you're working at a low-paid job, you'll be contributing to your own self-esteem.

Try to avoid giving up your education if someone is persuading you to do so. I once had a client who adored her husband, and still does. They met at university in Frankfurt, both doing degrees in German. It was decided that my client should quit her degree half way through its completion so they could become married and have children. This all happened and, twenty-five years on, Andrew is a high-flying Eurocrat and Adele is a housewife. But she is unhappy because they are no longer besotted with each other. They had three lovely children and own a big house inside Surrey's stockbroker belt but Adele has the feeling that there is unlived potential within her. She benignly envies Andrew and deeply regrets not completing her own degree. This has taken its toll on their relationship as they live now more as friends than lovers, and Adele is experiencing anxiety and depression. Her GP prescribed anti-depressants but how will they help reclaim her life? The relationship is more tarnished for the fact that Adele gave up what could easily have been within her reach.

The message here is simple. An education will insulate you from future life shocks and nobody will be able to take it away from you. Good looks and the ability to dance or model are evanescent. A degree will last you a lifetime. However, don't expect a degree to make your life perfect because it certainly will not; I'm just saying that you'll be better off with one than without one. Adele could quickly get back into the job market now her children are grown up and she has time on her hands, but her transition would be easier if she had finished her degree. Adele doesn't resent Andrew, she loves him. But she wonders what might have happened if she had lived more of her own life.

One cannot live life through someone else's lens. It may work for a time but eventually questions will be asked. In other words, you have to do your own bit to cement your own inner esteem. This doesn't have to be a degree but at least with a degree you will know you're a bit clever like the scarecrow in *The Wizard of Oz*. Additionally, if and when things go awry, you will be armed with a useful and recognisable qualification. Relying on others is one route to unhappiness because ultimately, you're on your own.

Love

'Love is the highest level of medicine.' (Paracelsus)

I think by now it will have become obvious that you need to be loved by significant other(s). I accept that some people enjoy living alone and are able to float their own boats and that's good for them if that is what they're happy with … it's their choice. However, most people like to be linked with others and enjoy giving and receiving love. Others prefer pets and the unconditional love that they seem to bestow. But are our pets in love with us or do they just want some tasty morsels?

JD writes:
"I just knew that this was where I wanted to be when I first tried it. It was as if all my insecurities disappeared and all my worries just melted away. It was okay at first and I could go to work all day and use it at night. I used to settle down watching a film and just inject the right amount to make me feel warm all over and at peace with myself and everything in the world was beautiful. It was great until the addiction kicked in proper and it just went out of control. But it was still great in the early days when I could handle it. After a couple of years I could see it ruining my life. That film *Trainspotting* says it all really."

The feeling that heroin gave JD was a feeling of warmth all over, of being caressed and being at peace, at one with oneself and the world ... what could be better? Nothing could be better if it wasn't for the fact that heroin usually ruins your life. To love and be loved would create those same feelings if only JD could have found love. He took the easy option and decided to mollify life's woes using a deadly chemical to bring on those feelings that could have been attained in love.

Unlike the rich, drugs often wreak their havoc on the penniless. In the article below, we read how someone's life has gone off the rails due to drugs. This story is not unusual in Britain and whilst drugs are seen as being cool and part of the subculture, deaths will continue.

It seems that a lot of people try to get that good feeling that can be achieved without chemicals ... the feeling of pure love can eliminate the paying of drug dealers and all the crime that emanates from drug use.

"All you need is love", droned John Lennon. The self-styled working-class hero might have had a good point. Perhaps his lyrics were the work of genius or perhaps he just hit a lucky strike at the right time. Lennon obviously had a few good lyrics about him and I think he was going the right way with *Imagine* and *War is Over*, however utopian. Lennon was rich enough to enjoy his love away from societal influences that would have undoubtedly affected his psyche.

This diagram shows Maslow's hierarchy of needs, represented as a pyramid with the more primitive needs at the bottom.

Maslow's triangle

Psychologist Abram Maslow argued that all human beings were trying to self actualise and get further up the illustrated triangle. Once our basic needs have been met, we have a better chance of doing this. Some of us stay stuck somewhere in the middle of the triangle and this is not unusual. The enlightened ones make it to the top. Clearly this triangle has nothing to do with money or being a winner in any society in particular; just the process of being and becoming a person. Carl Rogers, who was exponential in founding person-centred counselling borrowed heavily from Maslow's triangle. Others have made advanced Maslow's triangles and made their own shapes, probably in order to attain their PhDs, but I think Maslow has summed it all up. It includes the things we need and might want and seems perfect in its simplicity. Sadly, there are those in the world who don't even get their basic needs met and life is a continual struggle for these unfortunates.

You must be careful that your love is real and not a love based on co-dependency, a rife condition in today's emotionally impoverished society.

In getting involved with love, you have to know that your love is pure and not based on a need for someone or anyone; a desperate bid to stave off loneliness. Rather, you should be together but apart at the same time. Gilbran's writings in *The Prophet* says much of this and is a favourite reading at weddings. It encourages us to maintain our identity throughout our married lives; being together but having a life of our own that runs alongside. This way, you will always have something to bring to your marriage – something to contribute, not only financially, but intellectually and in every other way.

Perhaps more importantly you should try to ensure that your love is equal and there is a ying yang nature to the relationship. In the early 1990s, popstar Sting famously revealed that he engaged in Tantric sex; I believe that this is a kind of quality connection one might strive for … to swim into someone's eyes and lose yourself forever in their soul. Like Lennon, Sting has a lot of time to get involved with all this and you need time to develop your love with the right person. Sting, I imagine, doesn't have to be up at seven every morning, scraping frost off his car.

If you are unlucky enough to be involved with someone with a personality disorder, there are a few signs that you can look for. I mention these as such sufferers populate the offices of Relate and so if you are dating someone from this category, watch out … perhaps you should reconsider.

Perhaps you are the one with a personality disorder and you don't know it. Co-dependant people usually get involved with the wrong sorts all the time and mistake neediness for love. Assess that even though someone may look good in a short skirt aged twenty-two, will you feel the same when they are forty-two with a knife at your throat? Borderline personality disorder is one prevalent and easily hidden personality trait that I believe has permeated our society and deserves special mention. It is tied to co-dependency, so you have to evaluate whether you are in a soul-mate relationship with someone; someone who is your friend and shares your interests and laughs at the same things … or you just need them because you are afraid of being alone. In your evaluation try to immunize yourself from all pop song lyrics as you examine your situation. Co-dependency is about craven neediness and those who are needy put up with all kinds of abuse and ill-treatment because their self-esteem is low and they feel they don't deserve any better.

Although it is not always wise to label those suffering with a personality disorder (as it becomes a self-fulfilling prophecy) I have included borderline personality disorder and its link to co-dependency in *Broken Britain?* basically because these conditions are so prevalent in Western society. In a book called *Stop walking on eggshells*, Paul Mason and Randi Kreger (1998) set out the signs to look for in these conditions. The stop walking on eggshells bit, describes how you can regain control after you have lost yourself to another who has borderline personality disorder, so whilst the book is not actually for sufferers, Mason and Kreger make points and helpful suggestions that work both ways. The rise of borderline personality disorder is particularly telling to a society that seems to have forgotten how to raise children in a healthy way. This is also why I refer to their book in *Broken Britain?*

To define borderline personality disorder, you examine this list of common traits (not exhaustive) ...

1.   BPDs tend to 'split' and view people as either all good or all bad. Most of us are not all good or evil, but the borderline seems not to understand the shades of grey that constitute human life. It's almost like idolizing some people (until they inevitably let them down) and demonizing others. This may mean that, in the first throes of love, they are besotted; when this doesn't last, or if the lover transgresses, their ire and rage will become known to you very soon.

2.   BDPs like to project their own mistakes onto others as admitting to their misdemeanours evokes within them a feeling of horror (that they will be punished as they were when a child), so best to blame someone else.

3.   They may have little regard for others' feelings.

4.   They may feel paranoid about others, distrustful and suspicious that others are trying to do them down. Jealousy is a strong component of the BPD and partners around this irrational rage can suffer tremendously.

5. Not understanding their own emotions. An emptiness pervades their inner psyche and they want most of all to feel, but there is a numbness.

6. Impulsive behaviours that become out-of-control: spending, overeating, drink & drugs, sexual impropriety.

7. Create crises from nothing, making mountains out of molehills, and often turning to violence or quelling their rage with some drug or other.

8. Verbally aggressive towards others when they feel slighted, the over-reaction being out of kilter with the slight.

9. Acting in odd or irrational ways or over-reacting at perceived slights.

It is clear from the list that those suffering with BPD can be very difficult to live with or even placate. It seems that those brought up in chaotic ways, in regard to faulty attachment, are most likely to suffer from borderline personality disorder (BPD) and they also tend to attract partners who are co-dependent. Both needing each other in some perverse, unconscious way, they take their emotional toll on the battlefields of each other's lives. It is as if those with BPD want to reclaim control over their lives as a way of recapturing their out-of-control childhoods. As children, there was nothing they could do when adults around them were treating them badly or abusing them. Now they feel they have to keep a tight hand on the reins.

As well as control, adult BPDs are also very attuned and sensitive to the moods of others around them. They had to be like this as children because they didn't know where the next smack was coming from; they had to learn to unconsciously, and consciously, read the feelings of others. This can lead to paranoia too, so attuned becomes the BDP's radar system in picking up the moods of others.

They have a need to protect themselves from others by maintaining a distance, and in this distance they feel alone. But if they let anyone in, they feel vulnerable; it is a no-win situation designed to keep their defences intact. They have learnt that their inner selves, the self that they choose not to reveal to others, is so rotten that no one must be aware of it. This is why the intimacy of relationships and friendships threaten to destabilise the borderline's brittle shell.

So fraught is the environment created by the borderline, so tense the atmosphere, it sizzles with electricity. Typically, family members are worried what to say next lest they upset the sufferer. Many spouses lose themselves in the whirlpool of emotions and decide in the end that the relationship just is not worth the effort. And this can so easily happen to BDP partners, as they become engulfed in the quagmire and odd behaviour of their other half. They walk on eggshells so as not to upset the angry spouse and, in doing so, lose all their own sense of self and personal power. All that is left is a façade with families worrying and denying that a problem exists for even to confront it would create unrest. I am convinced that borderline personality disorder is on the increase in our alienating society and that left unchecked, figures will either continue to rise or just go ignored.

If you are a partner who suffers at the hands of someone with borderline personality disorder, it might be in your best interests to remove yourself – if you can – and with sensitivity. This can be very difficult as you will be trying to become yourself and stand alone in the midst of a storm. It is possible but not easy when borderlines send out completely mixed messages: you will end up feeling confused. One day you will feel loved and desired, the next, a despot! The question is: do you want to suffer like that and what are you gaining (if anything) from your suffering? These questions might best be explored in conjunction with a suitable therapist or counsellor.

It is well known that our health can suffer if we ally ourselves to challenging partners. In his outstanding work with terminally ill patients, Bernie Siegel (1999) draws parallels between the suffering we can experience in life and the illness this suffering can go on to manifest. Sometimes you simply have to get rid of faulty partners – even for the sake of your health. Many illnesses come about due to continued stress. This would be very hard to evidence but there is much anecdotal evidence to support this hypotheses. In other words, if you are under continued pressure, possibly suffering with a bad job or peculiar partner, your health may well suffer. If you are not happy, your health will suffer. The subconscious mind works in a very mysterious way but psychosomatic ailments are very well known and exist in fact. Sometimes you simply have to make a move for freedom in your own interests. It will feel bad at the time, but it will strengthen you in the longer term. In a way, you're on your own ... in many ways; and if someone won't change, that's up to them. Ultimately, it's up to you whether you leave a tyrant or tolerate them and suffer. The choice is yours, but don't wait for anyone to change because they never usually do anyway. They may swear blind that they'll change, and may even change for a few weeks or months, but usually, old patterns re-emerge. I have counselled many victims of domestic violence. Usually it goes something like this: (1) The wife does something to annoy the husband; (2) The husband flies into a rage (sometimes but not always) and hits her; (3) The wife cries and sometimes apologises for upsetting him(!) ... or if she sulks at her reprimand he may be the one to apologise: both want to return to the status quo; (4) He buys her a token of his apology and she cooks a special meal (depending on who feels worse or guilty); (5) Weeks or months pass until he's annoyed about something and he hits her again: if you are a victim of domestic violence – male or female – you can break the cycle by leaving the tyrant. And, more importantly, not returning. It usually happens again anyway and you know it will – it's only a matter of time. To believe that the person will not hit you any more you will be deluding yourself; believing what you would hope to happen. Teach your abuser a lesson and get out and stay out. Excuses will come thick and fast: ignore them. Be gone. And take your children with you. Many agencies today will protect you and support your decision – unlike yesteryear when violence in the home was put down to a 'domestic' incident and generally ignored. Today is not the same and there is help available for you. In removing yourself from a situation such as this, or any situation like it, you will be doing good for your health in the long run. Repressed emotions are never healthy.

A relative of mine suffered an abusive upbringing at the hands of her violent, unpredictable father. I could fill another book with a list of the outrages perpetrated upon his wife and children. After much to-ing and fro-ing in her twenties, my relative decided not to see her father again. This was mainly because he has never acknowledged the error of his ways or apologised. Perhaps he meant well! This illustrates that sometimes, reconciliations simply cannot be achieved. She is unwilling to visit his house and restrict the conversation to small-talk that avoids the buried issues, so there it ends. It is said that if you have one parent who abuses you and another one who doesn't take you away from the abuse, then you have two bad parents. My relative has maintained contact with her mother for whom she has compassion. Her father is now alone, having lost his eldest daughter, become estranged from his second daughter (at the time of writing), and unable to see his only grand-daughter. Sometimes, if you were abused as a child, and you are now an adult who hasn't received a sincere apology from your abuser, you have to ask yourself if your abuser ever really loved you at all. This may reveal a painful answer to you, but it is necessary if you are going to extricate yourself from the shadows of yesterday.

If you are a parent who knows that your other half is physically or sexually abusing your child or children, it is your absolute duty to leave the abuser. If you don't, the cycle usually repeats itself and is lived out in your offspring. This happens because your children see the interactions between their parents, or hear it through the walls when they're supposed to be asleep, and they learn that this is the way things should be. It is not how things should be and you alone have the power to change it. Grasp that power and do something about it. If you have no children, you owe it to yourself and may leave quicker with less emotional fallout.

Here follow some handy hints and suggestions that may help if you find yourself living with an uncontrollable tyrant who lacks insight.

If you have decided to go, try to detach with love, mixed with frankness. You might be faced with abuse and emotional blackmail but once you are free, this will diminish. The hardest part for you will be becoming free. The group Al-Anon talk much about detaching oneself from partners who are embroiled in alcoholism. Whether it's alcoholism or drug abuse or borderline personality disorder, the advice is relevant …

Detach with love

(adapted from *Al-Anon*)

- ❖ not to suffer because of the actions or reactions of other people
- ❖ not to allow oneself to be used or abused by others
- ❖ not do for others what they could do for themselves
- ❖ not to create a crisis
- ❖ not to prevent a crisis if it is the natural course of events

You are not responsible for anyone else's pain and it is not your job to repair their emotional scars. Usually, someone else's agony came from their childhood so how can you cure that? I have seen many clients stay with inappropriate partners in the hope that they can repair them like humpty dumpty. They hope that their influence will be able to put the egg back together and heal all the fractures, as if love will ever be enough. More often than not, this approach doesn't work and I usually see the damaged partner going on to damage the beneficent one. You may think that your love and hopefulness will repair a lifetime of chaotic parenting: it never does. By staying, you will probably be ruining your own life. You might then end up ill or on tranquilisers, or become alcoholic or get cancer. Perhaps you will decide that it's best to get out before any of that happens.

As mentioned previously, Gibran in *The Prophet* famously describes the entwined trees and the reason we have to stand apart in order to grow. With BPD relationships, soon there is no room for either tree to grow; parts of each tree die and neither reaches its full potential. This explains the many withered people that populate the earth and is one of the reasons for broken Britain.

We have all wondered from time to time how some marriages stay together, as if they thrive off the battleground that has become their way of relating. Often, there is an unconscious 'payoff' that each partner receives and that keeps the relationship going. This need not be a positive payoff, and usually is not if you are in a harmful relationship. A payoff can be what you always expected would happen and if your self-esteem is low, or expect no better, then you can be content in your disappointment. Obviously this applies to 'normal' relationships as well at BPD ones.

All this paints a grim picture of borderline personality disorder and, of course, the picture can never be pretty. So, if you are involved with someone like this, you have to decide whether or not you want to stay. This would apply to many personality disorders that you can read about in any psychiatric manual. Should you stick around?

In many ways, 'perfect' love should be like the following quote: *"The more I give to thee, the more I have"* – Juliet speaking to Romeo, from Romeo & Juliet, Shakespeare. This doesn't quite fit into the umbrella of co-dependency as it seems to be a purer love, and perhaps no-one has written better than the bard about love.

I have known few people who seem to exhibit perfect love. If they do, perhaps they keep it hidden. I say so much about love because I think it lies at the heart of all our strivings, although we often don't know it; it operates unconsciously and we are charmed if we ever know it. Psychiatrists' practices and counsellors' rooms are not peopled by those who have experienced perfect love ... unless they've suddenly lost it. The truly loved people wouldn't need much help as they would know, deep within themselves, that everything will be all right. We convey this message to little ones when they are tiny or they fear that they have transgressed in some way.

Many of us, having lacked this early warmth, grow up with emotional twists as we try to make sense of our turmoil. Insecurity can pervade our days and nights, causing us to drive away partners who really love us but can make no sense of our behaviour. This explains why some people become insanely jealous and obsessed with the whereabouts of a partner, or if someone casts their spouse an admiring glance. Jealousy is more about insecurity than love and people with lower self-esteem experience more jealousy. In 1948, Sokoloff was convinced that it was not love but fear of isolation that was responsible for irrational jealousy. A jealous person, because he has been left or neglected as a child, wants to cling in desperation to anyone who comes along.

Whether you suffer at the hands of an emotionally impoverished partner, or you feel yourself to be emotionally impoverished, part of recovery involves bringing this state into your awareness; knowing why you feel as you do and knowing why you do what you do. More often than not, you will find links to your childhood.

It seems that a whole host of personality disorders, that you can read about in the DSM IV[1], can be attributed to shattered childhoods. Whilst there is nothing you can do about the past, you can at least look at it and make an honest appraisal of your early life. More about this in the following exercise.

> Come to the edge.
> No, we will fall.
> Come to the edge.
> No, we will fall.
> They came to the edge.
> He pushed them, and they flew.
> *Guillaume Apollinaire*

Exercise

> Were you emotionally tortured as a child? Were you abused in any way? Did things happen to you that you felt were not appropriate? This can include sexual abuse or physical abuse.
>
> Are you one of the "well I had a good smack when I needed one but it never did me any harm" brigade?
>
> If your parents are approachable, and you feel up to it, perhaps you would like to ask them about your early life. Perhaps you could explore any early painful memories and see what they made of them. This takes courage and strength and

---

[1] DSM IV = Diagnostic and Statistical Manual. Ed IV of American Psychiatric Association.

you may find yourself alienated by your care-givers until they have become accustomed to the new you – the you who wants to change.

This new awareness will lead to a diminution of your angst. Eventually.

Your job

Do you hate your job? Are you only there for the money? Are you satisfied with the work you do? Or are you empty and unfulfilled? Buying new things might assuage your inner dissatisfaction for a while but what do you do when the novelty wears off? All too often, instead of seeking out a new life, we buy something else that we hope will do the trick or fill the gap.

Since most of us spend a third of our time working to earn money, no book like this would be complete without reference to this most important third. You might even spend more than a third of your life working especially if you have a BMW or a large house that you think impresses everyone. Here, I don't just look at jobs, but ambition. Many clients I have counselled over the years are malcontent and feel that they never became what they wanted to be. Many feel that their skills are not being utilised to the full and others think they are over qualified for the jobs they have ended up doing. Because of their commitments they feel unable to take the risk of moving or retraining and some simply work for the money – then retire – then die, realising that they've wasted their lives. "When you stop to dream, you die", a friend of mine once said. Dreaming is one thing, and doing is another and perhaps dreams keep our hopes alive. Many of the aforementioned commitments – mortgage, car, loans – are simply shackles and you must look at whether you have bought certain things in order to make you feel better about having to do a job you don't like. Here I will look at ambition and what drives successful people and look at some of their ingredients.

Ambition

Anthony King writes:

"Being something of an Irvin Yalom aficionado, I boldly approached the guru with a view to turning one of his stories into a musical. I am no stranger to musical theatre and could happily live out my days as a thespian. With naïve enthusiasm, and little else, I became involved in an email dialogue until it became obvious to the professor that I was not really Andrew Lloyd-Webber. He kindly put me in touch with his agent (for the 'rights') which fuelled my grand delusions to even greater heights. Subsequent emails followed and my dreams were filled with Irvin and myself watching the premier of 'our' musical on Broadway, attired in black-tie, in the company of Rollo May, Albert Ellis, and camomile tea. Later that night, my reverie was disturbed by an email from my hero. It read ... 'Anthony, let's see if you can write it first.' I was consumed with ennui!"

What shall I do with my life? Sometimes, indecision hangs in the air like the expectancy at a general election night, but without the outcome or intrigue. Procrastination can be the result and one can spend an entire lifetime flip-flopping around, steeped in indecision like a beached fish ... until you run out of air, get too old, and die. What a waste that would be.

But how would you go about embracing success or even knowing it if it presented itself? A lot of success is about belief in oneself, in fact most of it is about belief; that's why dullards seem to do well sometimes. Belief in itself is cultivated from an early age and comes from people – usually parents – telling you how good you are, how you're going to do well in life, and that you're an all round good egg.

Perhaps you really do search for riches and fame and recognition; or perhaps your search boils down to a quest for love. Love usually happens to be the common denominator. Love is like the psychosomatic illnesses discussed earlier in the book; it's hard to draw up concrete evidence so statisticians ignore it. We all crave it though even if this craving is outside our awareness.

Take music, as in the example from Anthony above. In the entertainment business (apart from comedy), musical talent is a matter of opinion and nobody seems to completely agree who is talented and what constitutes a good song. Moreover, management and marketing play a big part in the manufacture of pop stars, so if you want to be one, you really are taking part in a lottery. Having said that, I have yet to meet someone who denies Stevie Wonder's talent. He may well be truly exceptional and talent would probably always come out with someone like that, but what about those who have (or their canny managers/producers have) gone a long way on threadbare talent? Does Gerri Halliwell have the same heart-stopping emotion-inducing voice as Barbara Streisand? Is Kylie Minogue just a bum or is she as good a singer as Celine Dion? Is it not true that brilliant marketing has taken these icons to the top of their trees? But in addition to marketing, these people must also have belief or they would look nervous and inept and become incredulous. In short, they must have belief in the *fact* that they have at least some ability in order to be able to pull off a convincing performance.

Talent in itself is not necessary when it comes to being a successful pop star. I don't want to make a list of talentless singers who have become rich and famous. These entertainers are just good products like the Hollywood starlets of yesteryear and if anyone believes that these puppets have talent, then please know that there are a host of producers and directors who are pissing their collective pants. The movers and shakers and the controllers of the means of production know that the public will buy virtually anything if it is convincingly packaged. Every now and then, a puppet breaks free – like Robbie Williams – whose next talent was in teaming up with songwriter Guy Chambers. It seems that those who court and win success are not always the most talented – they are the most ambitious or needy or well-connected. Politicians and pop stars are good at pandering to the piper's tune and the casting couch and nepotism are legendary. Also legendary is the undiscovered genius of those who never pandered … figures like Karl Marx, Beethoven, Mozart – all died as paupers, but they were geniuses. Berry Gordy's talent was in nurturing Stevie Wonder's genius and that of his other lesser Motown stars. They say that fame is the mask that erodes the face within, but I wonder how eroded the face becomes in the absence of fame?

Even if we could agree who the best singers and musicians are, we would find that it is not often those people who gain the most success; the ones in the charts are the ones who have benefited from marketing and who know how to play the game; how to sell themselves to the market. Many singers are front-line puppets for music industry bosses who pull the strings. For example, the 'Tin Pan Alley' music-to-order writing service of Broadway's heyday, Berry Gordy and his Motown empire, Phil Spector and his obsessive control of his 'wall of sound', Stock-Aitken-Waterman and their canny ability to take relatively talentless TV stars and turn them into 'singers'.

Like Robbie Williams, George Michael was another puppet who broke free. Both were brimming with sex appeal and 'entertainability', and full of ambition. Both these stars perhaps believed in their own press and that their talents were based on concrete podiums. Before becoming a famous paedophile, pop mogul Jonathan King noted that, during George Michael's court battle with Sony in the early nineties, Michael would not even have been in the position he was without their grace and should therefore be grateful in having anything at all. This is perhaps the rub with popstars: they forget that many people in the general public could do what they do and begin to believe their own hype. This does not apply to George Michael because very few people could sing as well as he does ... I know some of my closest associates have tried for years, without success! George aside though, a lot of people can hold a tune and if you're a rapper, you don't even need to sing – just talk in time and buy some heavy gold, act as if you have talent and you're in.

In a 2007 Channel 4 TV interview with Chris Evans, George Michael is asked what he thinks when he graces the stage of the new Wembley Stadium? "That I'm a lucky bastard", smiles George. At least there's hope for him then and Britain loves humility. It's the other stars who believe they are there because of talent that I observe with interest. Clearly, reality TV programmes make pop stardom appear to be a desirable accolade and indeed, who of the sixties pop legends could get past the glare of Simon Cowell? Would Leonard Cohen have any chance of hitting stardom (apart from nepotistic chances)? *Just Jack*'s satirical take on stardom in their song 'Stars in their Eyes' neatly summarises the shallowness and incredulity of fame and its evanescence. Perhaps those who maintain their fame have a modicum of talent – or, perhaps more likely, an ability to play the market, but what of those whose stars fade?

Woody Allen quipped that 'you only have to turn up'! when it comes to academia and I suspect that this applies to some parts of the music business as well. Comedy is different because you have to make people laugh and you cannot rely on recording studio trickery like auto-tune or photographic air-brushing.

Usually, one only needs to be brilliant the first time. Ben Elton was great when he was a lefty champagne socialist comedian and as the writer of *Blackadder* and *The Young Ones*. Now he churns out fiction (which I have enjoyed!) and tribute musicals; he even wrote a musical with Andrew Lloyd Webber – about football, apparently without realising that your general musical-loving audience are not football fans; they are John Lewis-shopping, middle-class ladies wot lunch. Multi-millionaire Elton (Ben) is probably not worried though as he sees his gold accumulate in his bulging coffers.

Of course, some people are born into the right family, have a lot of money, contacts, are surrounded by eager plebeians and sycophants, set up a business and still see it flop … that takes some doing. I wish I could mention names but it's impossible even in a 'free' country.

Similarly, the crash of building society Northern Rock was under the chairmanship of aristocrat Matt* Ridley (educated at Eton and Oxford) who, to cut a rich story short, probably got his job because of his father, the fourth Viscount Ridley who was a past chairman of Northern Rock. Chairman Ridley's job paid £300,000 per annum – part-time of course – and one might have thought his hands were safe; but he was not an economist or financier, but a zoologist. No doubt the sub-prime USA market will be blamed for the crash. Crash aside, it just shows that there are some highly lucrative jobs around for those with the right contacts and you don't even have to do that much in order to be there. Just be born. Some 'owners' of businesses appear to do a great job and actually make their inheritances stronger, like Jacqueline Gold of the Anne Summers chain. Initially based on a porn empire, Jacqueline's father created an empire and his daughter has added to that great wealth. Perhaps it's easy if you have that elusive silver spoon hanging from your mouth. I suppose Gold could have made a complete mess of things and I think it is to her credit that her adult shops have prospered. Like all the silver spooners, Gold cannot help being born into great wealth.

[* Notice how privileged people abbreviate their names: Anthony Charles Linton Blair becomes Tony Blair, Anthony Wedgewood Benn becomes Tony Benn. Big cheese Dr Matthew White Ridley, DPhil (Oxon) becomes Matt. It is a device they use so they can come across as a man of the people. Conversely, notice how people from lesser places lengthen their names, often fabricating double-barrels when they marry or pronouncing their names in an unusual way. Mavis becomes Mahvis with the accent off the A and onto the M. They may remove the H from John. Recently deceased newsreader was plain old Tony Wilson in the seventies. Then, at the height of his Haçienda powers, he became known as Anthony Wilson; not content for long with this extension, he then added an H and became Anthony H Wilson. If he'd been an American it was only a matter of time before he would have elected for Anthony H Wilson III. The upper class do the reverse of this. It's as if the privileged want to play down their status and the poor want to create an impression of grandeur. I have a personal preference for being called Anthony, but no doubt I would want to disguise my elite background (if I'd had one) by asking people to call me Tony or Toe or even T: this would depend how esteemed my background was and the abbreviation is inversely proportional. That I like Anthony tells its own story.]

Unless you are a French revolutionary, there is not much you can do about nepotism and inherited wealth. Gone are the days of the guillotine and the British appear to be happy to tolerate their 'rich man at his castle, poor man at his gate' philosophy. A friend of mine suggested that we should lead a revolution, starting in Birmingham (the epicentre of England)

and riot. When I explained that apathy and contentment are too great in this country (as we are placated by white goods, computers, iPods, etc) to ever do anything like a revolt, he also added that if it was raining on the day of the uprising, not many people would turn out anyway. He's right, so the lucky have very little to worry about. If you are not to the manor born or your spoon is wooden, then you must devise another way ... your own way.

All this suggests that you might never have the job you want – to be the chairman of the board – unless you know the right people. However, it is important that our society *appears* to be a meritocracy or discontentment would be rife. It is true that some people work their way up from the bottom, but most people stay at the bottom. It is also true that some people win the lottery. However, we are encouraged to believe that our system is a fair one but it cannot be thus. When some people have more money and influence than others how could it ever be fair? And it's no use referring to communist countries that have collapsed because they were rife with greed and exploitation. One observes that the new Russian rich have done extremely well from the collapse of such a state; again, illustrating that contacts are all that really matter.

On transference

It seems to me that we now live in a world of transference: a world where reality is often ignored or neglected. Transference, in psychoanalytic terms, refers to a Freudian concept where we perceive new events, experiences or people as being some way related to things we have known in the past. For example, if your boss reminds you of a teacher at school, you will probably behave towards your boss in the same way as you behaved towards your old teacher. Whilst you know your boss is not your teacher, transference works unconsciously and so we are apt to put the faces of others onto new people. This transference also applies to experiences that remind us of something else. I wonder if the tapestries we live behind completely occlude the vision of truth. I have noticed that theme restaurants and theme nights abound. For example, in any provincial town, one can go to a local chain hotel for a theme night out. Here's what you'll typically get: you will be served with food that is pre-frozen and pre-packaged so that people can easily warm it up for you. Your ice-cream will come in a pre-prepared plastic mould that will be plopped into a glass. It gets worse. You will then see a tribute act ... perhaps someone dressed up and imitating Elton John and singing his songs. Perhaps he will be called something like Elton's John or Rocket Man. The act is no more real than your food. You will be experiencing this act, on an unconscious level, as reminiscent of the real thing, and an underlying part of you will believe that Elton's John is Elton John, especially if the act is a good mimic.

Comedy has gone the same way. Nowadays we can only laugh and cringe at a racist or office bore if they are contained within a character whom we can observe and, in some cases, pretend to laugh at. It is easy now for old writers to claim they meant to be ironic after all and claim that they weren't meaning to be racist or sexist after all. More recently we see Keith Chegwin's character in *Extras*, stating that: "the BBC is all run by gays and Jews". Ricky Gervais (in character) looks shocked and his (so called) genius writing encapsulates the revulsion we should all feel at Chegwin's politically incorrect statements – whether they are true or not. Gervais can get away with it as he has a beautifully crafted ironic umbrella, that perfectly couches today's zeitgeist. Gervais is a rich and clever one, as are the *Little Britain* creators. Both these modern, popular genre programmes rely on the use of an outdated character in order to say things that we are all supposed to cringe about, yet other viewers will undoubtedly enjoy on a non-ironic level.

But what we're really looking at here is a form of unreality or transference. It's okay to laugh at a joke if the character is ironic and twee, but if the comedian is 'real', everyone is offended or at least they have to appear to be. In other words, people are experiencing a version of reality that they want to see – i.e. something that resembles something else and not reality. They can only laugh at someone or something if the character is unreal or ironic. However, the joke is still the same whether it is ironic or it is traditionally delivered by the late Bernard

111

Manning. No matter how cool we think we are in laughing at the ironic characters in *Little Britain* or *The Office*, and how retro we might have become as we cast an askance look at the seventies and laugh, we are still laughing at the same thing and the result is a 'cringe' value, so beloved by today's popular writers. It's as if we have to take the piss in order to appear cool and above it all ourselves, whilst, in fact, many of us who laugh at these characters are indeed the characters themselves. Sasha Baron Cohen's Ali G was in fact so convincing that he became a role model for the very people he was parodying ... people who went on to refer to their girlfriends as *bitches* and *me Julie*! A misogynist is a misogynist whether it is cloaked in a character or comes to us as a Chubby Brown rant. You could even argue that Chubby is more honest.

Similar things have happened in the world of jazz. Jazz music is basically free form, musical improvisation and it is meant to be indulgent and creative. Of late though, jazz has come to mean *cocktail jazz* or *dinner jazz* and nothing really to do with creativity as branders have got hold of something free, tried to capture its freedom and package it into some grotesque consumer product. I thought this was most successfully done on a recent visit to Centreparcs. I like Centreparcs because it is scroat free, litter free, and (unlike Blackpool or London) you don't feel as if you're about to be stabbed at any minute. If this is a walled holiday, free from undesirables, I say bring it on. Anyway, Centreparcs have beautifully created, fabricated experiences that are absolutely false but credible. So you'll have a Chinese restaurant, Indian restaurant, Aqua Sana etc., but none of it is 'real'. It is a marketeer's copy of something real. Reality exists in Chinatown or Rusholme in Manchester and you know that's real because those businesses have history and you will be walking past homeless people and muggers as you make your way in. Branders and marketeers do not want us to analyse it though ... they want us to buy into it. We are now a people who are spun and branded everywhere we turn – it's as if everything has to be branded in order that people will consume and be interested. Even *Muji* is a clever, no brand brand: a sort of ironic spin on a spin.

In some ways, knowing how transference works, you often don't need the real thing, all you need is an adequate copy, and this is why you don't really need to have much talent to get on in life, just like some of the stars cited in a previous chapter. Or you could 'model' yourself on someone successful like the Neuro-Linguistic-Programmers suggest. Here, you copy someone successful and watch the money come flooding into your own gates. This is okay to a degree and can keep you occupied and hopeful for many years, until you realise that your modelee is related to or sleeping with someone important.

In many ways, our collective unconsciousness as a nation has become altered by advertisers and marketers so we don't know what is real and what isn't. Speaking of the collective unconscious, I am overwhelmed to see the success of Apple's iPod over the past few years. In the 1980s everyone had or wanted a Sony Walkman, so they would never be without music wherever they went. If you haven't got one, the iPod is much more flexible and probably highly desirable. However, it's not just what it does that makes it desirable; it's the fact that everyone else has got one. You can see people with them strapped to their arms in gyms. I suspect that nobody really is primarily interested in music; their main concern is how they look to others and how trendy they will appear if they have one. If anyone did want music with them all the time, the Sony Walkman would have never died out, yet there was a barren period in the 1990s when the Walkman was out and the iPod hadn't come in. Shock, horror. I wonder how people ever coped in this decade without the constant chatter of music … schizophrenics* would pay dearly to be rid of voices in their heads, yet the fashion conscious literally pay dearly to have their favourite music with them all the time. The music isn't the thing though! It's the statement they are making in having one. It could be turned off as long as everyone knows you have an iPod.

[* I use the term schizophrenics to denote people with schizophrenia. I know that the term 'a schizophrenic' is now thought of as a derogatory label and political correctitude asks us to say 'people with schizophrenia'. Observe how the government now use the term 'the British people' or 'the Iraqi people' rather than 'the British' or 'the Iraqis'. A new term does not forgive an uninvited war. I wonder how long it will be before we start using the term 'the millionaire people', or 'a person with many millions'. It is the ridiculousness of this new usage that makes me use the term 'a schizophrenic' and I mean no disrespect by it, as I would mean no disrespect by use of the term an Iraqi, or an American or a millionaire.]

Notice the latest rise in the popularity of the iPhone ... everybody wants one (except those who can't afford one and claim they don't like them). It seems that most people want to copy their peers or show off in some way. This is nothing new. Most people seem to ape each other just to fit in, seemingly more at ease with copying than origination, following rather than leading. This explains why so many people jump on the band wagon when a new product comes out. They buy things they don't need – and probably don't want – just because everyone else has one, like lemmings jumping off a cliff. Couple this with clever advertising and a pervasive superficiality in the general public, and bang ... you have a product that does a few fancy things, that nobody really needs, and sells in vast quantities. I think this is pure fcuking genius. But it gets even more beautiful. Just imagine if manufacturers and their advertising agencies could sell something so well that people were absolutely *convinced* that they needed the product. For this, they would have to ensure that their adverts were omnipresent (like Coca-Cola and their legendary multi-billion dollar advertising budget) and that they really infiltrated buyers' subconscious minds with seemingly *meaningless* straplines such as "Think different" (*Apple*). It has worked so many times and on such subtle levels that the buyer, convinced he can improve his life in some way, will rush out to buy his gizmo: ironically proving that he is thinking no *different* after all. Consider the *pure genius (Guinness)* involved in the marketing of FCUK brand. The agency responsible for the success of using the FCUK word spawned lots of T-shirts that rebelliously minded people could wear in order to shock others, the wearers gaining the satisfaction that they are a bit naughty and modern. When the FCUK brand was at its height, I noticed a modern Dad with his young child in Manchester's Trafford Centre. The father sported the words 'I couldn't give a FCUK' on his T-shirt. I wondered with disdain what message this gives to the child? Of course, the superficial pedant will be at pains to point out that the real word is FUCK and not FCUK but the subliminal and unconscious message is the same. This brand would have had absolutely no success in the 1950s but it is successful now because it incorporates the fact that people think it's cool to be bad and in displaying these obnoxious and offensive T-shirts they are telling others how bad – and therefore how cool – they are. I think this trend for cool badness originally started in America and coincided with rap culture. Role models who are deemed uber-cool (puff daddy [or whatever he is now called], 2-pac, 50-cent, Snoop Dogg, etc) all have had or are involved with guns and/or criminality and if these are our children's icons then it is little wonder that this country is in a scroat ridden mess.

More recently (January 2008) I was in the locker room of my gym and noticed a blingy belt worn by a young man who was changing near to me. Written in diamante-encrusted jewels within the belt were the words 'fucking criminal'. I wonder what message this conveys? He didn't actually look like a fucking criminal; he looked like a privately educated, white middle class lad with a strange *bed head* haircut, but my mind boggled at how rap and gangsta culture has permeated the echelons of Lytham St Annes' elite, to the point that anyone would wear a belt boasting that he was a fucking criminal. I notice with some mirth that *Viz* magazine are now selling shirts with CNUT on the front.

You've got to ask yourself, who are you trying to impress? Your other shallow friends who need these things because of the chasms within their souls? Then ask yourself: Would you have an iPod if you were the only person in the world? And: would you have a *boob job* if you were the only person in the world? You see, if you run about trying to please others you will never become happier within yourself. You will just inflate your credit card bill along with your breasts or your penis. In psychoanalytic terms (loosely speaking) these things are just extensions of the ego anyway. So, ask yourself: who are you trying to impress and why are you trying to impress them? If your ambitions are founded on impressing others, you must look within yourself to see what you lack and why you want to impress others. If this is your only motivation, then you can still have a go at *making it big*; it never seems to stop anyone who has appeared on C4's *Big Brother*, and some contestants seem to have made lots of money following their TV appearances. Here we see people with not even the pretence of singing talent being hoisted up for public acclaim and becoming famous. So, if you want to become rich and famous, and you have no talent to speak of, you might as well go for it. For this you need confidence and belief ... and *not* oodles of talent. This knowledge is important in deciding on your future career or even a change of career ... that is, knowing what you really want.

It may be that we strive forever looking for something or trying to please others, forever buying things, chasing rainbows, mating with the wrong people, only to realise that there is a pleasure in just giving up the dream or getting off the treadmill. There is some relief to be had from just accepting ourselves as we are, free from delusions or illusions; accepting the present moment and awakening in awareness. We can go on chasing dreams and chasing ideals but does it make us any happier or is the happiness in the chase itself? International Society of Plastic Surgery found that the UK is third in the world for breast enhancements performed on a yearly basis. America is first on the list, followed by Brazil (see www.isaps.org).

Topless models help newspapers sell thousands of copies with their attractive pictures emblazoned inside. It is a telling indictment that any society would accept such a ridiculous concept: a photograph of a young female showing her breasts in a newspaper! I am not saying that such a spectacle is not nice to look at but that the idea of it is almost appalling and slightly weird. Alas, this is the way society has gone and such newspapers that reside in the houses of young girls, show the youth the wrong message about women. This beautifully encapsulates our current 'tits-on-a-stick' culture. It is also interesting how the word 'boob' has become part of our language. It would appear that many young girls (under 25-ish) are so keen to emulate those celebrities who are famous for being famous that they get their *boobs* done as soon as they are at the legal age of consent, perhaps as an eighteenth birthday present. The shallowness of this is astonishing, but it runs deeper than mere shallowness. It means that the girl considering a boob-job feels inadequate in some way, as if she is not enough. Fashion magazines fuel their feelings of inadequacy and perhaps their partners would also prefer a bigger boob to fondle. Girls must ask themselves this: if your partner defines the relationship he has with you solely (or even partially) revolving around the size of your breasts, ask yourself if this is the man you want to be attached to. I know that some female readers will argue that they are having their boobs done for themselves but I would ask them to deeply analyze why they would need to enlarge their existing breasts. Of course, men are not exempt from enlargements. I understand that several clinics offer penis enlargement, especially in America. Who are we all trying to please? Is it inevitable that we will be left on the shelf if our breasts or penises are not big enough? You can also ask yourself if you have more to offer than sexual size because looks are fleeting and will eventually evaporate regardless of whatever surgery you might put yourself through. The key to unleashing yourself from all this torment lies in accepting yourself as who you are but I am very aware that this can be difficult. If you have been brought up as always left wanting or needing, you are likely to be prone to judging yourself harshly as you were judged as a child. Therefore you must look for a loving arm and a partner who appreciates you for what and who you are rather than what you look like. This way you will achieve a more lasting happiness as you will remain to be who you are long after your boobs have gone south (due to the weight of the silicone) and your penis is no longer proud every ten minutes.

Whether it's breast augmentation or botox injections or stomach staples or any so called enhancement, it all adds up to the same thing … short-termism – easy solutions that we can embrace and get a quick answer rather than looking at our inner angst and trying to achieve a more satisfying long term solution.

I'll try anything once

To live life to the full, there is an avant-garde maxim which states, "I'll try anything once". This ethos has a host of devotees as if it holds the openings to a fulfilled life. There are many things that you can try once, such as crystal meth that leads to dreadful addiction; or you could have a clandestine extra-marital affair, leading to divorce and bankruptcy and seeing your kids once a fortnight for an hour. Or you might try murdering someone which will probably lead to life imprisonment. I could go on, but clearly, trying everything once is not always a good idea.

Of course, you might be an idiot and try anything once, then wonder why your life has turned sour ... but you won't know why because you are an idiot so you'll be in a state of not-so-blissful ignorance. You might then develop regrets or guilt, even though guilt seems to be becoming less featured in modern Britain. (How can one harbour guilt when one is so angry with the society that continually deserts one, rapes one, continually demands money, spies on one, and then taxes one to death?) However, to make ambitions come to pass, you must indeed try your dream or you'll never know what the outcome might have been. If your dream is harmless and it hurts no-one else, why not try it? Then you will indeed be living a full life and diminishing any bitterness that might envelop you in later life should you never try.

The industry of a prime minister

During his tumultuous Premiership, I was a secret admirer of Tony Blair; not so much for his policies or the Iraq war, but more for the fact that he seemed very busy and got a lot done. I also thought he was genuinely funny. You need to be busy and get a lot done if your ambitions are to succeed.

Of course, Tony Blair and other industrious people rely a lot on others in order to allow them to go quickly through life. Had Blair been a *nobody*, his busy-ness would have soon been thwarted as he negotiated traffic jams, went online to pay congestion charges, stood for hours in airport queues, waited at bus-stops and so forth. However, successful people don't do this; someone else does it for them. This is about delegation, getting someone to carry your things, having a private plane so you eliminate airport queues, having diary secretaries, receiving précis notes and briefs, having speech writers put your ideas into words (if you have ideas). This would apply to Elton John in much the same way as it does to Blair. Noted for his speed in writing songs, Elton goes into the studio, bangs something down, then lets the band and a host of other people add to his work. Elton probably never gets involved in selecting a particular reverb for his vocal or worrying about which studio 2nd engineer to use. Both Blair and Elton are working at optimum efficiency and therefore their outputs are phenomenal: someone else is doing a lot for them. In this way, successful people can appear to be greater than they actually are. Everyone who is productive has a band of helpers. If you cannot afford a band of helpers then you need to find people who believe in you, who will work for next to nothing, just to be around you. They will gladly support you and pull your strings in the hope that one day they will bask in your glory.

Most people procrastinate endlessly and get involved with the minor details of life whilst rich people get someone else to do things for them. You could call this time management or delegation, but it's also the ability to see the bigger picture rather than just focussing on the minutiae or some other trivia. Rich people have the ability to see where they're going and be highly productive because they have a band of people and assistants around them, helping them achieve their goals, so they can do their work, be very efficient and succinct, then leave.

Successful people intuitively see what they should be doing in the smallest possible time in order to achieve the maximum results. The art of doing less and getting more. This process helps if you are in the *genius* category like Elton, but there are plenty of people who make quick strikes, gain great credit and big rewards, whilst seemingly do nothing; this is because they are surrounded by loyal (and paid) acolytes who are only too keen to bathe in the afterglow of perceived genius. Captains of large corporations have a genius for asset-stripping and cutting staff wages to the bone as they slurp on the cream at the top of the company.

Replacing Fred 'the shred' Goodwin is the son of an Oxford don and, himself an Oxford graduate, Steven Hester as the new chairman of the state-owned Royal Bank of Scotland. We hear in July 2009 that Hester is in line for a £10,000,000 bonus if he performs his duties well with RBS. I wonder what this performance will involve. Would that we could all perform so well.

I noticed with some sadness on the day that Blair resigned as Prime Minister that he was left to carry his own cases at a train station. Even for someone this great, things don't last forever. If your own ambitions extend to this level of stress or greatness, you need helpers, like Santa Claus. It's easy to elect to be a scroat, losing yourself in cheap cider, and a lot harder to become Blair … why not chose greatness since you only have one life?

Action makes dreams come true

"When you wish upon a star, makes no difference who you are, when you wish upon a star, your dreams come true", sings Jiminy Cricket in the evergreen Disney song from the enchanting 1940 *Pinocchio* film. However romantic this sounds, it is imperative to know that 'wishing' doesn't actually create dream fulfilment. In the many biographies I have read, it is very clear that action is the key to success and fulfilling one's dreams. I cannot stress ACTION enough. You could cogitate and theorise forever and never make a dream come true. We know all the clichés, such as 99% perspiration, 1% inspiration and perhaps such clichés are true, for without the necessary hard work, it is unlikely that anything substantial will happen. However, you've got to be pushing in the right direction, guided by an inner light, gut instinct, intuition, or whatever you want to call it.

However, you might be Paris Hilton and be able to afford to release your own pop record. Paris didn't make a bad fist of singing and, in my humble opinion, compares favourably with so-called *credible* singers. Should you give up? Well, it's sometimes tempting to throw in the towel and quit, but attention should be drawn to the famous tale of Ray Kroc – founder of the McDonald's empire. He didn't find his great success until the age of 52. He beavered away for years in business until this happened and then he became an 'overnight success'. Thirty years is a long night.

Plainly, Ray kept going and, whether you like McDonald's or not, you cannot help but admire what he achieved. Of course, if you do quit, you will be resigning yourself to being a loser. To be a winner you must put yourself into the losing frame. For example, a great snooker player who never competes will never win, therefore he must compete and be willing to fail in order to win. You must be willing to be rejected, scorned, pitied, ridiculed, and poor, if you are ever going to reach your goal; willing to place yourself in the zone of failure to be able to grasp success, for if you are not in the zone of failure, you will be in the zone of comfort and success never lies there. In other words, you have to be prepared to fail in order to succeed because failure and success are bed partners. For winners, giving up is never a real option and should just be a passing thought confined to down days. When you lie back on your death bed (if you have a relaxing death) you will at least know you tried rather than wishing you had. That will be a more fulfilling feeling of having a life that has been fully lived. If you have lived and tried, you will lie back in a satisfied repose. We are all prone to dying and so the key is to live while you can and try for your dreams. We never know when the reaper's grim finger will appear and it is always in our peripheral vision.

Life is unfair

Since death is only ever round the corner, a corner we cannot see, we have to acknowledge that life has very few truths or rules. The unfairness of life and death is a major tenet and realisation for some people and it must be embraced if one is to live in reality. Although successive governments promote fairness and equality, is this the actual reality of life or are they just paying lip service and spinning like ad men? How can life be anything but unfair? A child develops cancer. Someone else is born to rich, doting parents. Others are born in the gutter. Some are born with immense musical gifts. Others (to make a list would take too long) are not. Some make huge amounts of money based on the suffering or exploitation of others. Some work hard in two jobs to feed their kids and find that their ends still don't meet. Education systems strive to iron out differences in order that everyone will be treated fairly and equally, and these are noble intentions. (Ironically, most parents seem to want *their* children to do better than other children.) Marx wanted everyone to be equal, but as Orwell's allegorical *Animal Farm* shows, it doesn't really work. Observe the polarities that have occurred since the Iron Curtain came down. We now see super-wealthy oligarchs basking in the radioactive glow of Capitalism, and peasants who crave the return of the communist regime … at least then they didn't know they were poor; now they know they're poor and see all those things in the shops that they'll never be able to buy. Marx would now be turning in his Highgate grave to observe the inequalities that still exist in all modern societies and organisations. Nothing much has changed and, if anything, things have got worse than Marx may have expected. The poverty gap has not really altered and the wealth is still largely concentrated in the hands of the few who sell products and exploit their workers. It is still the fat cat who creams the profit and still the worker who toils for another's holiday in the Indian Ocean. For Marx, this was criminal.

The above kind of capitalism always seems to bring the beast out in the winners and the materialists; but there are many who do not strive at all and spend their lives shackled to a system that drains every ounce of life from them. Their efforts are rewarded by the minimum wage (if they're lucky).

Supermarket giants and all the other hugely profitable companies would no doubt infuriate Marx. Consider the billions of pounds of profit they make compared to the miserly amount they pay to the majority of their employees; wages that meander around the minimum wage. These companies argue that their workers are not just motivated by money, so they give them stars and little incentive schemes. As far as I can see, and with very few exceptions, wealth is never circulated fairly. This ethos is also reflected in 'fat-cat' wages. Add to this that governments conspire in colluding with these bastions of industry by offering tax incentives. Thatcher annihilated the mining industry and ruined their communities. Not long after that, the Conservative Government of the time were dead against awarding low paid workers a minimum wage. People like Michael Howard argued that it would be bad for business (Michael Howard QC, who would have an earning capacity of around six thousand pounds per week). The audacity of this is appalling and so very sad for those at the bottom of the wage scale who are just trying to get by. In some ways it's a good job Marx is dead so he wouldn't have to witness the fact that Britain has not changed … in reality it has worsened since his time as the poor/wealth gap is as wide but now more disguised. Exploitation is still rife and although we are ameliorated and appeased by Government placebos and gimmicks, the reality is that we live in an unfair, obnoxious society. I think that this explains the rise of scroatism; given that society is now globalized and forever changing, cohesion has disintegrated, so why should the young have any regard or respect for the society in which they live when it is all so meaningless and devoid of harmony?

Those who deny this have been blinkered by the media and are in denial because they have some paltry shares and believe that they are capitalists. They are obviously deluded. As in Marx's day, we still have to sell ourselves as prostitutes so that we can dance upon the capitalist's treadmill. When you realise that your 'star' awards are just pats on your tiny heads, perhaps the whole façade can be illuminated. But what is the solution? Well, unfortunately, there isn't one. If we think that we enjoy working in a call centre or at a checkout till, we have been brainwashed. Perhaps the minimum wage is all the balm we need. Nothing is fair unless one is taking an absolute share of the profits and the risk. Work is only enjoyable if it involves creating something or helping someone.

Rules

If you are one of those people who believe in playing by the rules and one of your core values revolves around fairness, you may have to take a hard look at your beliefs in order to become more relaxed. Does it annoy you if someone pushes in front of you in a queue? Do you become inflamed if a lottery winner squanders his booty on trash when you would have put it to better use? Are you derailed when you learn that someone of lesser ability than you has won a promotion or been left an inheritance that will enable them to pay off their mortgage? If you answer in the affirmative to any of these questions you may be living under the delusion that life has to be fair or that there are certain rules to which life should pertain. Perhaps you know this and project your blame onto certain groups who bestow benefits upon each other and 'use their own' and the ethos of 'It's not what you know, it's who you know'. Of course, being helped up the ladder by your group can mean that you require a modicum of talent. However, there are a great many well-paid jobs in television, politics, and the music business that require very little talent and yet multi-millionaires populate these industries simply because they had the right family group. It's amazing what you can do with the right contacts.

Sadly, you might have a lot of talent and no contacts: I suspect that this is more common than vice-versa. That is to say, if you have a lot of contacts and no talent, you're laughing all the way to the bank when one of your friends or family gets you a television job. This is when the unfairness of life comes to pass. Well, I say unfairness, but perhaps a better word would be reality. If I had the time to examine every successful person's biography to see how they *made it big*, I would probably find that most of them had an important connection that defined their career. As if this isn't enough, they then come to believe that they have talent, and go on to become uber-egos. I must say at this point that comedians seem to be an exception to this rule; this is because comics *have* to have a talent, so when one reads about Frank Skinner or Billy Connolly, they are often *there* on their own merits as raconteurs, oftentimes in spite of hugely traumatic early lives. For singers it's a lot easier … unless they are outstandingly brilliant, contacts come in very useful for the vocalist as they can *wing it* somewhat and don't have to be brilliant, because music is a matter of opinion. Comedy is not, so it simply has to be funny. (This is not to say that an average comedian couldn't become famous if his father was the head of entertainment at the BBC.) With only a paucity of talent, you have to know someone who will put you in the right spotlight, but beware ... there are those who will pretend that they have the power to change your life but they are demi-Gods; only you will know if your father is Michael Aspel or Michael Grade or Michael Winner or Michael Caine. These are serious Michaels... the big hitters.

In the introduction to this book I briefly looked at the career of my favourite author of fiction, Sidney Sheldon. He started his working life with the dream of becoming a writer. His real name was Sidney Schechtel and he was one of the many Jewish people who made it big in Hollywood. I suspect he changed his name to cover his Jewish identity as was the trend at the time but he claims that he changed his name to make it more easy to pronounce and catchy. Most Jewish people working in the film and creative industries at that time changed their names. Then, and to the present day and the foreseeable future, the Jewish contingent is overwhelmingly powerful in Hollywood. As mentioned earlier, it is not unusual for Jewish people to be great in what they do; they help each other out and, like all races, favour their own kind. In the first series of *Extras* Ricky Gervais uses the hackneyed character of Keith Chegwin to make the statement that the BBC is "run by gays and Jews". As a politically correct nation we are meant to be shocked and appalled by this statement and Gervais gets away with using the outdated character in order to make this point. The point can be enjoyed on two levels: you can either agree with Chegwin and believe that it is true, or you can be appalled and shocked at the anti-Semitic homophobic comments (which they are). Either way, there is some truth that the Jewish race seem to have done exceedingly well in entertainment both in the UK and across the pond. How can one be called anti-Semitic for stating the truth? This truth is not stated out of resentment and is just an observation, so the comments have no bad intentions. Have we become so touchy about what we can and cannot say that it is impossible to state that Jewish people are in charge of film, television, and media … is this not a truth? Unlike sport say, where you've got to be good and prove yourself, people in the know can often find themselves in highly desirable positions because they know someone who knows someone else. Again, if you are not well connected, this is something you might just have to accept. What choice do you have?

It is my own belief that society is richer for the Jews, especially their wonderful musicals: Rogers & Hammerstein (*The King and I, Carousel, The Sound of Music, South Pacific*), Sammy Kahn's songs, the Gershwins (*Porgy & Bess, Rhapsody in Blue*), Lerner and Lowe (*My Fair Lady*), Lionel Bart (*Oliver*), Leonard Bernstein *(West Side Story)*, Irving Berlin, Marvin Hamlisch (*A Chorus Line*). The world of film and music: Kirk and his son Michael Douglas, DeNiro, Barbara Streisand, Barry Manilow, Neil Diamond, Dean Martin, Peter Falk, Cary Grant. And then there are the film studios: Disney, Warner, Metro Goldwyn Mayer. The list is endless and there follows a vast array of current British celebrities and presenters who could be added to it: Tess Daly, Natasha Kaplinsky, Gaby Yorath, Jeremy Paxman, Bruce Forsyth, Bob Monkhouse, Alexi Sayle, David Baddiel, Stephen Fry – methinks the Jewish people are blessed with more than their fair share of talent. However, some people's (Jewish or not) only talent is the reading of an autocue; this is where nepotism comes into play and the fact that life isn't fair. My own field, the world of psychotherapy, has been greatly advantaged by the writings of Freud, Yalom, May, Perls, Berne, Ellis, Frankyl, Dryden … all of whom were/are Jewish. The Jewish influence on psychotherapy is the topic of a book in its own right.

I know I'm on shaky ground and I really don't want to offend anyone and I have to really stress that these aren't anti-Semitic comments, just statements of fact. I'm sure that a clever statistician could put shame to my claims and apply a spin on them, but this would miss the point. In addition to this, it is virtually *impossible* for me to be a racist since I myself am half-caste or mixed race or dual heritage, or whatever politically correct word is currently used. This means that I don't see races:

I see people. And I see that certain groups of people help each other get to the top.

Anyway, curiously, all the people who helped young Sidney Sheldon along his way were Jewish. Anti-Semites or even Muslims may be aghast to read this but hasn't it always been the same? Like minded souls always stick together – birds of a feather and all that. No one could argue that the Jews were under represented in the entertainment business and that's just the way it is. Similarly, and conversely, Asians are under-represented in the world of football. The Chinese are virtually absent from our British House of Commons. Groups form; some are powerful, some are not, perhaps power comes in numbers as Karl Marx would have argued about workers' revolutions. I am not singling out the Jews or any other particular group but rather highlighting the fact that you will get on better in life if you are part of a group that furthers your ambitions. If they were not shooting each other, wouldn't gangsta rappers be similarly nepotistic and introspective? Or the Masons, or the Oxbridge lot (Baddiel, Cleese, Palin, Cook and Moore, Alan Bennett, Blair, Cameron, Rick Stein, Fiona Bruce, Kristnan Guru Murthy – this is another infinite list). You could also argue that these are the most gifted and bright members of society, but I would suggest that they are the most advantaged due to their backgrounds. Perhaps those who attended Oxford or Cambridge are the best and cleverest folk in the world. Perhaps President George W Bush got there on merit too?

Is this unfairness? If it is, you will have to accept it! After all, what can you do about it? The Palestinians have found that strapping a bomb to themselves is no answer and it probably hurts a lot; same goes for the suicide bombers or 'freedom fighters' of Islam. There must be a better way than that. I think that the argument goes that the Jewish political lobby in the US is so strong in supporting Israel (the promised land) that the Palestinians have no real political option in the face of supreme Jewish power. In simple terms, some groups help each other out and create an impenetrable homogeneity that makes the group stronger and more potent, albeit closed. David Icke in his writings is often accused of using his Lizards as a metaphor to describe Jewish people but he claims not to be: who knows? His books are very interesting and complicated and if you like conspiracies, you'll love Icke. *Knowing* something that can't be proved (death of Diana, fake moon walk, 9/11 stuff, etc) won't improve your own life ... it'll probably just make you paranoid and bitter. You'll never know unless you are one of the 'powers that be' or the 'forces that work in this country' and if you are, you will claim that there are no conspiracies and there are no closed groups. Thankfully, some people appear still to be able to get up there without obvious affiliations to any group. This isn't such a long list. Billy Connolly ... erm.

Unions operate in the same way as groups but at least you don't have to be a certain creed or colour to join a union. I notice with some dismay how the unions have become more toothless since Thatcher's era and even those whom the unions were designed to protect appear to be against the union movement; again, this reflects the disintegration of society. There is no protection in this dog-eat-dog world and the scroat epitomises this state of affairs. Sadly, the scroat is a live apparition of all our broken dreams for in him lie society's woes made manifest ... almost like Jesus, he carries our can. This could all be very depressing if you aren't a brilliant Glaswegian comedian or don't belong to a particular group but you might take comfort in the fact that Elton John is not a Jewish entertainer, Eminem is not black, and Jung was not a Jewish psychologist. There are still spaces for the very good. But the 'outsiders' really have to be very good. Sometimes one hears similar comments from women who work in men's worlds, who say that they have to be twice as good as their male counterparts in order to succeed. Perhaps they are right, although in my own counselling field, I notice that most counsellors are women who appear to recruit their own sex.

The main trouble with groups is that they tend to engender hostility, envy, or scorn from those outside the group. When you're an outsider it's very easy to bleat but doesn't every group help its members? Would you not do the same in their position? Privilege is as old as mankind and as common as misfortune. Some members of the British Royal Family enjoy great wealth, never having to queue, always being protected, eating wonderful food, being chauffeured everywhere, flying in luxury, etc. At the other end of the scale, some children develop cancer at the age of seven and their lives are blighted as the pernicious disease eats its way through every crawl space in their tiny bodies. One of the tenets of rational emotive behavioural therapy (REBT) is that life isn't fair ... who said it should be? Where is it written that life should be fair? This is why we will never really live in a meritocracy: because we are all 'given' different hands to play. The concept of merit is usually attributed to Michael Young, stemming from his seminal work *The Rise of the Meritocracy*, written in 1958. Meritocracy is a utopian ideal where those with talents flourish. I think this is true to some small degree but many are left behind as there is simply not enough room for all the talented to prosper. This is why you see many people doing mundane jobs although they have degrees and many qualifications. It seems to me that no political system really works, democracy being the best of a bad bunch. Dictatorships and totalitarian regimes are often brutal and fall apart as soon as anyone sees a Coca-Cola sign. Communism should have worked, and socialism should have worked even better ... but neither of them did/have in the UK. Perhaps, mirroring human nature, people are all too keen to shaft each other with one-upmanship and so it seems that democracy is the best of a few other systems that don't work as well. Like a salty sea tale, there are two currents; the over-riding white frothy waves that beat relentlessly on the shore, denigrating the socialist model, applauding the collapse of the Wall and the expansion of Capitalism. The undercurrent is very different. An underlying theme of deprivation culture pervades the air, engendered by a government who seems hell bent on selling consumerism. In rock pools up and down the Western world, small groups of pond life make do with scraps from the wake of all this confusion. These are the prostitutes, the drug dealers, the disenchanted, the disenfranchised, the disengaged. They are the detritus that fall off the wheel of industry and they either get crushed on the rocks or they fight as best they can on the black market.

According to the sociologist Peter Saunders (1990) Britain is a meritocracy, enabling virtually anyone to achieve their goals and get to where they want to in life, through their own merits and hard work. In my opinion, this is an idealised view but it sounds good on the surface ... something we'd all like to believe in. If Saunders meant that merit suggested privilege then he's probably right about Britain since those with the greatest privileges seem to do much better in life. Look at how many British Prime Ministers attended Oxford University to highlight this point. I'm certain that most of them got to Oxford partly on merit but the merit started when they were born. To believe that *any* society is meritocratic is to be deluded. Ex-British Prime Minister John Major was very fond of the meritocratic system but I am still waiting to see it come to fruition and I'm not holding my breath. Politicians make great claims for fairness and strive towards eradicating poverty and trying to give everyone a fair chance. It'll never work because some people are gifted from birth but I think it's important to pay lip service to equality if only to fend off revolution! At least if politicians pretend that everything is fair the system keeps turning. It's when people feel they are being exploited that things go awry, á la French Revolution and let them eat cake.

It's not *what* you know it's *who* you know (or blow) – a cliché but true, like many clichés. Whether it's knowing or blowing doesn't really matter as long as the people with influence can make your life better. Until quite recently, it used to be a given that "the rich man at his castle, the poor man at his gate" was the norm, and never the twain would cross. In more modern times, the Indian caste system reinforces ideas like this whereby the rich marry the rich and the scroats marry the scroats. You might think this is normal but it serves to diminish social mobility and ensures that wealth is concentrated in the hands of the few. In truth, merit probably plays a very minor role in the story of success. You may find that 'old money' is safe and well and can be seen driving round in *Chelsea tractors* near my local private school.

If you were not born with a silver spoon in your mouth and not connected to anyone important, you may become despondent that life has dealt you a bad hand. Unfortunately, this is something you're going to have to accept ... the undeniable fact that life is not fair. When a child bemoans, "It's not fair", the appropriate adult response would be "I know, and who said it should be; I'm sorry for you". You might believe in Karma ... what goes around comes around ... but even if you live what you think is a blameless, guilt-free existence, you may still end up being riddled by some horrific disease. Conversely, you may be a total waster who has used everyone to meet his own psychopathic ends ... and then die peacefully in your sleep aged 95, as your 22-year-old lover slumbers exhaustedly at your side. Apart from a few self-created rules we concoct to make life more fair or interesting (and we construct them to make sense of a chaotic world), there really aren't that many rules or entitlements when it comes to the bottom line and reality.

If there are so few rules that govern order, and even fewer truths to back them up, then what remains must be chaos and this, in most people, can create an overwhelming feeling of despair; so unable are they to tolerate uncertainty. This uncertainty is at the root of most anxiety states. For myself, this anxiety about meaninglessness will eventually give way to Buddhism.

I have mentioned comedians who find success having grown out of inauspicious circumstances. The musician, Gordon Sumner (aka Sting) also found great success for himself and, according to his autobiography, his background was the epitome of normality. Sting fits within the pantheon of great British musicians and his book *Broken Music* (2003) is very inspirational especially if you are someone without a silver spoon.

The Sting

The rock star Sting, in his memoirs, appears to have come from nowhere and made it big. He had a modest early life with no special favours and no private schooling as far as I am aware. *Broken Britain?* so far has mentioned that one has to place oneself in the right location in order to become successful (or be born into the right place) and it seems that Sting had an inner guide that enabled his dreams to reach fruition. Sting has always paddled his own canoe, being a green campaigner before it was fashionable, and I think he is a credit to perseverance.

On his yearning to reach the top, Sting appears to have had a self belief that kept him fuelled throughout the hungry years. It was as if his fantasy of making it big actually fed his soul until his *inevitable* break occurred. Had it not occurred, I suppose he would now be the head of English in a school somewhere in England. He seems to have acknowledges the un-likelihood of becoming successful, whilst striving for that very goal. We learn that Sting placed himself in the right frame for success, whilst being able to tolerate failure. He made several trips to London before moving there permanently. Again, Sting was around the right people and, most importantly, he did not lounge around in Newcastle waiting to be discovered. This would never have happened. I know that almost everyone in LA who waits on tables is an actress or actor, but at least they've gone there to give it a go ... auditioning, not waitressing.

Sting eventually parted with his Newcastle band that would not shift to London with him, and made a break on his own. Here, we see that he was willing to forego attachments in order to follow his goal. This would be a painful sacrifice for many people. I know in my own life story that I was so attached to certain people that opportunities that presented themselves in my early twenties were wasted. I also lacked the confidence to follow them through. Sting had no such reservations.

He writes very eloquently about his decision to move to London and feels that it was absolutely the right thing to do: he was right. Virtually nobody gets discovered in a one-horse town; this is the stuff of fairytales and films. If you seek success, you have to literally place yourself where opportunities abound.

Again, guided by an inner voice and belief in his own significant abilities, Sting *knows* that he's done the right thing. You too have to *know* deep down inside that you too are doing the right thing. If it feels right, it probably is right. After a while, if you have no anxiety about your decisions, you will know you were right.

You can cultivate lots of self-belief – you might not even have much cultivating to do – this implies that you will have to walk a fine line between arrogance and humility, striking the right balance so as not to alienate those who could be useful to you. No-one likes a big-head, especially if they themselves are untalented, so, you must attempt to hook someone's interest then pull away, so that they follow you. This is almost like a striptease. I think Sting had the perfect ingredients, the right eventual connections (which he forged himself), and a perfect balance between self-belief and assuredness. If you have a strong self-belief, you are lucky, and it's probably best to keep it to yourself in order to protect yourself from those who will drag you down with their *comedic* put-downs or others who will knife you with their jealousy.

Who wants to be a millionaire?

Being a millionaire these days is no big shakes. Becoming a millionaire is a different matter. Sometimes it's easy … someone may leave you a big house in their will and you will become an instant millionaire. You might play the National Lottery at a 14,000,000 to 1 chance of winning the jackpot, and then win it. You might have a great idea like James Dyson, become a multi-millionaire in the process, and then move your workforce to Malaysia. You might write a book like *Think and Grow Rich* whose sales alone will make at least (the author) Napoleon Hill (1966) become a millionaire. Additionally, if you have acquired your million in these ways and you have it in a secure bank, you would have to be a fool to lose it all. To be a fool in this instance, you will buy expensive cars, develop a cocaine addiction, and generally believe that you deserve the gift of wealth. Perhaps you do deserve it in some way but if you only have say £1.2 million then it will quickly go unless you are a big earner who can continually add to your pile.

Trying to find answers to the question of wealth. I combed several money-making books and eventually came to a few conclusions that I will share.

Persistence seems to feature heavily in the lives of self-made millionaires, coupled with an unwillingness to quit; a bit like the American way. Mention was made earlier of McDonald's emperor Ray Croc who became successful only after the age of 50, at a time when most people are thinking of taking it easy. Croc was the personification of endurance. So we learn that perseverance is a key to the rich door. This makes logical sense doesn't it? If you give up, you won't get anything, and by trying, you will be living.

Belief crops up again. Believing that you can get rich seems to be half the battle. If you only believe in negative childhood introjections, you'll never become successful. Believe in your goal, believe in your dream. And of course, the belief has to be realistic. It's no use believing you will become an Olympic Gold medallist in breaststroke if you are fifty years old. Nor should you believe that you can save your way to millions if you have a *normal* salary. Until the recent credit crunch, property ownership seemed to be the road to wealth but there's still some risk involved. If you want to make a lot of money for doing 'nothing', get into property as soon as you can. You will have to abide cyclic market crashes but it will always come back to you. An acquaintance of mine inherited a lot of houses when his parents died and he has spent his whole life driving around in one of his cars, simply collecting rent. He didn't have to become academic or develop a great talent. Some might argue that spotting the right investment properties to buy, at the right time, is a great talent, but it's hardly comparable to becoming the great Arthur Rubenstein or doing a PhD is it? And if your parents have left you a portfolio of bricks and mortar, you really are laughing … money for old rope. The academics – those who have higher degrees – can find solace in the fact that they are cleverer than the property owning classes, but in a society that largely respects wealth above cleverness, even the academics are left flailing when asked to pay for a holiday to Mauritius. Fortunately, the academics can claim that real joy lies in walking round an old castle in Wales on a wet day. This might well be so, so I just mention this point to illustrate that you need not be clever or talented to reap great financial rewards.

Age need not spoil your chances. If you have been practicing to become rich, like a trainee millionaire, you may have a series of failures in your wake; failures from which you will have hopefully learned some valuable lessons. So your age need not necessarily be a barrier – far from it, as the evidence shows. Age would only be a barrier to becoming an Olympian but greatness can still be embarked upon after the age of forty and perhaps fifty is the new black.

Energy is required in order to fulfil daily toils. Your goal might take a lot of hard work. You also need the energy to ignore the people who will try to derail you. One has to be filled with zest in order to fulfil one's goals. Maybe you've been brought up on poor thoughts until the spectre poverty now haunts your unconscious mind. This in itself will fuel your negativity and lead you towards disaster. You must take calculated risks and try to eradicate the 'shit street' mentality you may have learnt as a child. I remember a family member often saying she would be in 'shit street' if this or that happened. She didn't have an easy life and so her imaginary street was always round the corner. I did not enjoy the charmed life of the lucky and this shit street mentality fed my inner thoughts, causing me to fear that disaster was imminent or inevitable. I have later discovered that this was never the truth, just a catastrophizing fear. A person who has experienced this childhood is unlikely to take risks, unless they have a lot of counselling and self-knowledge. However, to become rich, you must take a few calculated risks. I'm not talking about casinos here, God forbid … but more like Sting did in moving to London and risking his career as a teacher. He speculated to accumulate, gambling his teaching for bigger goals.

Security is not always possible if you are going all out for a big dream; you might have to invest everything you've got, and most people don't like that prospect. This is the difference between Sting and the band he left behind in the North East. They chose stability, he went for the big time … and won. I wonder how many go for the big time and don't win? I imagine that the streets of London are littered with dreamers who lost. In going for gold, one has to embrace the power of the unconscious mind and really believe. This is why dullards seem to do well sometimes; not because of any special talent, but rather a willingness to risk it all. Some achieve great things and this is usually down to belief. For this, the unconscious mind cannot be hampered by thoughts of *shit street* or *shit sandwiches* or *life's a bitch and then you die.* You've got to be up for it and you too have to be guided by your own belief and gut instincts.

There are many writers of *improve your life* books who encourage us to say daily affirmations in order to confirm to ourselves that we are about to live a better, improved life. The idea behind it is that your subconscious mind *hears* your daily bon mot and reorganises itself in accordance with your wishes. I believe that there is a lot to be said for this technique; you generally become what you believe about yourself and repetitive affirmations convince the subconscious to find opportunities and lead us to golden veins that we might mine. Talking to children in put-downs leads your child to have low self-esteem and the Church of Scientology and the psychotherapy school of Transactional Analysis make much of the choice of language. In the way of a self-fulfilling prophecy, if we continually hear that we are no good – whether it's as a child or an adult – we generally become no good. If we are perpetually ridiculed, we become ridiculous. Conversely, if we give ourselves positive messages, we are meant to become greater. If you are surrounded by people who put you down, perhaps you should review your list of friends; why should you be the butt of anyone's joke? If you want to be successful, you are best to avoid those who scorn or ridicule you.

Perhaps the best known of these self-talk affirmations is the one by Emile Coue ... *Every day, and in every way, I am getting better and better.* There are many variations on this theme; I like: *I am healthy, wealthy, and wise.* Whether or not you are healthy, wealthy, and wise is not the point ... the point is that you are trying to become so. Also, by giving yourself this message, you are training your subconscious mind to think in a positive way; it will then guide you towards your dreams.

You can create your own affirmation if this appeals to you but try to make sure that it contains no negative words. For example, if your affirmation is: *I don't want to be fat any more*, you are using negative words like *don't* and *fat*, and the sentence itself is downbeat. You would be better redefining the affirmation into *I will be thin* or *I am slim* or something like that. This way, your subconscious mind will assimilate the positive message.

You may find that your life will improve as you become more focussed on your affirmative message to yourself. If all this makes you feel a bit anxious, bear in mind that you might as well be anxious about doing things that will improve your life than anxious about doing nothing. Boredom can also be stressful so you might choose to live life at the cutting edge. If you're going to be excited instead of frightened of stressors, you might as well be anxious or excited at the top of your tree, living your dreams. Where there is no risk there is no pride, so there can be little happiness.

Some *think gurus* suggest that we should visualise our goals, pretending that they already exist, seeing how they feel. It was said that *Queen* front man Freddie Mercury behaved like a star before he became one. I can believe that, but I also wonder how many people behave like a star and never become one. These people don't tend to write autobiographies. Many books have been written about creative visualisation. This involves allowing your subconscious mind to 'experience' an event before you actually achieve it ... in your imagination. In this way, you program your mind to expect success, using a series of imaginative meditations. The selected biography at the back of this book will suggest books for this purpose.

Many self-help authors invest great hope in the power of the subconscious mind. This can be harnessed to alleviate anxiety and many other symptoms (as we shall later see) but also to fulfil one's ambitions. This is not only about the power of the subconscious mind, but also using intuition. 'Knowing' and 'seeing' comes from within and cannot be evidenced ... sometimes we just know. None of this can be scientifically proven and in our increasingly 'evidence based practice' medical model of care, intuition and what we feel can and does take a back seat. However, it is possible to ask oneself a question (for example) before going to sleep and the mind will work on finding an answer in the night ... it's that good. Not only does sleep "... knits up the ravell'd sleeve of care", (Macbeth, Act II, Sc.II), and ease our woes, but also provides answers from the subconscious mind.

In addition to all this, we have to realise that <u>action is the key</u>. Without action, nothing will happen and the best time is now. We can sit and theorize forever and fill our minds with theories and philosophies and become armchair thinkers. If you 'know' you will succeed, don't be worried about making a fool of yourself or what others will say; just do it.

Montaigne advised that to succeed, you must act like a wise man and look like a fool! Elton John was a perfect example of this when he first splashed onto the scene in his outrageous outfits. But Elton was also rare and so his value increased. Verily he was no fool ... and still isn't.

So, if you're about to do something that you 'know' will lead to success, and you have decided to embrace your intuition, your subconscious mind, and act, then go ahead. Make sure it is something you enjoy and that won't get you into trouble. And you can't just want money. You have to do something else to achieve it unless you are a bank robber. Then you might well lose your liberty and spend twenty years in jail regretting that life has passed you by.

Remember that you might fail repeatedly before finding success – and this will be a learning curve for you; you will know what not to do next time. You must be in the zone of failure in order to find success ... this is very important. Hopefully, repeated failure will lead to success ... eventually. If you hide away from failure you will never find success because they are flip sides of the same coin. Nobody aims for the bottom yet, as I said earlier in *Broken Britain*? most people end up at the bottom or thereabouts. The idea is to harness your powers (assuming you have any), retrain your subconscious mind, rid yourself of possible parental put-downs, and avoid negative people who will drag you down or mock you. You might end up singing in a hotel bar, but at least you'll have tried. I personally know many hotel entertainers who could quite easily have been stars and, a lot of times, it's not through lack of trying that they end up singing for seventy pounds a night. They would say it's about breaks ... I would say that you have to make your own breaks if you have no-one to make them for you.

Ideally, you will get to know people who can make a difference for you. If you want to be a pop star, perhaps you need a proper manager, otherwise you will be sending off demos right, left, and centre, to no avail. If you're in a more normal job market, perhaps you need an employment advisor, and if you have no contacts, perhaps they do … of course, this will come at a cost. "…Who do I know? Nobody!" sings Fagin in Lionel Bart's film adaptation of Dickens's *Oliver Twist*. This is the crux of the problem if you want to get somewhere in any job. You need to get to know influential people.

When you're on your way try not to let a fragment of doubt derail the train of achievement. It is so easy to quit and go for a job in a supermarket stacking melons. Is that what you want?

Exercise

Are you working in a job you don't like? Are you fulfilling your potential? Do voices from the past haunt you?

I would ask you to list all the things you would like to have been and then assess whether or not you think any of them are possible. Having read the section about ambition, is it possible for you to alter your life so that you are more in tune with your purpose in life or dharma? Only you will know if you are truly fulfilled and whether your purchases are just placebos that hide the fact that you feel empty. If this is the case, you must decide what is important and then ditch the deadwood.

Addictions

Anthony King writes:

"I sit in a bar in Salou, Northern Spain (or perhaps Catalunya), sipping my humble diet coke and contemplating life. Nearby, a man with a large, loud family teaches his children how to drink alcohol. His teenage son is wobbling but trying to look macho as he imbibes his Stella, copying his father. The mother is drinking pints – in the spirit of girl power – and wears tattoos, multifarious earrings and a navel ring. They all have red faces, not from embarrassment but from too much exposure to the sun and all the other elements that consumerism has bestowed upon us."

Since the introduction of 24-hour licensing – which gave British bars the option to open round the clock – little has changed in the binge drinking habits of Britons. In introducing this irresponsible law, the new British Labour Government was keen to spin on the notion that since bars did not close there would not be a glut of drunken people piling onto the streets at 2 a.m. on a Saturday night. This law, in my opinion, was made with total disregard to the liver health of drinkers. Another spin was that perhaps the UK would adopt a more continental style café culture; this hasn't happened either and it probably never will. The supermarkets are no better and there is a correlation between cheap alcohol and binge drinking … the cheaper the beer, the more people will get drunk. Supermarkets are keen to get us through their doors so we will spend on more expensive items or do our weekly shopping at the place which sells the cheapest alcohol. However, when their spokesmen and women appear on TV to justify their cheap prices, they never admit it's about making more money for their shareholders. This is the worst part about it: the sheer hypocrisy. Readers might remember the furore caused by Gerald Ratner when he spoke about the "crap" his jewellery chain were inclined to sell.

Perhaps no one wants to hear the truth. Perhaps no one wants to tell the truth. Whatever the case, you can rest assured that it's all about money … money for supermarkets and taxes for Governments. It really is that simple. Alcohol is very cheap but it is also poisonous. Due to its content – ethyl alcohol – it probably should be banned but it is so entrenched in Western culture that this will probably never happen. So you have to make a choice for yourself. Do you want to become a slave to a poison? Or do you want to be free? In making your decision, bear in mind that most people who appear on TV will be spinners with a vested interest in making money out of you. Ratner spoke his truth then suffered for it.

They say that the apple never falls far from the tree and I cannot help but marvel at how teenagers copy the smoking and drinking patterns of their modern parents. Verily, the sins of the father (and mother) are visited upon the young. Although drinking alcohol and smoking nicotine does absolutely nothing for you, in today's permissive society however, it is shocking to see how many people do not actually care about their health. Additionally, alcohol is not seen as a 'sin', so keen are advertisers to ram their messages down our throats. Because many of today's parents are 'mates' to their 'kids', it follows that these kids will copy the behaviour of their mates; after all, mates are peers aren't they?

Since modern parents (and particularly scroat parents) are so ill-equipped to deal with setting an example to their children – and they would probably set a bad one anyway – their kids learn only laziness, apathy, addictive behaviours, sloth … and addiction. At the extreme, we see the mother of kidnap plot girl, Shannon Matthews, epitomising the behaviour at the worst outcrop of Britain under new Labour. The mother, Karen Matthews, had seven children by five different partners and had never worked a day in her life, relying on benefits instead.

The late, great American comedian Bill Hicks, in one of his rants about 'cracker spawn' and 'trailer trash' notices that liberals are all too keen that we shouldn't judge these low-lifes. "It's a judgement call, and I'm making it", says Hicks. Who will break political correctitude in this country and make the judgements now? The underclass have plainly lost their way. They are ill-educated and misinformed about almost every aspect of life. Morality is low and they seem determined to fulfil their own child-like fantasies without regard to any cost to themselves or society. I don't blame governments or schools for this. It is obviously parental responsibility – but there lies the problem … there is no responsibility and the ones who won't cast judgement are guilty of condoning this abhorrent behaviour by being silent and not judging these miscreants. In other words, by not judging, one is permitting the behaviour. If they were judged, they may feel some guilt and desist – without this guilt, what is to stop the clueless from leading carefree, damaging lives? Nothing … and this is why scroatism is everywhere.

In October 2008, the *Lancet* reports that every year in Britain, around one million children are subject to abuse … 'hitting with an implement, punching, beating or burning'. It goes on to say that 15 per cent of girls and 10 per cent of boys are exposed to sexual abuse which 'ranges from being shown pornographic material to penetrative sexual abuse'. One can readily observe soft-porn in national tabloid newspapers and so-called 'lads-mags'. Whilst the internet has revolutionized information, it has also brought pornography into almost every home that seeks it. The question is not where you draw the line any more, but where is the line?

Bringing children up today is like an all-inclusive holiday or an all-you-can-eat buffet ... you have to know when to stop. So keen are some people to have their senses blitzed, they do not know when to stop or how to stop, and they may not even wish to stop. With choice comes responsibility – one must be responsible in what you teach children, what you show children and how you act in front of them. I have counselled so many clients whose lives have been blighted by aberrant, useless, chaotic parenting. With children, we have to know when too much choice, and the purchase of that choice, can be bad for them. I have been on all-inclusive holidays where everything is included in the price, as the name suggests. Most children choose everything that is bad for their health given this smorgasbord of desire yet I observe that parents seem not to care what their children consume – mainly because they do not care what they themselves consume. In the light of the deprivation that clouds their normal lives, some people, free from usual restraint, go crazy like a bull in a China shop, rather like the children in *Lord of the Flies*. This is why your children are not your mates; they need boundaries and the boundaries need to be imposed by a responsible adult ... you! Parents (or mates) or even real friends (or mates) show younger ones what to do ... sometimes unconsciously and, in my opinion, this is how addictions are born.

It seems to me that we stuff things down our throats in order to compensate for living in the present, not living the way we want to do; sometimes we want to do something but don't, so we make up for this with compensatory behaviours, usually addictive substances, sometimes hedonistic thrill seeking. We may realise that our life is a mess and decide to lose ourselves in addiction. These behaviours temporarily quell resentment and dilute the unlived life, until one realises that time is passing and the behaviours are counterproductive. Smoking is more than addiction – it's a pacifier. Alcohol is poisonous (a fact you rarely hear in our society) yet we sit around quaffing away. Most indulgences are deferring the gratification that a real life could bestow and serve as alternatives to real living. The addictions come to fill gaps so revealed in Life Tree. This is controversial as many people would argue that they really are living if they are imbibing their poisons when in actual fact they are killing themselves. Some people describe smoking as a 'slow suicide', as if we are compelled by the subconscious mind to go and top ourselves. I don't believe at all that smokers are trying to kill themselves (subconsciously or not). Rather, I see that we are in the grip of addiction and it can be broken. Ironically, it can only be broken through interacting with the subconscious mind. All addictions can be combated.

Tamzin comments:

"Coke just seemed normal to me, like an everyday thing. I started off doing it at weekends but it felt so great that I would use it during the week whenever I was feeling low. I took coke like my Mum drinks wine, just as a normal part of my life. I once gave up for about three months and I was just miserable the whole time. Sure, I could see the world how it really was but who wants to? I started using again last month on my 25th birthday when my boyfriend brought some round for me. He taped a small bag of it in my birthday card as a present, and then I realised what I'd been missing. To be honest, I can't see anything wrong with it and I'll probably give up one day and settle down ... but not just yet. Everyone does it."

To learn more about present day popular drugs, I will look at the past.

Wartime attitude to food

During the Second World War (1939-1945) food was scarce. 'Luxury' foods were hard to come by, unless you had the right black-market connections. This meant that because of their scarcity, foods like chocolate became even more sought after than they already were. Anything that is rare becomes more desirable and its price escalates.

During this time, an attitude about food developed whereby people did not want to waste anything. This is very understandable since tasty commodities cost a lot and you wouldn't be seen throwing anything away unless it had turned rancid. Wartime was no time for being picky. One simply licked the platter clean.

Subsequently, children brought up in this period were strongly encouraged to eat everything up lest food, and therefore money, should be squandered. This was a time when you ate what you could, when you could. However, as anyone who's got children knows, children don't eat or think like that. They usually want to nibble a bit here and there until they're satiated, and then leave the rest. In this sense, like the cat, children intuitively know when they are full and will stop eating.

This attitude of eating as much as possible probably came into being long before the war, perhaps it existed since stone-age man brought home his first brontosaurus for a family bucket feast. Whatever the cause, we can clearly see how a relationship between food and emotions could have been built up when food was scarce. The underlying message is: "if you eat all your food it will please Mummy"; "I've cooked this for you and if you were grateful you would eat it up"; "I don't know where the next meal is coming from so you'd better eat this one". In order to not evoke anyone's ire, children were strongly encouraged to eat what was on their plate, and indeed, some would have wanted to anyway even if the plate contained only gruel. This would mean that the child growing up in this mid 20th century would have to ignore her feelings of 'fullness' in order to make the adults happy. In the extreme, perhaps some children were tortured in some mild way if they did not acquiesce.

Moving on to present day, since most people do things without much thought and are inclined to act upon their innate 'givens', what we now see is a transmogrified version of the wartime attitude. Where once mothers encouraged their children to eat everything because of food rationing, we now see the same encouragement to eat everything but for no apparent reason. Surely, once the food is bought it is 'wasted' and 'used' anyway? Sit in any gastro-pub or chain-style-reheated-from-frozen restaurant and you will hear mothers and fathers saying things like:

"Be a good boy and eat it all up."

Question: Why is Johnny a good boy if he eats it all up? It might be good if it's a super-food like broccoli (which it usually isn't) and he is out to mop up free radicals, thus reducing his risk of cancer, but to call him good if he eats it is to imply that he's bad if he doesn't. Perhaps this goes some way to explaining the fact that Britain has a growing obesity problem. Overwhelmed by a mother who judges her son's goodness by the amount that he eats, Johnny goes through his adult life trying to eat everything up until he becomes bloated but knows not why. He is unconsciously pleasing his mother in her earliest and most influential introjections that she has planted unwittingly into his tiny mind. Johnny too will probably encourage his own offspring to eat all that's on their plate as well, and so the cycle perpetuates – unless he gains awareness. More darkly, perhaps Johnny's mother is encouraging him to gorge in order to cover her own gluttony, so she doesn't feel too bad when ordering *Death by Chocolate*? In this way, the entire family will balloon and the family explanation will be that they are 'big boned'. The mother is unconsciously fulfilling her own childhood introjections that were born out of the war but are now no longer appropriate in wealthy nations. However, as stated, most people just say things without much thought and therefore these erroneous messages go on and on from generation to generation ad nauseam … literally.

"Eat up your chips then you can have an ice cream."

I recently heard this one in a faceless chain-café where the brand is strong but the menu is awful. In this instance, the father was encouraging Caitlin to finish all her French fries (carbohydrate and fat) in order that he might reward her with ice cream (sugar and fat). What sort of treat is that? I appreciate the fact that it's so easy to get into this trap with children as the 'desirable' foods are so heavily advertised that we are now unconsciously programmed to associate chips and ice cream with reward and happiness. In a society so bereft of happiness per se, the advertisers don't even have to do as much as they do in order to sell their stodge. The popular McDonald's *Happy Meal* is a good example; how happy can a meal be? And why is the meal happy? Are we really any happier after having eaten it (after the carbohydrate rush had subsided)? Are we any nearer to spiritual nirvana when we have consumed a McCain 'chip from heaven' or listened to their 'chips, glorious chips' advert which trots out the line only 5% fat etc. (Fat isn't really the problem as it's carbs that cause the most weight gain and chips are mainly carbohydrate, but nobody seems to get this fact.) So, Caitlin's father gave his daughter an admonishingly bad look until she finished the last chip then he went back to the counter and bought her an ice cream. She smiled and he plainly felt like a good parent. For sure, he's a better parent than Fred West, and he obviously had no malicious intent, but this is why British bellies continue to expand at an alarming rate, soon to catch up with our burgeoning US counterparts. (Although I think it's a bit different for Americans who I believe eat a lot out of their constitutional 'right' and believe that they are living personifications of liberty and freedom. I am free and therefore I will eat as much as I want. No-one will stop me. I shall carry a gun and shoot any motherfucker who denies me my rights. This me me me society however is probably here now anyway.) In 1965, the psychoanalyst Winnocott spoke of 'good enough parenting' … but this simply is not good enough and leads to a lifetime of problems and mixed messages that are hellish to sort out.

If we allow our children to give in to every desire, they are bound to become fat, especially since they are bombarded with advertising slogans day in and day out. This is freedom gone berserk and parallels an underlying process in our society that encourages hedonism in every aspect of our lives.

It is easy to see how food and love have become linked and this is further worsened by the fact that our children are often left in the care of non-parental hands. In a society so bereft of time and love, McCain hit the nail on the head, and their advertisers are surely very intelligent in knowing that our current society has a deep void of love. Conspiracy theorists might argue that the Government wants our kids to be in nurseries so that women can work and neglect their kids. There are many wrap-around nursery providers and many babies are left in private nurseries when they are only weeks old. One of the leading lights in Attachment theory and child rearing was John Bowlby, who did extensive work on child/mother bonding. Bowlby believed that poor bonding led to all sorts of unfortunate events to occur later in life and it is quite obvious and logical to see how this happens. Of course, mothers who leave their children at these nurseries aren't deliberately damaging them and the spinning is quite good, so mothers and sellers of child care places and governments who encourage such practices, can argue that it's actually good for children. It is not. (Hey, where's the evidence, Anthony? Look around you; some things cannot be evidenced.) Faulty bonds in early babyhood and pre-school lead to emotional impoverishment and cravings for love that advertisers can work on … sell more products … more money for the materialists and the government. This situation turns the wheels of industry and is good for capitalist societies and good for government coffers … everyone benefits except the 11-year-old who sits either in front of his telly or *X-box* all day and cannot run because his legs won't carry his weight as they scrape together in the middle. They sit there wanting to be cuddled, having never formed a bond with their BMW-craving mother, stuffing a chip from heaven or a Happy Meal into their mouths.

We are bombarded by advertising. It is impossible to hide or become immune from it. The statements presented by advertisers just have to be a bit credible. This can be seen in almost any advert you care to observe. And it has, through advertising propaganda, strongly influenced our thoughts and deeds throughout the past seventy years, with deleterious effects upon our offspring. Most of us are hooked by desires that advertisers create within us and they are very deft in anchoring our emotions in order that we will spend on things we don't need. In order to do this, they need to make us feel inadequate in some way. Desire for these things causes misery that we hope a new product will relieve.

In *Simpsons – The Movie* (2007), I noticed a banner advertising the fictitious *Duff Beer*, the favoured brand of Homer and friends. The strapline on the banner said 'binge sensibly!' I was overjoyed that the talented Simpsons' writers had comically identified the rich irony that occurs when products allowed by governments encourage consumers to be aware of what they're doing. You will see advisory guidelines on different foods and RDA (recommended daily allowance/intake) guidelines on lots of products. Perhaps this is as far as legislation can go in a free society as they couldn't ban products altogether could they? Binge drinking itself is a popular pastime enjoyed by many Brits, usually in town centres and cities, and is most evident at weekends when binge drinkers hit the streets (during the week people binge at home). It seems that Britons like to get 'shit faced' or 'rat arsed' as often as they can afford and many enjoy drinking to forget that they are in a job at a call centre, 'tied' to a phone and VDU all day (the modern day equivalent of a factory), in a job that has no prospects, pays badly, and causes alienation. Additionally, these corporate slaves may have been raised without that much love and so, rather than face all these hard truths, they like to go out and get blind drunk. This applies to both middle- and working-classes (who have recently merged as the middle classes are too embarrassed to appear superior and it's not cool to be clever since the Oasis/Madchester revolution). Our bar culture is populated by late-teen and under-30s showing their *boobs*, baring their arses, simulating sex on the floor, vomiting in shop doorways, hurling racial abuse to take-away shop owners (who are foolish or greedy enough to stay open) and generally having a great time. Often, these drinking binges are accompanied by E tabs or poppers, cocaine or crack (depending on what's available). We are encouraged to consume more and more and a successful, rich society like Britain relies on consumerism in order to function. If we are free, we are also free to abuse ourselves ... we also need to know when to stop but because we are all basically animals, we don't. The sociologist

Emile Durkheim described modern industrialised societies (like ours) as a 'disorganised dust of individuals', which, for me, calls to mind Margaret Thatcher's comment that "there is no such thing as society". This disorganised dust is the fragmented, broken society in which we now live.

Living in one of the capitals of debauchery (Blackpool) I often take my life into my own hands and wander around the puke strewn town centre on a Friday or Saturday night. It's not a pretty sight. Without wanting to sound like Noel Coward, I recently left my local theatre with my 12-year-old daughter, on a Saturday night, at 10 p.m., in the middle of Blackpool. I didn't know which way to go back to my car for the best. In one direction a group of women dressed as nurses were bending over and mooning at passers-by, two of them pulling their thongs to one side in case anyone had not seen enough. In another direction two gangs of males were vying with each other and pushing each other, spoiling for a fight. This is typical town centre behaviour and Blackpool is perhaps no worse than anywhere else; I've seen it everywhere, except in Stratford-upon-Avon – but that's another story. It is well known that the age of deference has now died and with it has gone respect. I believe that low-paid alienating jobs, lack of respect, bad upbringing, lack of love, and a notion that 'we are free to do whatever the fuck we please', has caused a rot within British society that is impossible to repair. Yes, I said impossible and I believe that there is no going back.

Writing this and witnessing such scenes make me feel like Edward Woodward's character in *Wicker Man*, where there is no morality and all around seems so shocking. I suspect that the current vogue in 'dogging' mirrors this societal shift in morality. Is this neo-paganism? I suppose it is, but without the need to worship anything but the God of materialism. I think that we now have a more heathen life than paganism because at least the pagans had some belief in nature and the elements. If religion imposes shackles upon us, then dogging and swinging must be the antithesis of this. Dogging and swinging would not in themselves be a problem (as long as they are not harming anyone else yada yada yada) but questions arise for me when I contemplate how the influence of the swingers passes down to their offspring. Undoubtedly most doggers would deny that their children are influenced at all but I believe that this is impossible, even if the influence is only subconscious. Initially, religion sought to suppress all this aberrant behaviour and make us into diligent workers (Protestant work ethic) but now, with increasing secularisation, the boobs are out. As thongs proliferate our psyche, God takes a back seat in the new town centre Sodoms.

It appears that the once laudable brand *Stella Artois* has now become the favoured drink of the lager lout (*Newsnight*, BBC, 2007). But it doesn't matter whether it's *Stella* or *Grolsch*, or *Budweiser* or *Becks* or the newly emerging *Magners*. Obviously, they all contain alcohol and this is where the problem lies. People just drink different brands because they have bought into the advertising and they believe that they are making a different statement to their friends; they wouldn't admit this because they don't know it and it acts unconsciously, but I do notice with some wry amusement that *Magners* is the current drink to be seen with. Anyway, to encourage us to drink sensibly, misses the point. The ones who don't drink sensibly never will as they are not bothered about messages from the nanny state. The best thing to do would be to not drink it at all. Who of these binge drinkers will go into a *Weatherspoon* pub and, having seen an advert to drink sensibly or stay within 21 units per week, decide to have one and a half pints of low strength lager and then walk home nicely? Will he choose to do this instead of having ten pints of Stella with Jack Daniels/Red Bull/vodka chasers? Who will? The truth is that these types of binge drinking consumer don't give a damn about what governments have to say anyway; they all know that governments lie and manipulate and evade and spin and take us into illegal wars that don't have UN resolutions based on dossiers that are sexed up by megalomaniacal rulers … so why should they listen to these people who are so very wrong about big stuff? This is why the *Duff* advert to Binge Sensibly is sublimely perfect.

Peter writes:

"I started drinking initially to quell my anxiety about living alone in Huddersfield. I was doing a degree and my girlfriend left me and my life seemed to fall apart when she went. Don't get me wrong – she was hard work anyway and a bit of a paradox; she wouldn't sleep with me but was happy to go with others behind my back. I think she was just young and mixed up but it broke my heart, especially when she would bring boyfriends round to our shared house; it sounds ridiculous now but I tolerated it just to be near her. I guess you'd call me co-dependant … I certainly was at the time.

Then after leaving University I got a mundane job that was well below my abilities. It was here I started drinking a lot. I thought at the time that I liked the taste and everyone else would drink too much as well. One night after leaving work drunk, I drove into the back of a parked car and fell asleep still impaled into its boot. It got that bad. I woke up a few hours later, reversed out and pissed off.

Everyone around me was drinking and appearing to be enjoying themselves but I know now that it was a shallow façade. By this time I had a big mortgage and a job I didn't enjoy so I guess the beer just gave me a respite from the responsibilities I didn't want. I was always planning to give up alcohol and I made a few futile attempts but I soon realised I couldn't do without it until I changed my life.

> I could write a book about my embarrassing escapades with alcohol but the stories in AA's Big Book tell other people's tales that are similar to mine.
>
> When I stop drinking for periods of time I am compelled by the desire to gobble chocolate, which I believe isn't unusual for recovering alcoholics. At least I won't lose my driving licence eating chocolate!
>
> I have suffered with anxiety for twenty-five years and I think the downside of alcohol initially fuelled the anxious times. I think I'm also hypoglycaemic."

"It's me genes."

"Your genes didn't run to the fridge" ... as the joke goes. It might be that you have a genetic predisposition to a vast array of conditions and ailments but, as yet, nobody has found a *Cadbury* gene. More likely, it is the way you have been brought up and the influence of advertising that makes you view certain foods as a treat. One often sees an obese family bearing the same degree of overweight as each other; usually if the mother is three stone overweight then the father and children are as well or mirror a ratio thereabouts. If they're all morbidly obese, the same applies. It is easy for such a family to use a defence mechanism of denial and projection so that they can cast ownership of the problem onto someone else's shoulders. How does this work? Well, firstly, they deny that they have a problem at all, claiming that they are cuddly and that all the family are the same, and they always have been. Men will say that they prefer their wives to be overweight but they don't use that word ... they say things along the lines of "I like a bit of meat on a woman"... they are relieved that J-Lo has a *plumper* derrière. This may be actually true but it may also make them feel easier about their own burgeoning waistline. J-Lo isn't at all plump in the British sense of being size 20 and to think she is a salad-dodger is to delude oneself. Neither is Beyoncé or Shakira. Women also feel more relaxed if their spouses are overweight as they think it stops the spouse looking elsewhere for a slimmer model (the assumption being that the slimmer one wouldn't be interested in a beer belly) and they can roundly deny that they have an eating problem. This attitude will spread down towards their children who will copy the pattern set by their parents, gorging on take-away pizza and chocolate every night in front of the TV (presumably to watch more food advertising). When little Calvin or Kylie returns from school one day to say that so-and-so had called them fat, the mum and dad will say it's either in their genes or go to the school for a fight.

A word on projection. Many of us project our bad feelings onto others. It keeps the bad feelings away from ourselves. For example, if you feel hard done to by the government (your pension may be inadequate), you might project the bad feelings you have towards the government onto a minority group such as (commonly these days) Eastern Europeans. This allows the Eastern migrant to carry your anger and you can blame them for taking benefits that you think should have been yours because you've paid into the system all your life. This kind of projection is a classic defence mechanism and allows you to get rid of uncomfortable feelings. On a simpler level, this explains why many dogs look like their owners and represent characteristics that the owners are proud of. Behold the pit bull terrier with the angry young scroat; the dog has short hair and a short temper and his testicles hang for our viewing amusement. Look at the little handbag dogs or the poodles. All dog owners choose a dog that they unconsciously believe suits their own personalities and their looks ... they are unconsciously projecting their own emotions onto their mutt of choice. Some psychoanalysts would argue that everything around you is a choice of your projections ... your fancy coffee table, your car, or your untidy office – all reflecting your inner state and the unconscious choices that you have made.

Following on from this, the parents, and the children to a lesser degree, will then project the blame for their obesity onto others. This means that instead of seeing fault in ourselves, we blame others for our weaknesses. This family might blame thin magazines for not accepting them as they are and then castigate the magazines for using thin models. They might blame shops for not selling their sizes – although this is changing as our population grows in girth. Comfortingly, balloon waists are now available. I wonder if these should be branded Fat Jenes? Instead of losing weight for the sake of their health and longevity, they will look to others for answers when the answer lies firmly in what they put into their mouths ... not their genes. It would not be so bad being overweight if it did you no harm but the scientific evidence is overwhelmingly in favour of being the 'right' height to weight ratio. I must stress here that there is no merit in aspiring to becoming a Kate Moss either. As far as I gather, usually in the red-tops, most *super models* are addicted to one thing or another.

I'm not sure Gok Wan and his *How to look good naked* programme really helps either. I admire his strivings to build his guinea pigs' self-esteem and make them look better, but he himself was a man with an eating disorder and was obese as a teenager. If he was as content then as he wants chubby women to feel about themselves now, he would surely have stayed the way he was? It's a bit rich to teach women to accept their flabby proportions yet lose lots of weight yourself. He is paper thin. Additionally, in promoting women to be overweight and accepting of it, he is emphasizing the proclivity for this nation to grow. I believe that this will have a disastrous effect (if anyone believes him) yet I can see why it's good for him as a businessman. A thin man telling fatties to be happy is like a fat dietician advising people how to diet isn't it?

In both sets of denial and projection, the eating problem becomes further entrenched if it's someone else's fault, someone else to blame. This is even more the case in our current blame culture. Having said all this, there but for the grace of God go I, because we can all easily pile on the pounds if we lose control of ourselves and allow advertisers to lead our lives for us.

When it comes to giving things up, it's best to give up everything at once if you can, as advised by Dr Lefever in his addiction tome *Break free from addiction* (2004). In other words, as I hope Life Tree illustrates, it is desirable for inner peace to give up as much as is possible. It's no use giving up alcohol then continuing to smoke or giving up chocolate and then taking heroin. The idea is that one addiction shouldn't replace the other.

It's no use trying to step off the treadmill of addiction and keeping one foot on the hamster's wheel ... your foot will become grazed. Try to get off it completely if you can. This is very difficult though and you might have to accept that you are the sort of person who needs to maintain one addiction, even if it's coffee. Town centres all over the world are full of addiction centres and well meaning agencies who can help you get off the wheel. Alas, I am advocating as much abstinence as you can handle. Withdrawal from illegal drugs, withdrawal (if medically feasible) from prescribed medication drugs, withdrawal from alcohol, caffeine, chocolate, soda, hydrogenated- and trans-fats, sugar, nicotine ... the list is endless and includes avoiding advertising messages. (Look at Jim Hagart's www.subliminalworld.org to observe the subversive horrors of advertising. Also see a *Columbo* film called *Double Exposure* (1973) to observe, in an entertaining way, how *subliminal shots* work).

If you are not going to live on a mountain in Tibet, it is impossible to avoid advertising altogether, so you might want to temper your abstinence by trying to buy things you haven't seen advertised, or buy them because you need them, rather than because you think you might look as cool as the advertiser's chosen anchor. *Police* sunglasses make David Beckham look cool because he is a talented, international footballer/model and really has nothing left to prove. Why would you want to look like someone who you'll never be? Beckham would probably look cool in the old NHS spectacles of the 1970s and I bet that if he wore them, everyone else would copy. I had them in the seventies and I didn't look too cool. Look at the latest 'pob' haircut which women all over the place are currently sporting. It is arguably ridiculous but because Victoria Beckham and Sarah Harding (Girls Aloud) have the cut, everyone else has dived in. This of course is nothing new. I guess that people want to unconsciously identify with their idols (although wearers of pobs would disagree that these stars are their idols) ... such is the power of the unconscious mind and how it motivates us into doing the most ridiculous things with scissors.

Television counselling psychologist Dr Linda Papadopoulos, in *Mirror Mirror* (2005), suggests that it is a good idea to take emotions out of food (She also writes very wisely about the 'pornification' of society in 2010). "Holidays are coming ... always Coca-Cola" advises the song in their wonderfully filmed Christmas advertisement. All advertisers enjoy hooking our emotions with their anchors; it's the best way to sell their products as they create a nice warm feeling in our bellies. Of course, they know that most people don't have a wonderfully warm beautiful Christmas but when it comes to selling products, our unconscious emotions are the entry point. Papadopoulos's suggestions are nevertheless a good idea but it's hard to take the emotions out of food when our emotions and the impact of food are inextricably linked to blood sugar levels, and therefore physiological. This means that when we do eat, we feel differently because our body chemistry has altered with our intake of food. Glucose levels have changed and the brain changes accordingly. On Christmas morning, why not try a high-tar cigarette, a full sugar cola, and a Mars bar, and see what a warm feeling hits your emotions. It will not be pleasant, but many British kids will do this not only on Christmas morning but on every morning before they go to school. The rising suicide rate could be inversely related to this Christmassy feeling as Bing Crosby bewails his epic *White Christmas* hit whilst loners prepare their nooses.

Sugar

Special mention should be made here about sugar. In recent years, sugar has gone a bit quiet; I suspect it's because there are so many other things to worry about. In the 1970s a seminal work was written by John Yudkin called *Pure, White & Deadly*. This book, and many others that followed it, makes it very clear that nobody at all *needs* sugar (as a sprinkly addition) and the myths about it are legendary and endless. Sugar is a major ingredient in most processed foods as well as many others, and commonly masquerades under a variety of different names which often end in -ose.

Hundreds of years ago, sugar was regarded as a luxury because it was a special import from faraway countries and only the rich could afford it. This undoubtedly added to its scarcity value but as well as being rare in those times, people who were lucky enough to sample it, liked it very much and soon developed a craving for it ... our tastes became accustomed. This was years ago and now, in the 21st century, sugar is omnipresent, in almost everything you eat that doesn't naturally occur. There is a myth in society that sugar gives us energy, a myth that has been helped by years of adverts like "*a Mars a day helps you work, rest, and play*". In simple terms it's like this: you eat a chocolate bar and you have consumed a bar of fat and sugar ... those are the main ingredients regardless of how manufacturers present and advertise their wares. As soon as the product hits your belly, a chemical reaction occurs that causes insulin and glucose to be released via the pancreas and liver. This reaction destabilizes your blood sugar levels temporarily because the refined sugar you have just eaten comes as a shock to your system. The glucose will give your brain a bit of a jolt (as will the caffeine that is also present in most chocolate bars) and you will feel *charged* or get *a buzz* for a short time. This will be a subtle feeling but most people will be aware of it. After this *short time*, your blood sugar levels will drop dramatically as your body compensates for the initial boost – there is a down after the high, rather like cocaine. During this down, you can either take in more chocolate (to maintain the buzz) or suffer the low that inevitably follows. Again this low may be subtle but you will be vaguely aware of an uneasy feeling or fatigue. You may not attribute these down feelings to soda drinks or chocolate bars, but they will have been caused by them and all things like them.

The same thing would happen were you to take coffee, or indeed, almost any refined carbohydrate food or drink. This *simple* chemical reaction is enough to make most people keep on eating these kinds of foods ad nauseam, not really knowing that they're on an addictive cycle. I wonder if the emergence of coffee houses would be so great were it not for the fact that caffeine is highly addictive. We might as well have opium dens. Anyway, you might not blame your chocolate for the subsequent down feelings because the same bar initially gave you a lift and helped you to energize ... albeit for 25 minutes. But, like cigarettes, these high sugar *treats* also relieve symptoms they create. I will repeat this: cigarettes, chocolate, alcohol, cake, heroin, cocaine, nicotine and all its by-products etc relieve the symptoms they themselves create. This means that if you have a cigarette or anything on my list (and many things too numerous to list), you will want another one sometime afterwards. This begs the question … is it worth it? [There is a lot of astonishing information about smoking in *Nicotine Trick* (2002) by Neil Casey (who exposes what nicotine is all about and gives readers a neat way to relinquish the weed by using the subconscious mind) or 'How to stop *smoking* and stay stopped for good' by Gillian Riley (2003) which is good for different reasons.]

You have also got to bear in mind that sugar is 'empty calories' and of no nutritional value whatsoever. In fact, sugar in itself is completely meaningless as far as health and nutrition are concerned and should never play a part in a good diet. All this can mean that if we chose to ingest addictive substances we are satisfying addictions that have been created or lie within us, rather than satisfying any real need for food. We are satisfying a desire that has usually been created by advertisers who simply want to make their paymasters wealthy, for this is their job.

I have heard many clients say, and believe, that they 'need' sugar in some way, in order to function: this is just a myth but one that many people are misinformed about. It is beyond doubt that this misinformation is behind the thinking of the majority of obese people in the world. It's true that sugar gives one a short term boost but it causes so many other problems that it's not really worth bothering with if you can avoid it. However, avoiding it is one thing and then being addicted to it and having your subconscious desire it is another. This is the but …

The brain itself does not need sugar … it needs glucose. The brain will not thrive or do anything in a better way because you have drunk six sugars in your coffee. There is absolutely no reason whatsoever to 'use' sugar in the hope that it will give you energy. It might well inspire a quick boost, but this will inevitably be short-lived as the insulin/glucose cycle takes place. After this, you will go low again and look for your next fix. I would agree that it's not as bad as the craving for heroin and I have never heard of anyone mugging an old woman to feed their toffee addiction, but sugar is addictive nonetheless and I suppose you have to decide whether you want to be a slave to it or not.

Yudkin (1988) argues that high-carbohydrate foods are the ones that cause obesity and if we could stick to meat, fish, and vegetables, we would naturally lose weight because those are the foods that satisfy hunger. The craze that swept the world at the turn of the 21st century was the Atkins diet (2003): this has now been almost vilified out of existence but Dr Atkins made some good points. However, these points were largely against the multi-national corporate bodies whose vested interests are in selling manufactured, hi-carb, processed food. They want these foods to be addictive – although they would obviously claim otherwise – and through advertising, they push them down our throats at every opportunity. Typically, hi-carb foods such as chips are sold on a low fat ticket, but it's not the fat that's the problem; it's the carbohydrate/insulin response that ensues as a result of eating chips and the fact that hi-carb foods are usually stored as body fat if they are not used in energy. So, a low fat chip doesn't mean you won't get fat; it's how carbs are managed by the body that makes you fat so if you eat a lot of low fat chips you will get fat. As well as playing with their Wiis, the British seems to enjoy lolling around being lazy, and this is why they are getting fatter. But the carb/fat myth runs deep. The lazy lot will readily gobble their 5% fat chips believing that it's the fat that puts on the weight. This is largely a fallacy. It's the carb that encourages weight gain and not a lot of people seem to know this. It is one of those untruths that pervades our society and is perpetuated by advertisers who are only too keen to serve their big clients … after all, this is their job. You can take it as a fact that eating too many chips will make you fat, regardless of how they are presented to us and whatever spin the advertisers use. Didn't we always know that chips make you fat? Low fat doesn't mean you won't become fat; this is just a clever play on words because it's more likely that the carbohydrate contained within the chip will make you fat. Owing to the relentless bombardment and bamboozlement by manufacturers (owners of the means of production) and advertisers, I believe that there is a vested interest in keeping us ignorant of the fat and carbohydrate myth. This has led to what Marx would have called 'false consciousness'. Although he was, strictly speaking, referring to class oppression, it applies nicely to how we regard food groups. This means that myths are perpetuated and the ruling class (in this case manufacturers) don't want us to know certain things. I wonder how long it will take for this penny to drop and false consciousness can be replaced with honest consciousness. Such is the power of brain washing. I doubt it will ever happen.

The Hypothalamus – part of the brain that links the nervous system to the endocrine system via the pituitary gland and maintains homeostasis – works by determining the amount of glucose in your blood. When those levels of glucose go too high, the excess gets converted into fat. You push the level too high by eating refined carbohydrates (cakes, crisps, biscuits, ice-cream, etc) or going too long without a meal and then scoffing a lot. The simple solution to this, apart from desisting from refined carbs, is to eat some protein with every meal, especially breakfast. Protein is more satisfying and when did you last gobble a fillet steak and then eat another? Steak doesn't work like chocolate and with proteins, you will feel full for a lot longer, thus eliminating the desire to binge and the cravings that develop thereof.

So you know what you should eat for a healthy life, or, more specifically, what to avoid. Whether you follow the advice is up to you, but always remember the impact that sugar and refined carbohydrates will have on your system if you choose to partake. Lots of refined carbs and sugar itself is quite simply not a good thing to consume and will send you on all sorts of subtle but life changing spirals … at least now you will know what's caused it. In her sagacious book *From here to longevity* (2004), Mitra Ray states that CALORIE COUNTING IS ONLY NECESSARY WHEN YOU EAT PROCESSED FOODS! She suggests that if you eat foods that go rancid (not that *are* rancid!) you will be on your way to a healthful existence. Buy one of those ready-meals that you warm up in the microwave and observe all the strange ingredients it contains: then give it to someone you don't like. Or do you really want to eat all that odd sounding stuff?

In a way, your body intuitively knows what it needs but it doesn't know so well what it doesn't need. It will obviously eat and digest what you give it – within reason – even if it is poisonous like alcohol. However, part of the idea of Life Tree is to raise the level of consciousness or, in other words, become aware of what we are doing to ourselves when we feed. What is the point of living if we don't know what we are doing or just consume blindly at every counter or sweet stall?

It is this blind consumerism that gives rise to a host of problems if we simply capitulate to our desires and whims or are led to the trough by every advert we have ever seen. Addiction comes into this category, so keen are we at times to follow our unconscious desires. We can choose to ignore consciousness when we form addictions and become addicted to alcohol or drugs or whatever. Of course, we are trying to mollify our inner turmoil when we become addicted to our crutches, but this never happens ... except temporarily. Will alcohol ever make our situation better – whatever the situation is? No. Our bad feelings continue unchecked even if we manage to forget for one night in the midst of our addiction. Then our problems grow worse because we then have two problems: the initial problem and the drug problem! Because most drugs include the development of tolerance, we need more and greater amounts to keep us satisfied. This certainly goes a long way to explaining addiction – initially through advertising and external influences, then we become inveigled into liking sugary, sickly things until we are addicted. Addictions usually start out as a subconscious effort to avoid feelings that are uncomfortable.

This is one facet of addiction, but you may be one of the unlucky ones who has deficient brain chemistry (though this is very rare, hard to research, and improbable), in which case, you might be seeking drugs or addictive substances. However, let not these words be a cop out and give you excuses to remain addicted as there are other things you can do to boost your happy brain chemicals rather than shoot up with heroin!

Many current addiction interventions are performed in the hope that freedom from a particular substance can be achieved. The trouble is that such interventions (meditation, keeping a journal, breathing techniques, chamomile tea) are subtle and experienced unconsciously ... unlike cocaine. It's a leap of faith to swap cocaine for a brisk walk. There are no magic solutions, just reality for us to face. It is impossible to assuage feelings of anxiety or depression with an eating binge (for example). It just won't work and you'll always be wanting more. You have to work on the root causes of your dismal feelings. Advertisers know this and use anchors to promise a subconscious thing that can never be delivered, hence more consumerism.

Salman Rushdie created a work of genius not only with his acclaimed books but with his seventies slogan: 'Naughty but nice'. Those three words beautifully encapsulated the sugar and naughtiness debate and led many to the chocolate éclair.

Anchors

Neuro Linguistic Programmers (NLP) have used the word anchor to explain the way we relate objects to emotions and experiences and vice versa. Psychologists call this association. So you might associate a certain smell with a particular experience or a certain person with an emotional state such as happiness or fear. Advertisers commonly use anchors and associations to sell products. Typically, something sexy is utilised; for example, a young female model will sit astride a motorbike or be seen near a car. This image is accepted into the subconscious part of the brain and associated state of mind will act in the future so that when the car is seen without the sexy girl, at some level, the male will think of sex and be inspired to consider buying the car or bike. The use of celebrities in anchoring is a brilliant device because they come with their substantial baggage. Take Kerry Katona and her *Iceland* adverts: Kerry is known to have had a chaotic life and struggles with one trauma after another with children and different boyfriends and there are lots of rumours about her. Iceland, being a budget frozen produce shop know the demographic of the majority of their shoppers and want to maintain and attract shoppers like Katona; in other words, Iceland's shoppers will identify with Kerry. Think of David Beckham and his Gilette adverts: when you buy 'the best a man can get' you are also buying unconsciously into Beckham's glory days and, as you make the purchase, you will be unconsciously experiencing the '02 Greece goal. Think of any advert and observe the chosen celebrity and how the perceived attributes of the star fit comfortably with the advertised product.

How can it help? How can eating a chocolate make you less angry or less lonely? It can't, but we reach for these things as a result of advertising anchoring and social conditioning. The best idea is to work on the root causes of your despair; whilst this is not always possible, it will do you more good to attempt this rather than to simply mask the uneasy feeling. Sugary foods and high-gl-carbs always seem to be moreish and so can lead us to fully blown binges as we go about satisfying our addictive desires. It is essential to know that, just like the adverts that encourage certain behaviours and purchases, any addiction is in large part, automatic and unconscious. All these things can be broken with sustained work and new neural brain pathways can be formed given time. This means that any addictions we may develop can wear off eventually.

It would appear that wherever you turn, sugar is present and it is so common that we no longer notice it. It's as if heroin is one problem, alcohol is another, but sugar is not only pure, white, and deadly, but also ubiquitous, addictive, invisible, pervasive, and yet nobody really knows how great an impact it has. Manufacturers would like everyone to go around in ignorance of the impact of sugar but its effects on our health have been well documented over the past thirty years. Even if the initial symptoms caused by eating too much sugar are not life threatening, I wonder if years of over consumption actually lead to diabetes, obesity, and other serious health concerns. Amongst these other concerns is hypoglycaemia.

Hypoglycaemia

Hypoglycaemia is one of those invisible conditions that cause a feeling of illness and a host of seemingly unexplainable symptoms. The condition is a result of eating too much sugar or refined carbohydrates and the impact these foods can have. Over the years, the hypoglycaemic condition can cause subtle changes in the personalities of sufferers, again with them not knowing why they are suffering or what to do about it. Sometimes, a few simply dietary changes will remedy the whole situation. Sugar and spice and all things nice is not part of the hypoglycaemic condition. Symptoms include:

Feeling tired and unwell
Having no stamina
Confusion and an inability to think straight
Cravings for sweet foods or alcohol
An inner shakiness
Being irritable with others
... and many more, mentioned later

You have to know that a low fat diet – which is so popular and has been for many decades – usually means that you have a high carbohydrate diet. The way carbs are metabolized can be causing you to gain or retain weight. Doctor Atkins (of the diet fame) knew this and I suspect the thinking is slowly changing although this will take some time. Avoid 'bad' fats such as saturated fats and hydrogenated/trans fats and cut down on carbs. This way you will see weight loss if this is what you want. 'Good' fat does not mean fat will appear on your body; hi-carb does ... it's as simple as that, broadly speaking.

Too many calories need not always be the problem with weight gain, unless you are consuming way too many. Usually the problem will be refined carbohydrates and packaged/processed foods. We know that refined sugar is a 'foodless' product and a complete waste of time if you want to be healthy; not only that, it rots your teeth. As mentioned earlier, by eating foods that can 'go off' or 'natural' foods we will be preventing ourselves from consuming too much sugar and additives and other nasties.

Perhaps we all know about the link between diabetes and sugar and the late-onset diabetes caused by being fat (caused by too many carbs and too much sugar), but there is another side to diabetes ... hypoglycaemia, that is just as upsetting. It is evident by now how sugar and carbs play their parts in this ailment. Put frankly, too much sugar and carbohydrate messes with your pancreas so you eventually become fat then diabetic. Before this, your adrenal glands start to become exhausted.

Whether you have developed hypoglycaemia or you have exhausted adrenal glands, if this is the case, you will feel lethargic, irritable, morose – your body's chemistry will be out of synch. If your adrenal glands are overworked, your liver will be slow to convert glycogen to glucose; you will become sluggish and may suffer from blood sugar 'spikes', that may subsequently lead to panic and anxiety spasms. Additionally, the adrenal hormone cortisol regulates blood sugar levels and if cortisol is low, all the other symptoms mentioned above will be worsened. As well as panic and anxiety, you may feel wooly-brained or become confused ... all because of what you've eaten.

Because hypoglycaemia is caused by eating the wrong foods, the condition can usually and simply be reversed by eating the right foods. This means (you probably know by now!) avoiding sugars and refined carbohydrates, eating natural foods (and protein with every meal), and improving your life in other ways through exercise and connections with others ... more of that later.

Because sugar and chocolates are supposed to make us feel better when things go wrong (do they?), we can often turn to those foods unnecessarily in the hope of finding an answer. Usually, life stressors are at the root of our despair and so a strawberry cream chocolate is never going to sort that out. Since stress causes your adrenal glands to work overtime, you might consider deploying some stress management techniques in your trickiest situations and see how they go. If you couple stress to wonky eating patterns and eating refined carbohydrates or avoiding protein and 'good' fats, you may well be heading for hypoglycaemia and a host of other disorders.

Who can resist a Cadbury's Crème egg or a Crème egg McFlurry. Or, if you're at the higher spending scale, some tasty Belgian liqueurs, or perhaps a black forest gateau? Is your mouth watering? There's a chocolate for every pocket and every class. I spent a very enjoyable day with my daughter at *Cadbury World* in Birmingham and when we left, our arms were festooned with a cornucopia of scrumptious goodies from the confectioner's factory. So much is available for the Western belly.

Jason Vale in *Chocolate Busters* (2004) makes some excellent points in his well written book (which is an Allen Carr-esque romp through *chocoholism**). Here we see, in layman's terms, how the sugar cycle works and why you might like to avoid it at all costs.

[*chocoholism, alcoholism, spendaholism etc... I don't believe in the disease theory of these 'isms'. As it makes clear in Life Tree, you cannot catch these isms. I think that these isms are taught, learnt, carried out, and obviously have a hugely deleterious effect on the lives of many sufferers, but I don't believe that disease is in any way involved. You can, and will, get over it by using some of the techniques contained within Life Tree. Awareness and knowledge is the first step.]

Life Tree aims for a more holistic approach to health and wellbeing rather than just blaming sugar for everything. You may well have a highly stressed life that has nothing to do with eating problems. Other chapters of Life Tree will therefore be more appropriate for you.

Smoking guru, the late Allen Carr, in most of his books (smoking, alcohol, weight, drugs) encourages readers to give up their addictions by celebrating the fact that they're free from their addiction. Carr creates a very effective metaphor of a pitcher plant in his book about alcohol; he posits that anyone who uses alcohol is at some point stuck within the (metaphorical) pitcher plant ... sometimes users can fly away from the plant with sticky feet, others get stuck completely and fall to the bottom and get eaten by the plant. This is the tragic nature of addiction.

Children are wittingly and unwittingly encouraged to eat sugar almost from birth. Sugar could make cardboard palatable; who really enjoys *Shredded Wheat* without putting sugar on it or adding a bit of granola (as I do!)? This cereal is one of the few that contains no sugar. Most of the others are laden with it. Parents used to dip babies' dummies in syrup and we are told "Christmas is coming ... always Coca Cola". A can of (non diet) cola contains about six spoonfuls of sugar. We hear that 'a spoonful of sugar helps the medicine go down'.

But don't despair, you can be free of all this in twenty-one days and your system will have recovered and rejuvenated itself. You just have to make a decision and then stop. Armed with Life Tree you will be able to do this because you will know why you want to stop.

On your next shopping mall trip, observe how fatness seems to run in families. We know why ... because they all share the same lifestyle and faulty eating patterns. And we now know what causes most of this problem: sugar and refined carbohydrates. To summarize ... a gap in the soul, sugar consumed as a baby/child, family problems, advertisers leading us into temptation, more addictive substances, more sugar, obesity, type 2 diabetes, hospitalization...?

It's as if the human organism is not complete and therefore always striving for a feeling that it believes does not exist within. Every society is known to use some sort of drug or psychoactive substance in order to change the way it feels. This is a grim indictment. I mention this to some people who look down their nose at drug abusers, only to discover that their own larders bulge with cakes and crisps. Perhaps our job as a society should be to come to terms with accepting that drug use of all kinds is rife. As a people, we seem to need a fix of some kind, which usually begins as a 'harmless' trial among peers but can end up with terrible addiction.

Similarly, weddings and almost any other event are doused in alcohol and one is often thought of as strange if one doesn't drink alcohol. I would imagine that the same is true for any mood changing drug if all your peers are snorting away (or whatever is their drug of choice) and you are the one left out if you don't partake. I suppose that this is about belonging to your associates, peer pressure and all that. *Carling* adeptly realised this in their 2007 Christmas advert which showed a silhouette of a few friends in the pose of brothers in arms, and the word BELONG is written on the advert in Carling style letters. What do Carling want us to belong to? For sure, they know that the society is disparate and that people want to belong, in an increasingly alienating world. How better than to belong to a group of peers, swilling lager, having a town centre fight and ending up in the gutter showing your arse. Belong. Human companionship is a strong selling point for advertisers who know that we desire to belong but have no time to actually develop our social networks (not websites). With most of us experiencing social fragmentation at first hand, in the form of divorce, social mobility, nuclear families; belonging is something we cannot take for granted. Beer aside, whisky and alcopops belong themselves to the same band wagon. But who are we encouraged to belong to? Other binge drinkers. And this belonging is supposed to decorate over society's despair and disintegration. Perhaps our need to belong and be part of a wider group – a need that is increasingly ignored – neatly summarizes our penchant for drugs. As I said earlier, if most people would do better dreaming of becoming toilet cleaners than pop stars, then when this reality bites, perhaps we need something to soothe our egos. This is about broken dreams and need not have been a troubled early life. Who had a lovely early life? It's a very rare thing to have had a happy childhood. Of course, you can kid yourself that you were happy and that the smacks never did you any harm, but I wonder how happy you were at the time and how happy you are now about visiting the same brutality onto your own offspring. Most of us have been hurt in some way or another; whether that is during childhood (commonly) or later on (usually broken career dreams) we must some day acknowledge that the scars we carry can only be healed from within ... this will be the day when we no longer need cake or heroin.

As well as hypoglycaemia and diabetes, there are other, even more troublesome diseases one can develop, perhaps due to a faulty diet, in the spirit of 'you are what you eat'. I now finish this chapter by looking at these...

No one can have escaped the cholesterol message over the past couple of decades. GPs routinely screen for raised cholesterol levels, believing that they lead to heart disease, diabetes, and stroke. If this is the case, it's no wonder that we are becoming more and more concerned with getting our levels under control. Malcolm Kendrick (2007), in *The Great Cholesterol Con,* writes about cholesterol problems and their consequences. His writings are not the traditional advice one reads about cholesterol and the clue lies in the title of the book.

Like Allen Carr and Jason Vale have done with smoking and chocolate respectively, Kendrick explodes the cholesterol myths. Around the globe, millions of people have been prescribed statins in order to treat cholesterol problems. However, Kendrick argues that aspirin can be almost as effective as a statin.

Kendrick (2007) covers the fat and carbohydrate debate I have already written about and corroborates current, modern thinking. He goes on to say that it is not fat consumption that raises VLDL cholesterol levels, but eating carbohydrates. This is largely what Dr Atkins was talking about and a point that Life Tree is keen to emphasize. So, it seems that fat is not the culprit in heart disease. This might come as a surprise. Since the general medical advice is contrary to much of Kendrick's well researched writing, much of his data comes as a shock to traditionalists. It's as if a myth surrounding cholesterol has developed around medics, encouraged by the pharmaceutical industry, and that myth is what we should all believe unquestionably. Kendrick also states that people with low cholesterol levels are more susceptible to cancer! This isn't just a willy-nilly statement but it appears that Kendrick has undertaken major research in his book, much of it harvested from www.pubmed.com , so you will have to buy his book or have a look at that website if you want to know more. Importantly for Life Tree, another myth explodes before our eyes.

Kendrick seems to be saying two main things: Firstly, that eating carbohydrates increases cholesterol and affects the adrenal glands, and secondly, that stress (which also affects the adrenal glands) also increases cholesterol. He looks at major surveys of displaced populations and finds that those people such as émigrés who have found homes in cultures vastly different from their own, have experienced a higher rate of heart disease and stroke. This ties in with my argument about social cohesion and the fragmentation of society. Perhaps we have been looking in the wrong place to find an answer to raised cholesterol levels. Perhaps fat is not the culprit after all. If we are all social animals who want to be loved, imagine going to a new country and then being spat upon and taunted in the street by the indigenous population ... that can't be very good for your heart.

With all this, I don't want to paint the picture that all fat is good – life is never this simple and all fats are not the same. I think it is important to know that fat in food does not mean fat on thighs or belly. Although the words are (confusingly) the same, they don't mean the same thing. I think this confusion lies at the heart of our fat avoidance in food. It is becoming clear that refined carbohydrates and sugar cause us to gain weight. I will now try to differentiate between good fats and bad fats.

A book which covers nutrition, like *Broken Britain?* would not be complete without mention of trans-fats and hydrogenated vegetable oil. Arteriosclerosis and other heart diseases can be caused by eating certain foods with too much fat in them. These would be saturated fats like the stuff you find around red meat or chicken skin; fat which is solid at room temperature. Trans-fat is probably the worst kind of fat. The same applies to hydrogenation. Chemically, they are incomplete compounds which contain anatomically 'jagged' edges that can do untold damage within your veins and arteries. Trans-fats are artificially manufactured fats that are found in many processed and fast foods. (They may be called 'inverted' or 'partially inverted' or 'hydrogenated' or some other compound word which will have been created by the time *Broken Britain?* debuts.) Trans-fats and hydrogenated fats are cheap and they extend the length of time that a product can sit on the shelf without spoiling. But what's good for the companies that make this food isn't so good for the people who eat it. Trans-fats increase the amount of fatty plaques in your blood and may also stiffen your arteries. Researchers at Harvard University believe that trans-fats, alone, are now responsible for the death of at least 30,000 Americans every year. (Schlosser & Wilson, 2006, p.167-169.) I have noticed that some recent products are labelled 'no hydrogenated fats' and so I suspect that the zeitgeist is changing as we get more consumer savvy. If you are going to avoid any fats, avoid saturated, hydrogenated, inverted, and trans.

Even if your addiction runs predominantly to fast foods, you will not be doing yourself any favours if you ingest trans-fats or whatever they may masquerade as. One has to look into what your addictions are trying to fulfil. Many people with eating disorders don't eat because they're hungry; most blame boredom, anger, sadness, etc and this can apply to any addictive substance, whatever your predilection happens to be. As we devour a chocolate bar, or a chip, advertisers have already planted the emotional hook of the *chip from heaven* or the now even creamier chocolate, so our gullible brains only have to put two and two together unconsciously and bang ... you're on the road to fully blown addiction, bingeing, comfort eating, shopping to excess. The key is to try to identify whether you are eating or drinking or snorting because you *need* to, or you are responding to an emotional hunger to fill the prevalent gap in society and in our souls that is known and cleverly exploited by advertisers. These gap fillers are known as compensation behaviours by psychologists. To make up for unacceptable stuff in our lives, we compensate with alcohol, drugs, food, smoking, gambling, and other compulsive behaviours ... just to fill our gaps.

The thing about food is that you can't just stop eating like you might with other addictive substances. It figures that manufacturers are making every effort to make their products more addictive, primarily due to the use of sugar, the insulin response, and the effects of the carbohydrate/glucose cycle. Since we need food in order to survive, the best we can hope for is an awareness of its pitfalls and a knowledge of how food manufacturers attempt to deceive us into buying their adulterated trash.

If food can spoil it's probably okay ... this means that it hasn't been tampered with or doctored or added to or processed. Recently, we have been advised that we should avoid products which contain additives that we can't pronounce. Eventually I would expect that bananas will be laced with sugar before being sold. We'll see. *Coca-Cola* used to add cocaine to their drink, hence its name. This was at a time when cocaine wasn't thought of as being particularly harmful. You've also got to be a bit careful when shopping and try to read the labels. Manufacturers are becoming wise to our quest for health and currently branding new products with a spin on health: perhaps the product will contain a fragment of a healthy word within its name, such as bene- or vita- or nutri- etc. Or perhaps it will have a latin sounding name which has become popular following the success of the Harry Potter books. This way you will be cleverly eating well; clever for eating latin sounding things. These products tend to be full of sugar – just to make them edible.

Remember that hydrogenation is used only to prolong the shelf-life of products and should be avoided wherever possible. They're bad for our health. You can read a lot about the chemistry of all this in *From Here to Longevity* (Ray, 2004) and why scientifically they're bad for you. Quick-type products are tainted with them, particularly cakes, chocolates, sauces, and dips. As mentioned previously, some manufacturers even boast that their products contain no hydrogenated oil, only to see them labelled in another guise on the ingredients list. Caveat emptor – buyer beware. Sugar is prone to the same spinning and this too appears in various guises – honey-coated, glucose, raw cane, etc … all of it causing the glucose and insulin response that can lead to fatness and diabetes. As previously cited, the book *Pure, white and deadly* (Yudkin, 1998) list the many woes of eating sugar which is virtually worthless nutritionally but it serves to make bland food taste edible … that's why cereals are coated in the stuff. You really don't need it for energy, except perhaps for a quick boost in extreme circumstances. Nikki Waterman's *Sugar Addicts' Diet* (2004) details how you might get rid of it and feel a lot better after you've weaned yourself off. Waterman uses her own temptation of Pick'n'mix sweets and how she broke free.

Fad diets can also be a façade for the internal yearning for love. The diet industry is a perpetual treadmill that feeds fat on its own obese profits. *Weight Watchers* and other slimming clubs provide social stimuli and a nice night out with other *sufferers*. Weight loss can be a ruse that covers the fact that the overweight really want love and attention … as do all addicts … as do we all for that matter. In comfort eating, one is really trying to fill a void of love, a gap in the soul. Hence a *chip from heaven*.

It doesn't help that beer is punched into men at every opportunity. Beer and alcohol in general are very high in carbohydrate and calories. The sign 'binge sensibly' in *Simpsons – The Movie* says it all. The drinks industry know that most people don't drink sensibly. After all, they are selling a legal but addictive product. The drinks industry would deny this allegation but they are legal drug peddlars so they would wouldn't they? How can you be sensible at all if you drink alcohol when ethyl alcohol is poisonous? Being sensible and drinking alcohol is an oxymoron.

TV soap operas are no strangers to perpetuating binge drinking; almost every character involved in them overindulges, and the ones that do not drink are portrayed as weirdoes. Again, these messages act on an unconscious level but they still permeate our senses. I have read and heard people say that advertising has no effect upon them whatsoever, but its effect is often subliminal so whilst you might consciously deny its effects, the messages are still going in. Interestingly, although *Coronation Street* promotes the fact that social life revolves around the pub, in actual fact, this is becoming less true as more people seem to sit at home watching porn on the internet, playing on their Wiis and binge drinking indoors … this way it's cheaper as the supermarkets have grabbed pub goers with their insipid price cutting. So, whilst pubs are dying (except gastro pubs where you can enjoy a frozen meal warmed up by a teenager on a minimum wage) people are still drinking more than ever. One only has to look around modern Britain to see that men over 30 (sometimes even younger) have bought wholesale into the idea that it is normal to drink too much and suffer for it and talk about it to their friends. Additionally, since *Carling* and *Carlsberg* seem to have cornered the market on football advertising, as in 'A Taste of Britain', the beer bellies are growing and growing as men unconsciously buy this putrid myth. Ask yourself, how is *Carling* a taste of Britain and in what way does it taste like Britain? Also ask yourself why alcohol companies should be allowed to sponsor sport.

The way I see it, we live in a soul-less, predominantly immoral, culturally diverse, fragmented society. We search for answers then realise that there aren't any outside of ourselves so we use pharmaceutical solutions to dull the yearning ache and fill the gap.

It is this lack of satisfaction with life that makes each of us vulnerable to addictive substances. When we are sad or hope has disappeared we are prone to look for easy solutions. When we feel we have nothing or are low in self-confidence, we often turn to the bottle for a boost in the form of dutch courage. It might feel better at the time but in actual fact, if you have too much dutch courage, you will be repeating yourself, boring everyone and embarrassing other people. We need good connections with others; people to talk to, to love, to bond with, to share our sorrows with. But be aware that your connection with people should ideally be a healthy one and doesn't steep you in the mire of further addiction. If your friends are just drinking or line-snorting friends, perhaps you need new friends. If it's only drugs that bond you, this will reinforce your addictive behaviour. Once you become clean, and people get to know about it, you will soon discover who your true friends are. They will be the ones who don't encourage you to carry on drinking. As someone recently said to a client of mine: "Andrew's not the same since he stopped drinking; it's not our Andrew any more". Comments like this undoubtedly inspired George Best to carry on drinking even when he was well into his second liver ... leading him to his death. Of course, your *friends* will be jealous of your freedom but they will never admit this. They will try to drag you down to alleviate their own desperation. Your real friends will support you and make no negative comments. Then you'll know. In the early days of your freedom – say, the first three months – you might want to avoid the *bad* friends as they will make it difficult for you. When you have got some time under your belt, you might have established new friends that are not bonded to addictions or, better still, work on the Life Tree and the points raised herein.

In a way, you need better things to do than your addiction. So go out, wise up on information, get educated, make friends who aren't linked to addictions. Get a life! And remember that, whilst watching television, you are bombarded by adverts which can encourage further addiction and, over indulgence, and slobbishness.

Observe the losers in a lottery queue ... you might see me there! I say losers because most of the people in the queue will lose their money. As with everything else, you must make your own decisions ... the Government won't help you because they promote choice. Legalising 24-hour licensing and the National Lottery and Super-Casinos won't help you to stop drinking or gambling. It's almost fun to watch the Government spinning these vices into acceptability ... fun if it wasn't so harmful for so many gullible souls. Blackpool (my current abode) craved a Super-Casino as a lifeline for its ailing fortunes, as did Manchester (my former abode). How sad is it that both towns have to await such a lunatic scheme in order to attract investment for their areas. Why not go the whole hog and legalise Super-Whore-Houses as well?

Gambling has never excited me at all, but I have stood at fruit machines after having bitterly lost £5, and watched a friend of mine put in over £100 from his very hard-earned wage packet. This friend did an unenviable, low-paid job and, although I tried gently to stop him, I could see he was compelled to carry on with the wretched machine.

Legalising 24-hour drinking, gambling dens, brothels is all very spin-able for governments so you alone must make the choice as to whether to engage or not. Poker is the new flavour of the month and notice how it is creeping into our collective unconsciousness and gaining a veneer of respectability through TV shows such as *Celebrity Poker*. The normality of poker will eventually invade us just as lap-dancing bars have. Behold the oddness of lap-dancers having to smoke outside their brothels: we now have a society that allows young girls to show their genitals but forbids them to smoke indoors.

The whole concept of gambling, or any other addictive behaviour, revolves around filling one's gap by promoting hope; hope that doesn't really exist. Apparently, gamblers are not losers per se, for if they always lost they wouldn't continue gambling. Gamblers are nearly winners, always striving for the big win that they think will change their lives. More often than not, the big win never comes, so they keep on going, wasting more and more money with often bigger and bigger punts. This hope and eagerness to win, I think is reflected in society at large, a big win offering a lifebuoy against the mundanity with which we all have to live. Casinos and the like have created a world that runs a subtle counterpoint to reality where the illusion of escape is forever available – as long as you keep on spending. When we get caught up in addictions such as gambling, we can go into a kind of trance; people with eating disorders say the same thing; the desire grips them and they go for it regardless of the consequences. As we stuff our faces or put money into machines that <u>inevitably</u> rob us, we must ask ourselves: is this real pleasure or are we compensating for a lack in another area of our life?

When people perform a behaviour over which they have no control, and they behave this way consistently, repetitively, as a way of escaping from profound feelings of worthlessness, profound feelings of helplessness and powerlessness and anxiety, this is the way to avoid and escape from what's going on inside and what's going on outside in their lives. Eventually we find that we are avoiding everything as our addiction reaches greater heights.

Eventually, what is known as the contemplation stage takes place. This is where we are thinking about changing as we realise that we cannot do without our various addictions. Some people never reach this stage and happily mediate their ways through their problems; others are more radical and decide to stop altogether.

First of all, we realise that the addictive behaviour is not getting us anywhere, is costing us money that would be better spent elsewhere, and is perhaps injuring our health. We may claim not to care, but most of us want to live. You might develop better things to do and join a 12-step-programme such as AA in order to become free. You may avoid situations and people that will drag you into your old harmful behaviours, until eventually: you are free. New neural pathways will have formed and you will no longer be an addict. I do not believe that one has to be addicted for life, but I do believe in total abstinence. Why? Because to have a bit of this or that is to play with fire and it is too dangerous if you are the sort of person who is not content with a little bit. We have conquered addictions if we can leave our vices alone, content in the knowledge that although we were once trapped, we are now happily free.

Chick-lit author Marian Keyes, herself an ex-alcoholic, in an interview with Simon Mayo (BBC Radio 5 Live, 2006), mentions a day when everything seems okay and when she seemed to be at peace with herself. This day comes and you won't know when, but it will. Then you'll know you're free.

In addictions we never find completeness or happiness; just an illusory sense of these notions. Genuine happiness does not lie in a bottle or a syringe or a tub of ice cream. In using various substances, you will be travelling further away from where you want to be. By using nothing you will become nearer to calm and contentment if you are able to address your underlying issues and demons.

Therein lies a paradox. You want affection, connection, love, and a relief of anxiety but you self medicate with drugs or alcohol or gambling. Only by changing your social environment will you be able to manage your addictions. Many clients I have seen who are 'addicts' in one way or another, are really seeking love. We are all seeking love. When we find our search goes unrequited we, as a human being, try to mollify ourselves with other things. These other things never help. They just appear to at the time. What could be better than being told you are loved and supported, no matter what – by someone who really means it? When we find this, our need to self medicate evaporates and if it doesn't, we have not found what we are looking for. You might take to reading Eastern philosophy about this which, as far as I can learn, suggests that the answer always lies within ourselves and within acceptance of our human condition.

All roads point to changing your life and getting a set of people around you who are not involved with abuse of any kind.

Exercise

Is there anything you can't do without? What ten things would you take to a desert island if you had to live there for a year? Make a list. As always, let your thoughts run freely and write whatever comes to mind. You will know what you need.

From this list, is anything harmful? Is there anything there you would like to do without but fear you couldn't on your desert island? In real life, have you tried to give up anything and failed.

Don't despair. If you really want to get rid of these harmful things you can. It won't be easy but it is possible. You were not born with these vices and you need not die clinging onto them. If you have failed in your attempts to quit in the past, please remember that within repeated failure lies the opportunity of success. If you keep trying to quit, you have more chance of being successful than if you stop trying. Repeated failure will enable you to find future success. Ignore any people who will try to mock you for trying … they are pointless people. The philosopher Schopenhauer thought that only one sixth of all people were worth bothering with; a sentiment I can thoroughly agree with.

If your list includes one bottle of champagne to enjoy with Kelly Brook – who you also have on your list – don't worry about it!

Your hobbies & interests/fun, holidays

In order to be 'real', you need to have fun and try to feel young again; this will be easier for you to access if you had a happy childhood. I know there is the stereotypical dad dancing at a wedding and I know that people in this country are so keen to ridicule others in order to deflect embarrassment from themselves. But, if you are going to have fun and become freer, you are going to have to learn to care less about the opinions of others. This being real also involves deep thinking as promoted by Vivienne Westwood in her *manifesto*.

You might like to draw or paint. You might consider going dancing or learning an instrument. However, the more you can engage with others, the more enjoyment you will get out of the activity. I know this will send shock waves through some shy people, but it really is the best way to get over yourself, enjoy life more and see the bigger picture and all that. Remember that once you've got over your initial embarrassment you will find that recovery (from inhibition) lies in the places you avoid. There is no better way to make yourself 'whole' than to mix with others. This does not mean sitting outside a pub getting pissed for four hours whilst your kids play in the gutter; on the contrary, it means doing something functional and wholesome. Perhaps you'd like to do something in the community. Find something useful and something that interests you or something you once enjoyed. The list is endless but always try to ensure that it involves a connection with other people. Importantly, if you believe that they are judging you, it is because you are judging them and yourself ... you are projecting your thoughts and feelings onto them. So get over it and get on with it. In doing this, you will be relegating a 'what if...' into a 'so what...' and this holds the key to a happy life.

This short chapter is about freeing your inner child and quietening down the parental voice in your head. When you are laughing authentically and free from *scripty* (see Eric Berne, 1967) or game-playing behaviours, you will be free. Try to let yourself run riot, dance and sing. No one will mind, and if they do, that's their problem not yours. Who shall judge you? Who is fit to judge you? The ones who pour scorn on your levity will be jealous of your freedom. This section is deliberately short as I don't want to tell anyone how to have fun; I will let Templar's *Rules of this, that, and the other* ... books do that. Enjoy what you do. Laugh.

Exercise

If you are lucky enough to have a child of your own, you can live your own fun vicariously and you may find yourself in enjoyable situations simply because you are entertaining a child. This means that you will be able to have a good time as a result of having a child with you ... it's a good excuse. Perhaps you are a god-parent or aunt or uncle and can borrow a child for a day out at the zoo or a wonderful week at Centreparcs? Thereupon you can discover freedom and allow them to take the reins in educating you in what it's like to be young. Try not to be too pedantic with the child. As long as they're safe, let them show you what to do; in allowing them to lead, you will be building their confidence as well as learning from them. Try to tune into them. Try out something new with them – all the usual activities such as swimming and football as well as new ones can be challenging and enjoyable, once you've got over any inhibitions you might have.

After your excursion(s) is over, write down how you felt – good or bad – and try to analyse why you felt these things. Being with children is an opportunity for growth in an adult ... adults who may have had their own childhoods frozen by a persecutor or just a frosty faced old fool. It's now time to thaw out.

Your offspring: sons & daughters

"I believe that children are the future, teach them well and let them lead the way…" sang George Benson and (some years later) Whitney Houston in *The Greatest Love of all*.

If you have children, you are in part responsible for the future as they are future citizens. You therefore need to teach them the skills that will equip them to be able to enjoy a fulfilled life and make them aware of things that might destroy their lives. All too often, parents take out their frustrations on their children. I regularly see mild forms of physical child abuse all around me. A local mother, who my daughter names "Grip Jaw Annie" is seen squeezing her four-year-old daughter's face as she demands that she does as she's told. Red marks adorn the child's face and you can see that her faith in her mother is being drained away with every brutal clasp. But this mother is no different from anyone else who severely admonishes their child. It seems to be a popular pastime.

Perhaps it is easy to forget that we can easily ruin the future generations by torturing our children. They are young and oftentimes simply do not understand. Nor should they be used as whipping boys or handy receptacles on whom to visit our existential angst. They will carry these scars of betrayal forever. They look to you for guidance and unconditional love – ideally. I know that unconditional love is not always possible and that children need boundaries and guidelines, but I never believe that they need smacking. This doesn't mean you should beat yourself up if you feel you have been remiss. I have not been the perfect parent by any means. Who is? From this day forward you can improve, even if your subjects don't believe you to start with.

It's never too late to make amends and rectify yourself and this should be done with actions and not empty promises. If it is in your power to make things better, do so. You will be changing the future.

Little ones are not to be trained with a rod and a whip ... even if you are an evangelist or a creationist and you believe that pummelling your children is all right in the name of God. (Do bible-punchers at least get the irony of this?) As a parent, you need to know about *theory of mind*. This is a human developmental stage where young children of under three(ish) years old cannot put themselves into your position and so do not know how you feel. Their brains are not capable of this task. So this means that they won't understand you if you shout at them in a supermarket for knocking something over. They will fear your rage, but they won't know *how* you feel. This cannot be smacked into them. All they will experience is pain. Similarly, if you are a tyrant and you hit them (which, in my view, is always wrong), then they will not know why you have done it. In other words, they cannot experience your anguish and know how you feel. Shouting at them and hitting them simply won't help; you will just store up resentment in them for their future. Sure, you will say that the odd slap did you no harm, but that is because you are not in touch with your inner pain. Every slap degrades your faith in humanity, whether you can admit this or not. Often, the slapper feels worse than the slapee so what is the point in venting your own rage on those you love? What message will you teach them through the use of violence?

Jessica writes:

"Dad used to hit me nearly every day. This was the seventies and the police just put it down to a domestic. The neighbours used to phone them if the screams got too loud but they never did anything. It was like that Suzanne Vega song 'Luka'. My Mum was useless because she never protected me and he used to hit her too. She eventually lost herself in the bottle and is still there now. There were three of us siblings and he'd treat us all very bad at different times. I think it was a power trip for him because he'd do it for no reason. He wasn't a drunk or anything. Sometimes he'd make us stand up to eat our dinner and just smack us in the face for no just cause. Aren't mothers supposed to protect kids against this sort of thing? In a way, they were as bad as each other. I remember he once cut my hair off when I was fifteen ... my hair was my pride and joy and he knew it. He wanted to take everything away from me. I'm pleased to say that I don't see the bastard any more."

Neglect is not a very politically correct word and many people would be offended were anyone to suggest that they are neglectful parents. Perhaps some of them would sue you for defamation. It is evident that many modern parents believe that giving a child material objects constitutes a well cared for child, but it does not. We are surrounded by placebos for love which are meaningless when compared to love. We seem to neglect those at the polarities of age – the very young and the very old. By no coincidence, these are those who are economically useless and have perhaps become a burden. We are busy running round, trying to decide what luxury car to buy next, whilst our loved ones lie craving our attention. Very often, the answer lies in the voices of those we ignore ... the old and the young. The young don't care what car you drive and the old have become wise enough to know it doesn't matter at all; and I really mean it doesn't matter at all. It only matters to the eyes of others who you think will be impressed – those who you fear will see you for what you are unless you drive the latest model. Perhaps you are a fake, but you will spend a lot of money trying to impress others into believing that you are not a fake until one day you realise none of the things you have bought matter to anyone except you. So we run around spending and neglecting, thinking that our careers are more important than our offspring. At least we turn the wheels of industry and capitalism.

While all this is going on there is no fathering or mothering. We are fooled and encouraged to believe we can have it all yet this concept only exists for a minute fraction of the population. Most people have next to nothing and certainly not it all. But we still persist in running around and trying, showing off in a childish way until our walls cave in and we realise that all the things we've bought are meaningless.

How many people can devote themselves to the job of parenting and how many would want to? Would we rather sit the young in front of the television and have them brainwashed by the adverts that show them how to become the next generation of consumers? It's easier to do that. We fill their young minds with relentless activity that is television and video games then wonder why they become drug addicts later on. Perhaps real, boring, mundane reality is not enough for them. When the lies of childhood have dissolved what do they have left? I see older children and late teenagers stood in front of gambling machines in my local 'amusement' arcades. Their faces are dead; they are looking for something they will never find. These are broken Britain's left over children: the hoodies, the young offenders, the scroates, the misinformed. The neglected children of people who never cared.

Exercise

Do you carry regrets? Have you done things to your children that you knew were wrong? This could include smacking (which you might mistakenly feel is right), beatings, or sexual abuse?

If you have older children do they remain in contact with you and is this contact close and one you could describe as quality contact?

Some children don't want to see their parents any more but don't tell them this for fear of hurting them, so instead, they emigrate to Australia to be away and make a fresh start.

Can you make amends for your behaviour?

Do you tell your children you love them?

Do you actually love them or do you regret the day they were born because you feel they have blighted your life by their very existence?

Do you think that your life would have been better without children and you could have been this or done that without them?

Have you got children you have never seen?

Religion & Spirituality

If you pray very hard for something, it might not happen … everybody knows that. And everybody also knows that many things happen which you didn't pray for at all. For example, when we ask God for money, *they* say that he does not simply send down a wad of cash to your doorstep, but rather gives you the intellect and wherewithal to help you to help yourself to make the money. Religious people would argue that God gives you the power to act.

I would say that religion is about being connected to others – fellow worshippers – and connection to the universe. Whilst people like Richard Dawkins decry religion it seems so depressing to be without the belief that 'there must be more to life than just this'. This perhaps explains why people like

Deepak Chopra and other luminaries sell millions of books and CDs about this so called connectedness to something bigger. Who can say who's right and who's wrong? In fact, being right or wrong doesn't really matter and it's not the point. The point is that you feel connected to something to insulate yourself against the knocks of this abrasive life. Dawkins has his intellect to protect him so let him celebrate. I can't quite buy his arguments because perhaps I'm not brave enough to face his 'truths' … are you? Of course, in the spirit of postmodernism, there really are no truths and it's all about beliefs, so why not have some if you feel like it? Unless you are a crazed fanatic, believing in an afterlife will do you no harm and it will almost certainly cosset you against your impending death.

Again, this is a short chapter and one that you have to fill in your Life Tree journal. I am not a preacher and only you will know whether or not religion and spirituality are important to you. I could write on and on about religion and even do that clever sermon technique where you take a bit of a biblical quote and then interpret it in such a complicated way that no-one understands it. Because there is no proof about the existence of God, why write anything at all? I considered leaving a couple of pages blank for this chapter but that's all a bit art-house isn't it? Therefore if none of us know for sure about God, who can write and who even has the authority to preach?

I know and accept that some people need something to believe in ... for some it's God, for others football.

Spirituality is a bit like religion but even harder to define or write about – not that that ever stops anyone. In fact the harder it is to write about and the more vague the topic, writers can have a field day, knowing that their writings cannot be disputed and that there is no right or wrong answer to any of it. As far as I can see, spirituality is about being a bit mystical and being aware of senses that are often ignored in our fast paced world.

Whether you are religious or not, you will probably find the following exercise beneficial.

Exercise

Be away from any distractions and disturbances. Sit or lie in a comfortable position, relax your shoulders and become aware of your breathing. Breathe in to the slow count of 7, and breathe out to the slow count of 11 … for about three minutes. Drift and float but don't fall asleep!

<u>Meditation</u>

Imagine yourself as a tree. Your feet and legs are your new, solid roots, very strong and firm. Your body and head are the trunk, solid, perfectly formed. Your hands are your branches, stretching out but not being shaken by the winds of change or any weather they may experience. Your branches reach towards the sun and a light nourishing rain adorns your leaves.

Hold this image in your mind; be at peace with yourself and who you are.

Know that no matter what changes occur, you are still you and you are doing your best, whatever that means to you.

Say these words as many times as you feel comfortable with: *I am me and I am in this world and have a right to be here. No matter what changes I will stay unchanged within myself. I am who I am and this is the way I was intended to be. I have a unique connection with the universe and its spirit is flowing through me. My roots are now strong, as are my branches. My life is unfolding with many lessons and the answers will come to me as I ask.*

Count down slowly from 10 and come out of the meditation with a deep and refreshing breath.

Part 4 – Your Trunk/Core

It will have become evident by now how your past can influence your future. This isn't always the case but, more often than not, we are all too prone to replaying scenarios from our past and then we are mystified as to why our future doesn't change. This can lead people into saying things like "with my luck, I'll never win", and "I can never lose weight", and "you can't rely on anyone out there", and "it's a dog eat dog world", and a whole array of defeatist self-talk that has been created from events that have happened to us in our distant and not-so-distant pasts. As we replay the past in our futures, this can lead to us being with wrong partners, making choices that are bad for us, failing in our endeavours … simply because that is what we expect of ourselves. Of course, no-one sets out with an ambition for failure or doom, but these things happen to us because of our expectations and they are almost always unconsciously driven. This means that we don't always know what we're doing but always seem to get ill-fated results. In fact, all too often we blame fate, destiny, genes, or God for these things without acknowledging that we play the main role in our own lives.

If you look at your own tree or the tree at the front of this book, it is plain to see how our roots lead to the tree we will become and how our core or trunk gets formed. The core is the inner part of you that never changes and I have based this concept on the part of you that cannot change no matter what you do. The core is the part of you that you may like to keep hidden and think that no one knows about – perhaps they don't. It is the basis of this idea: you are not your actions; I am not what I do. This means that you are not defined by what job you do or what exam results you may or may not have achieved. You are also not your behaviour; so whatever you do is not you. Inside your core is the precious part of you that has been created from your past and on your core are your branches that you have probably created yourself. The core is permanent and whilst it is as unique as an eye-print, it can be affected by the winds of change and the forces of society, which I shall come to later.

Many of us will have met people who say that although they are forty years old (or fifty, or seventy) they still feel the same inside as they did when they were twenty. This is part of the core, your essence that is timeless and part of you forever.

In your independence, I would ask you to regard the cat. You may have such a pet and, if so, you will know how independent it likes to be. The cat has its own life within your life. Consider how the cat grooms himself and keeps his fur clean; consider his independence as he goes out hunting or looking for a mate. Most cats fall into the right body-mass-index weight ratio so we can assume that he has his diet right; cats usually leave food on their plates if they are satiated. They may return later for another nibble. Consider how cats like to be stroked as they purr, but it's on their terms ... when they've had enough they wander off. Like lions, they look proud because they enjoy a natural life that affords them quite a lot of freedom. Most of all, watch how they enjoy stretching out in front of the fire on a comfortable rug. They even do yogic movements that keep their spines supple. You could do worse than to emulate the cat. Some people are allergic to cats, but that's their problem, never the cat's. Consider this metaphor as you regard the cat.

The winds of change

Unusual is a life that is never affected by times of change. If there is no change there is no life. There are two kinds of change: welcome and unwelcome. For example, you might be considering leaving the UK to start a beautiful new life in Sydney, Australia, in the sun. When you get there, you might learn that the ship containing all your treasured belongings has sunk, so this is an unwelcome change you will have to deal with. Often, and encouragingly, change is a time for personal growth and development, even though you may not see it like this at the time. Adapting to change is an essential part of mental wellbeing if we are not to become derailed by its impact. If we cannot adapt we often become ill.

Whether change is welcome or unwelcome, it often produces an amount of anxiety within us. Anxiety is experienced by most of us and in varying degrees throughout the course of our lives and, like change, it can present us with an opportunity to learn something about ourselves. Like a tree blowing in the wind, we have to adapt to change as best we can and allow for its effect upon us. Unwelcome changes can cause depression; a feeling of helplessness and malaise. More often than not though, it causes anxiety. Changes have to be manageable and in bite-sized chunks – too much all at once can lead to our undoing.

This chapter is very important as I believe that many of us suffer from varying degrees of anxiety. As well as change, many variables fuel anxiety and anxiety levels have never been higher than today in fractured, angry Britain. This is for the reasons stated in previous chapters but also involves a nature/nurture debate as well. Perhaps more importantly, anxiety manifests itself in common ailments. This is nothing new. Conversion illnesses, somatoform[2] illnesses, psychosomatic ailments, backache, headache, hypoglycaemia, eating disorders, panic attacks, obsessive compulsive disorder, nightmares, and even certain cancers have been linked to anxiety. I will look closely at anxiety in this chapter.

What is anxiety?

First of all, to know whether you're suffering from anxiety, you need to know what it is. The psychiatrist's 'bible', *The diagnostic and statistical manual* (DSM IV) is *the* reference book of choice when defining mental illnesses and conditions. The book you are reading now is meant to bring together contributory factors that give rise to anxiety (child rearing, society, the Gap, addictions, etc) and they are all linked. Life Tree is meant as a holistic examination of these conditions in the contexts mentioned.

As far as the brain is concerned, and as far as I can make out, the anxiety cycle goes something like this. First of all, a

---

[2] Illnesses that result as a bodily manifestation of an inner distress.

threat is perceived. You might be walking in a dark alley in a rough area and see a group of hoodies coming towards you. Or you might have just received your tax bill. Your eyes see what appears to be a threat. In your brain, the thalamus, receives information and the amygdala reacts to this information by sourcing stored data from your memories of similar previous experiences. This all happens in one-hundredth of a second and before any conscious thought can take place*. The amygdala responds immediately to the threat and prepares your body for fight or flight by sending out messages to release action hormones, mainly adrenaline. This can almost close down your pre-frontal cortex (your higher thought centre) and you won't, at this point, have chance to rationalise. At this juncture, all your conscious intelligence goes on hold as you prepare to run or do battle.

> * This is a subtle but crucial point and suggests that a host of cognitive behavioural therapists have got it slightly wrong. CBT relies on the fact that the way you think affects the way you feel, and this is true to a degree, but it's not the whole story. The fact is, our amygdala gets going *long* before we have time to start challenging negative thoughts or applying rational thinking. In an emergency situation our brain's emergency response will go into gear before our cortex has time to calm us down. Obviously, if we are under threat, we need instincts like this in order to get away rapidly, so it's probably a good thing. If the threat isn't one of violence and it's *just* a big tax bill, you might want to sit down and take a few breaths, let your initial panic subside and then your cortex will be ready to offer solutions for you.

If we suppress our basic instincts by rationalising all the time, we will cease to be fully human and who wants that? More importantly, we would lose the ability to express our emotions. To combat anxiety, you don't have to relinquish your humanity; it will always be there for you. With a step back, you can then decide whether your responses are appropriate, after your amygdala and the consequent hormones have run their course.

As far as anxiety symptoms are concerned, the DSM IV lists the following common feelings and emotions:

First of all, anxiety itself is sub-divided into the following categories: panic attack, agoraphobia, phobias, obsessive-compulsive disorder, post-traumatic stress disorder, acute stress disorder, and generalised anxiety disorder.

Anxiety itself, and all its ramifications, includes the symptoms: palpitations, pounding heart, or accelerated heart rate; sweating; trembling or shaking; sensations of shortness of breath or smothering; feeling of choking; chest pain or discomfort; nausea or abdominal distress; feeling dizzy, unsteady, lightheaded, or faint; derealization (feelings of unreality) or depersonalization (being detached from oneself); fear of losing control or going crazy; fear of dying; paresthesias (numbness or tingling sensations); chills or hot flushes. (DSM-IV-TR.)

Sufferers commonly report the following feelings and symptoms. The list is long and can include any new or strange feeling. The list is not exhaustive.

> 1. sweaty palms – clamminess for an unknown reason.
> 2. trembling hands or jelly legs – this is part of the adrenaline response where your body is getting ready to fight or flee. Your muscles are being prepared for action and it feels like this.
> 3. prickly heat – running down your spine or legs.
> 4. urgency to use the toilet – for either urination or defecation. You might want to have a 'final' wee before making a speech or you may have irritable bowel syndrome. IBS can be affected by what you eat, but it is often the result of stomach nervousness and tension. Many sufferers plan their lives around the nearest toilet so they are not caught short. Upset stomachs and diarrhoea are part of the anxiety quagmire.

5. butterflies in stomach – a churning or rasping in the stomach.

6. dizziness – or giddiness is one of the more frightening symptoms as sufferers fear that it is a sign of something more serious ... perhaps MS or a brain tumour!

7. general nervousness – feeling on edge all the time. Being startled by the sound of a banging door. Other sufferers are *made* nervous by certain people or dread social situations. Unsympathetic ears play no part in the recovery of the anxious person, nor do those who would judge you harshly.

8. mind going blank – as adrenaline seeks out every crawl space in your body the mind goes blank. Again, this is because your body is preparing for battle, so reading or precision tasks become immaterial to the troubled mind.

9. obtrusive and unwelcome thoughts – a fatigued mind or sensitized nerves can play their own games with us. Sufferers describe thoughts of harming others – usually loved ones – or themselves in some way. These thoughts are abhorrent to the sufferer and they try to push them from their mind – this makes things worse and the thoughts just pop up again.

10. sticky thoughts – these thoughts are intrusive and tend to 'stick' in the mind for no apparent reason.

11. desire to escape one's surroundings – sitting in an aisle seat at a cinema, just so you can get away without embarrassment; running out of a supermarket without your shopping, unable to wait in the queue.

12. irritability – and inability to concentrate. Getting angry with people without just cause; snapping like an ex-smoker.

13. mood-swings – one minute happily crying with joy, the next minute completely distraught.

14. memory loss – not remembering where you're going or what you went out for.

15. palpitations – get these checked by a doctor. Adrenaline directly affects the vagus nerve that runs alongside the heart. Many sufferers think that they are about to die if their heart 'misses' a beat or they get a sinking feeling in their hearts. More often than not, this is the action of adrenaline.

16. blushing

17. inability to swallow

18. inability to take a deep breath

19. tension or busy-ness in the head, like a constricting band.

20. tightness in the chest

21. feelings that you and/or your surroundings are not real

22. greyness of vision

23. tricks of vision – the appearance of things moving that aren't.

24. feeling that people are watching or against you – mild paranoia.

25. fear you might faint

26. fear that you will embarrass yourself

27. fear that you will lose control

28. fear that you will say something awful

29. fear that you will harm someone

30. fear that you will vomit

31. a feeling that the ground is moving

Some of these symptoms may very well indicate a more serious disorder so it's advisable to get checked out by your doctor. If he says it's *just* nerves you'll be okay. With this plethora of symptoms it is small wonder that those suffering with anxiety can develop hypochondria and agoraphobia. Unfortunately, as many of the symptoms are present in more serious ailments, sufferers can become convinced that they have MS or a heart problem, further exacerbating their woes. They also add second fear to their existing anxiety by worrying about when the next anxiety or panic attack may occur. Here they set up a self-perpetuating cycle of fear that feeds off itself. Fear of fear develops and a cycle is set in motion. Happily, all these symptoms can be treated with astonishingly simple interventions.

The DSM has a huge array of personality 'disorders' that you can read about and frighten yourself. The legal drugs agencies must be pleased about this as the more problems we have, the more they can medicate us. Anyway, the above are the general symptoms and you will get the idea. Some CBT practitioners, trainers, and psychologists are obsessed with the DSM and categorising everything and everybody, but life is not like that. We are all a mixture of 'disorders' and it is only the degree of our disorder that makes us either sane or mad. In my experience as a counsellor, and as a person, I have found that we are all many shades of grey, not just one thing.

I must point out here that I am not a great adherent to the DSM as it tends to medicalize a vast array of conditions which are really about the existential angst of living in itself. Anxiety is about existential angst. This medicalization of relatively 'normal' states, such as social phobia (or shyness) means that the condition can now be treated ... with Seroxat or other anti-depressants. Hopefully, Life Tree will show that antidepressants are not always the answer, if they are ever the answer, and latest research questions the entire efficacy of antidepressants. However, the DSM (and the ICD10) has a role in categorising more organic mental ailments and I list the above symptoms so that we are all clear about what we are referring to. If you would like to read an excellent account of modern psychiatry, and the obsession with pigeon-holing people and their states, have a look at Dorothy Rowe's book *Beyond Fear* (2007).

The other main problem with the DSM is that people are people ... human beings. If we were studying quantum physics, it would not matter that all our data was gathered quantitatively and our research would not need to be 'touchy-feely' in any way. However, in the counselling world, our particles are people and I think that the human element in research often gets lost in researching actual people. Consequently, since the DSM is interested in medicalizing and quantifying, I think it misses the whole nucleus of psychotherapy; namely that there is a person suffering at the centre of it all.

Obviously, you won't feel too good if you experience any of the above anxiety symptoms and they are physiological, not 'all in the head', although adjusting your thinking and rationale can alter most of these states. The symptoms themselves may sound familiar, in varying degrees, to many readers and are also similar to the symptoms of hypoglycaemia (low blood sugar) which has already been mentioned in Life Tree. Moreover, if you live in a broken society, you are bound to feel anxious occasionally.

Of course, worry is nothing new and probably since time began, humankind has worried about getting its basic needs met. However, in today's society getting one's basic needs met is not usually a problem. We worry about many things that are not worth worrying about and indeed, most of the things we worry about don't actually happen. This means that we can find ourselves in a state of worry about meaningless things and then perhaps we might also become worried about being worried all the time; this is a well-known and common state of affairs that can lead to a self-perpetuating state of anxiety, where the adrenal glands never seem to be at rest and they become exhausted.

Interestingly, anxiety has existed as long as man has existed; indeed, in many ways it exists to keep us safe from our attackers. Philosophers have long mused about anxiety and Kierkegaard believed that creative people were prone to experience deeper levels of anxiety. The reason for this is that those involved in original and creative pursuits have to explore unknown areas in order that their work is authentic. In exploring these unknown areas, a person has to experience the unknown and step into uncharted territory. This can evoke an anxiety reaction as the creative person explores new depths of meaning. Nietzsche also said that: "One must have chaos within oneself in order to give birth to a dancing star."

In his informative book, *Staying Sane* (2001), the eminent psychiatrist, Raj Persaud, offers some golden nuggets about anxiety and its treatment. He suggests that anxiety can be the beginning of obsessive compulsive disorder (OCD) and cites Howard Hughes's anxiety about money turning into a compulsion and fear of contamination. To prevent this, Hughes became a recluse. When stress decreases, anxiety decreases and the likelihood of OCD diminishes. Persaud maintains that we don't inherit our relatives' tendency towards anxiety but they may pass on their predisposition to react in certain ways. In this respect, anxiety seems to be a learnt response to crises and changing the way you think can certainly inhibit anxious responses.

Chloe writes:

"In June 2005, I finally gave up smoking and drinking alcohol after several failed attempts and a huge amount of reading. Shortly after that momentous date, I developed palpitations and was so worried I went to the doctors. I have suffered with anxiety for the past twenty years, on and off, so I was aware it was probably that anyway. Interestingly, all the symptoms began after I stopped smoking & drinking! I think that's a bit ironic. After a battery of tests at the hospital (bloods, liver function, blood pressure, cholesterol, 3 X ECGs, sugar, thyroid, etc...) they said that I had a slight arrhythmia and I concluded that since the numbing effect of alcohol had gone away, I had probably, unwittingly, raised my own anxiety levels. These palpitations have been coming and going for the past 6 months and, even though all seems well in my life, it seems odd to have anxiety related symptoms. However, 2005 has been a year of big events for me, as I believe in pushing myself, so I've appeared on a TV quiz show and been on an adventure holiday; all stuff high on the stress rating scale. The trouble with the palpitations is that they drain my self-confidence to such a degree that I just want to run away and hide from the situation I'm in when they happen, rather like a panic attack. I usually feel great, then I get a reminder of an anxiety spasm and I could run away and cry. Even though I tend to do anxiety-provoking things – and my work life as a teacher and musician means that I'm 'on-stage' all the time – I have considered other possible causes for my malaise. Those include blood sugar levels and I'd thought of having the big glucose tolerance test. Although the hospital said I wasn't diabetic I fear I may be hypoglycaemic. Or could I have low blood pressure as I often go dizzy when I

stand up quickly or go into a sauna. At the moment it's all a confusion as the symptoms are very similar for all these conditions. Last month I had a big public speech to make and began smoking again! So smoking is back in the equation too now, although I've proudly stayed off the booze; it wasn't that I was an alcoholic, I just drank too much too regularly and when I realised I was becoming too fond, I got rid of it. Chocolate has also become a feature in my life since my teetotalism which I know gives me a boost and for all the wrong reasons. It's just that when I've had a normal evening meal, I get such cravings for chocolate that I find it hard to resist; either chocolate or smoking anyway. All these 'addictions' are a mystery to me – chocolate, alcohol, tobacco, coca-cola – but I just want to be free of them all and without the cravings that cause me to seek out these insipid vices. But there just seems to be such a gap in my life without them; I don't think meditation will do and I'm just glad I never tried illegal drugs or I'd probably be a crackhead in some gutter by now! Other strange phenomena include palpitations after eating a meal (especially chocolate) and sometimes when standing up too quickly there's a slight dizziness. (When I mention palpitations here, I mean a fluttering in the chest, sometimes 'missed' beats and sometimes a sinking feeling; all classic anxiety symptoms I think?) Like everyone, I'd like to stop smoking, if only I could take something to ease the cravings and I think that could be connected to irregular heartbeats etc.

Apart from that, I'm 40, quite happy with the way my life is. According to the Body Mass Index/scales/height, I'm a stone overweight (although I've lost 3 stone during the past 2 years on a low-calorie diet) and I go to a gym 3 to 4 times a week and have done for the past ten years. I'm at a loss to know what's causing the palpitations – sometimes they come after eating or when I drink coke or smoke – so you might be able to find some clue in this writing? Maybe hypoglycaemia? I'm at a loss to know!"

Chloe's letter to me (via my website) is typical although it contains a host of symptoms. Like anyone with serious health concerns, she has sought medical attention and been given a clean bill of health. This reassurance does not assuage her anxiety though and her symptoms seem unwilling to abate. Chloe has a lot going on and she is something of a high flyer and even a bit famous, but there are other things that Chloe does that contribute directly to her anxiety. Although not specifically, the rest of this chapter discusses Chloe's state, a state which affects most Westerners from time to time.

"Present fears are less than horrible imaginings" – says Macbeth [Act 1, scene 3] who obviously didn't live in today's fast moving society. Today, present fears can be as bad as horrible imaginings and often inextricably linked, but it's probably true to say that we can always imagine things to be worse. To say to an anxious person that their state is 'all in the head' is to miss the point. The symptoms are not in the head. They are real enough, but often caused by the way we see things and the stuff we consume.

Anxiety itself is our protector, linked to the fight or flight mechanism, so, in this respect, it can help us get away from danger or stay and fight it. French philosopher Michel de Montaigne wrote: "Sometimes fear puts wings on our heels; at others it hobbles us and nails our feet to the ground" – and made much of his imaginings about fear and the fear of fear and not knowing what to expect. You may have heard the expression 'paralysed with fear' yet this is quite unusual ... more often than not, we either run away from a danger or we confront it, depending on how we rate our chances. In modern times, we are rarely called upon to physically fight for our lives yet a tax demand can cause the same adrenaline response just as if a mad devil dog tried to get its salivating jaws around one's gonads. The fear response can be the same and often, the rational mind doesn't have time to make sense of the occurrence ... it simply has to act. So, first there's the fearful object (tax demand or devil dog), then we have an adrenaline rush (the brain asks itself whether to fight or flee), and, depending on our chances, a host of feelings are switched on. These feelings are described on previous pages from the DSM. However, if we get a tax demand

and have a panic attack, this may not make sense. At least if we were running away from a pit bull terrier, we would expect to feel shaky, tense, and all the other DSM stuff. The tax demand has the same effect and it can all happen in a split second.

You can read much about fear and anxiety from a branch of psychotherapy in a book called *Human Givens* (Griffin & Tyrrell, 2004), who make much of the brain's amygdala and how it creates an emotional and very rapid response to a feared or threatening stimulus. *Human Givens* differs somewhat from the Cognitive Behavioural Therapists' view of how our anxiety taps are switched on, but, for the purposes of Life Tree, suffice to say that they are sometimes switched on inappropriately and for automatic reasons. Ironically, this means that you can also feel very bad, with a plethora of upsetting symptoms, and the cause will not be much to worry about and the symptoms you feel will not kill or hurt you in any way. This is the thing about anxiety – the symptoms aren't harmful although they feel awful. Even if you feel you are about to go mad – you don't. Anxiety is about feeling rotten and that's as far as it goes. With anxiety, the presenting symptoms are often more harrowing than the actuality and so the key to overcoming these symptoms is to embrace the monsters they are.

One of the most upsetting and derailing aspects of anxiety is the panic attack. Panic attacks are a manifestation of anxiety and often feel worse than they actually turn out to be. Because panic feels so bad, and can take us unawares, it can be very shocking, especially one's first panic attack.

Writing forty years ago, Dr Claire Weekes (2000) was probably the leading author in anxiety and panic and acknowledged worldwide as the foremost authority. Her books demonstrate a reader-friendly, self-help solutions guide and are peppered with interesting case-studies; books that are enjoyable and comforting to read. Sometimes, in the spirit of bibliotherapy, I suggest that my clients read a Claire Weekes' book as the knowledge contained within its pages is often enough to effect a full recovery. They are essential reading for the nervous, anxious, or panicky person. Importantly, many people presenting themselves to GP surgeries or even A&E, as suffering from some form of anxiety but don't always know it; they turn up with a specific symptom and think that this is their problem, which it is in a way, but anxiety is often at the root of it (at the root of anxiety is some upsetting life event or change).

Essentially, it is crucial to know that if you are suffering from panic or anxiety, it is the fear of having another attack that maintains the symptoms and makes matters worse. So, there is the actual panic itself, then you develop a fear of having another attack which turns on the adrenaline tap and so a cycle of panic is set up. Panic and anxiety exists within a person who has been under stress and anxiety can be our reaction to this stress. Sometimes the panic itself comes at a time when we least expect it, perhaps on holiday, and this is why it seems like a mystery as it appears often not near the stressor, but after the stressor has disappeared. A panic attack is a surge of adrenaline through (often) tired nerves which causes us to feel 'off' for a while. How we react to this sensation is extremely important as it is the reaction to the panic attack which decides how upset we become and whether it will ruin our lives. If we did not react, it would lose its impact; and again it is the fear of a further attack that maintains the adrenalin cycle. If we did not fear panic, it would not matter and, in fact, it need not matter.

The symptoms of panic are like those described about anxiety in the DSM book listed above. However, panic is usually magnified and feels more intense, causing sufferers to flee from certain situations, fearing they will lose control in some way, go berserk or hurt someone. Other symptoms include the sensation that the heart is missing beats of galloping, light-headedness, dizziness, tingling in hands/feet/lips, feeling sick ... naturally, people suffering from these symptoms often misdiagnose themselves as having (commonly) multiple sclerosis, a brain tumour, or some other gruesome condition. After repeated visits to their doctor, they are (sometimes) reassured that it is 'just' nerves that is the problem and that they will heal with rest and the right nutrition. Sometimes, patients don't believe their doctors and pay for private medicals and MRI scans just to be assured that they're not going to die. We can see then how upsetting panic and anxiety can be.

This perfectly describes Chloe's condition. I have had many clients who experience the whole gamut of symptoms and wonder how they are still alive. They are alive because panic and anxiety in themselves don't hurt us; they just feel rotten. We cannot stop the adrenaline fight or flight reaction when it gets going unless we change our state in some way and try to relax and accept that we are off kilter for a while. It is important therefore that you learn how to relax through a choice that feels appropriate for your self. Popular relaxation methods include and incorporate yoga, breathing techniques, tai chi, or simply unwinding in a hot bath whilst listening to gentle music. At these points you will not want to listen to the television news as good news is rarely reported. TV news in itself can exacerbate your symptoms by hearing about things you can do little about. This can put you in a negative state of mind which is a mood you don't need when you're anxious.

It is at these times when we are low that the anxious mind seems to pile more things on us with which we have to cope. Everything can seem worse than it actually is, and we may feel we're at breaking point. Feelings, colours, and sounds can become exaggerated and we become engulfed in the quagmire of distress, piling adrenaline onto adrenaline and anxiety onto anxiety, thus perpetuating the cycle. Here we feel our emotions in an exaggerated way, more intense, and more upsetting. It is as if every emotion becomes larger than it should be. Buried memories may come to the fore leading us to ruminate over guilty pasts and the like.

You might think that shame and its accompanying sense of guilt is dead and gone in the young of today's society but you might be wrong. A couple of years ago, the Irish comedian Graham Norton hosted a Channel 4 TV programme where members of the audience were shamed in front of their peers. This was done by secretly gaining access to an individual's computer and having a look at their history file of websites they most visited. Not surprisingly, most of the sites were pornographic and this was revealed to the ashen-faced and severely embarrassed audience member, on television. Their shame, it appeared, knew no bounds as they blushed and tried to deny their exposure. The audience made much fun of the victim without, it seemed, acknowledging a glimmer of 'there but for the grace of God go I'. Watching the victim's shame was very interesting as it demonstrated that guilt and embarrassment are still alive in the *noughties*. Even more interesting, a hundred years ago Norton himself would have been arrested for his homosexual activities, assuming that he is an active gay male. Whilst the stigma of gayness has disappeared, anxiety and guilt about private computer pornography obviously hasn't.

So guilt doesn't help because what's done is done and you can only move forward, perhaps making amends.

It is not unusual for sleep to become affected by anxiety: sleep is a highly prized possession when you've missed it for a few nights. Again these are the exaggerated emotions of the troubled mind that finds itself in the grip of anxiety. There is a misconception that obsessions, compulsions, and phobias are separate illnesses but they are always linked to anxiety … they are anxiety's language of choice. It is as if anxiety and inner turmoil need an outlet and often the outlet is a phobia or an OCD which becomes a physical manifestation of anxiety ... something real and visible. Additionally, gruesome thoughts may abound, leading sufferers to think they are one step away from insanity. Some sufferers with these sticky or obsessive thoughts fear that they will stab their new born baby or poison their husbands. These thoughts are abhorrent to them and this is why they think they are going round the bend. In actual fact, the thoughts are (more often than not) simply the product of a fatigued mind and nothing to worry about. If you have these symptoms, the best website I have found is www.nomorepanic.co.uk which explains all the symptoms and their various manifestations. The website offers comfort to many sufferers, especially those who are afraid of going for tests for fear of what they may find.

Weekes (2000) offers deceptively simple remedies to anxiety and these can be seen in her books. One of the major tenets in overcoming anxiety involves acceptance of the feelings you are experiencing and accepting that you are a bit out of kilter. Also, the knowledge that the symptoms of anxiety won't kill you is of great comfort to many clients. Weekes (2000) suggests accepting, floating, and letting time pass to be the keys for recovery. I think this would also be the Buddhist way to recovery as well and having worked with many clients, I can agree that these simple tenets often hold release from nervous suffering. One has to let go and go with the feelings that arise. If you're really aware, you can ask yourself what these feelings are trying to tell you. I have found that many clients who try to maintain control get more and more upset. The art of letting go means turning a 'what if?' into a 'so what'. If you try to maintain uptight control, you will demonize the symptoms and they will increase their power over you. Accepting the symptoms means accepting yourself. Things in life don't feel perfect all the time and if you are stressed and nervous you will have to accept that you will be off sorts for a while. It is in this acceptance you will find the heart of recovery.

When suffering from nervous type illnesses it is easy to become slightly agoraphobic, preferring the comfort of one's home to the terror of going out and feeling bad. However, if we hide away from our fears, we make them worse. The best thing you can to is to get out there and face it in the knowledge that the symptoms of anxiety and panic are harmless. To clients and patients I cannot stress this enough. Whether it's phobias, OCD, panic or virtually anxiety of any type, recovery lies in the places we avoid. By facing our fears and embracing the symptoms within us, we diminish their importance so that they gradually lose their hold and power over us. I know someone who has never been outside Greater Manchester, never been abroad, and only shops at known, comfortable places, lest her panic arise should she venture from her comfort zone. Quite simply, if she went with her horrid feelings and fear, into the unknown – in the knowledge that panic would not kill her – then she would eventually recover. This poor woman seems unable to do this. Of course, she is not literally 'unable'; she just thinks that this is so. If she ventured out many times and often, she would find that her symptoms would eventually subside. When you can live out and accept that the feelings no longer matter, you will be well on your way to a full recovery.

Don't wait for a perfect day so you can go out. Go out anyway and the day will become perfect because you've been out ... or at least bearable. Moreover, you'll be proud of yourself. I have known sufferers wait for this, that, and the other so they can go on holiday, forever making excuses, seemingly without realising that it is their fear that's stopping them. To relieve yourself from the clutches of fear, you just have to go. This is easier to write than actually do, but it is possible. And you'll be pleased you did. In fact, you might as well suffer and go out than stay in and suffer; if you're going to suffer anyway, why not suffer whilst you're out?

Usually, underlying all these fears, phobias and anxious thoughts is a fear of death (whether or not this is consciously expressed). Also there is an inability to self-soothe which was perhaps taught unconsciously in childhood. Accepting anything that arises in thought is one way of accepting ourselves and therein lies the key to freedom from terror. Like birth, death will take care of itself so why spend one's life worrying about it.

I think these sentiments echo many of Dorothy Rowe's (2007) writings and are based on strong ancient philosophy, especially those of Marcus Aurelius and his 'meditations'. Underlying most of our anxiety lies fear and underlying most of our fear lies the fear of death. But who of us will know where or when the reaper will appear?

If we follow Nietzsche's maxim to 'become he who you are', we can hardly do this by hiding in the shadows, waiting for life to happen, living on our knees. We haven't got that long here on earth in which to procrastinate. So, in actual fact, you might as well live life and be anxious whilst you're living rather than hide away with your panic attacks (which won't kill you). Don't let life pass you by. We can observe in Tolstoy's wonderful *The Death of Ivan Ilyich* (2004) how an unlived life can end in bitter disappointment and death. Herein lies a warning for those who hide. But don't be ashamed of yourself if you have hidden thus far ... just get out as soon as you can and choose life.

Because depression and anxiety are so prevalent, the above advice can apply to both conditions. If you don't get anxious about being anxious or depressed about being depressed, you will eventually recover if you are fully able to accept your self and your thoughts.

I mention many times to very anxious people that an amount of protein with every meal will probably help their symptoms. Some believe me and try it, to find that they feel much better. Remember that most manufacturers are keen to sell us hi-carb, low-protein food simply because the former is cheaper for them to package, preserve, market, and sell. This doesn't mean that it's good for us. Try protein and reduce your carbs and you will see a difference both in panic/anxiety as well as your waistline.

Don't fear going over the edge into madness as there is no edge. It's the same with going round the bend; there is a bend but it's a crescent and eventually you'll be back where you started and fully recovered. Like a wave, anxiety will recede because that's how adrenaline works. Anxiety, and the emotional turmoil it causes, is not a psychotic illness nor does it lead to insanity. Although 'neurotic' is not a pc word any more, anxiety is a neurosis and so madness does not lurk around your corner. Our thoughts and emotions can be so closely tied that when we establish a pattern of anxious thought, emotional reaction can be triggered so quickly, it seems almost reflexive. Let not inaction ensue in a moment like this as lethargy will set in, leading to further inactivity. At this stage, try not to take strangeness too seriously as a walk in bright light and a protein snack will almost always affect feelings of recovery. If you suffer from nervous illness, find out what your inner voice is saying by listening. Face it. Stress need not always be unhappy ... it can be a great time for self-discovery and growth.

All this means that you don't need to suffer constantly like the aforementioned client and so many others. In learning that panic will not kill you, anyone should be able to step into the unknown and then prosper even if it feels awful at first; you will find that your newfound freedom will be worthwhile. Life is too short to live on your knees. Why die with unlived life inside you?

At the end of this book you will find Britain's simplest diet and lifestyle list ... *Anthony's Karma Life Diet*. Following this is easy and should lead to a great reduction in anxiety, an improved outlook on life, and some weight loss as well. I am no dietician but I know what works.

As well as eating the right things, one can do various things to reduce anxiety. Action is the key to this as action teaches the subconscious brain that bad things don't usually happen and therefore repetition of a feared circumstance (what psychologists call habituation) usually leads to a decrease in anxiety. Since anxiety is largely controlled by our subconscious thoughts, it is action that usually re-teaches the brain that bad things don't necessarily happen. If we therefore face up to our fears, and face up to them a lot, we will see a gradual reduction in the power they have over us. Hiding away from battle will never make us stronger. Many people use drugs (street and legal) in order to remove or allay their anxiety, but if you want to see a reduction in your own anxious state, consider the following statements:

"An unexamined life is not worth living" postulated the philosopher Socrates – I think that by this, he meant that we really have to look within our selves to see what we really want, experience what we really need, ask ourselves sometimes difficult questions, and find out who we really are. This is the aim of Life Tree and it should be unique to you. This should be done alone or perhaps with the help of a counsellor, and certainly without the use of artificial stimulants. If we become anxious in doing this, we must ask ourselves why. Only then will we discover the secrets of our hidden selves.

"We can only move forward when we look into the dark", said Jung, and I think this follows on neatly from the last paragraph. It is this darkness that many people are uncomfortable with. Some of us do not wish to see inside ourselves for fear of what we might find. This darkness needs to be examined, again, with sober eyes and mind. Sometimes darkness is masked by superficialities such as small-talk, being the life and soul of the party (to mask insecurities), getting blind drunk, describing oneself as bubbly etc … usually these are masks (or defence mechanisms) that we all use in order to cover our true selves. This is all very well as one wouldn't necessarily want to bare one's soul to all and sundry, but be careful that you're not hiding from your own self. In looking into your dark, you will probably find things you don't like, past hurts that have encumbered you for too long, ambitions whose flames have long died, lost loves, distant longings, repressed urges. Then you've got to be honest with yourself and decide whether you live your life by masking these things and have lost yourself along the way. If this is the case – and only you will know – these hurts will bubble through from the unconscious every so often, in the form of anxiety or depression. Perhaps they will appear as dreams or nightmares; sometimes they appear as panic attacks and phobias. When you look into Jung's described darkness, you will be able to find out what makes you tick and whether you need to remove some of your masks in order to live a truer and more fulfilled life. What do you really want?

The importance of sleep

"Goodnight, sweet prince, and flights
of angels sing thee to thy rest."
(Hamlet)

As well as earning a living, for those of us that have to, another third of our life is spent asleep and, like the world of work, one should endeavour to have a quality sleep in a quality bed, alongside quality people if this is your wish. Much has been written about the importance of sleep and the lack of it. William C. Dement, one of the world's biggest authorities on sleep, stresses its importance – many times – in his highly researched tome, *The promise of sleep* (2001). There is little doubt that we should at least spend about a third of our lives asleep to maintain good mental health. Sleep is a time for processing the day's events; this is done in dreams, whether we remember them or not. To sleep well, you need to be as stress free as possible and a low-stress existence can undoubtedly lead to a good night's sleep; they are interrelated. But who has a stress free existence? Comfortingly, sleep will also rejuvenate a flailing nervous system or exhausted adrenal glands.

To sleep well we need to be calm before retiring to bed. This can be achieved through the normal hot baths, relaxing music, nice-smelling candles, etc; but nothing creates calm more than peace of mind ... this can be a harder quest. Although not an answer to all of life's ills, meditation can provide balm for the troubled mind, perhaps bringing some temporary but much needed relief. It is my own view that meditation can be an excellent precursor to sleep and I have known some clients to report that they have fallen asleep during their meditative states. There is a great deal of literature available in meditation and so I will not go into it here. I usually suggest Buddhist mediations and have been known myself to join Buddhists for this very purpose. Active meditation with others can be an excellent way of getting one's life into perspective and this too can pave the way for relaxation, a quietening of the mind and subsequently a better night's sleep. It is important to know that with meditation, the more you do it the better at it you become. Popular meditations include the 7/11 breathing technique mentioned earlier, just-sits, observations, chanting to a mantra ... and a seemingly endless variation on such themes. A Google search will equip you with a vast array of suggestions and meditative themes. Meditation itself need not be complicated and you need not be some sort of guru to get involved in it. I mention meditation in this sleep section because, like sleep, meditation brings to us an altered state of consciousness. If we wish to remove ourselves from the busy-ness of everyday life for a while, then sleep and meditation are excellent and cost free!

Learn to Observe

Find a place where you won't be disturbed
Switch off any noise and your phone to silent
With your eyes open observe what is around you
Feel it and see it
Accept it
You are not attached but part of the flow of life
You do not judge what you see or feel
You accept
If you become distracted accept that ... observe it ... ignore
Just be and listen and see
You have the real you – your 'trunk' or core
You are beyond the material self
Sit and be
The more you observe the more aware you become

This meditation is all about embracing (and even finding) the inner you that might have become deluged by the demands of daily living. We all need to become reconnected with inner truth if we are to accept ourselves and move towards self fulfilment of even enlightenment. We just have to be conscious or 'awake'. Freedom from bullshit is a very hard thing to attain when we are surrounded by it in the West, but the freer we become, the less we are engaged by it and the less we need to be involved with it. This is true freedom and leads to peace.

There is a recent vogue in cognitive behavioural therapy (CBT) called mindfulness, which seeks to marry person-centred counselling, yoga, and CBT itself, perhaps to make CBT more 'friendly'. The scientific talking therapy that is CBT takes on board mindfulness which is an Eastern concept and involves existential philosophies and experiential awareness. As you may know, CBT is the current therapy of choice and is not to be confused with counselling. It is interesting that there is a CBT intervention for most ills, including sleeplessness and as CBT now embraces mindfulness, we shall see if the therapy favoured by NICE can be truly effective in treating insomnia.

If you sometimes find sleep hard to achieve, meditation will soothe your soul. Since breathing is the key of life, you will find solace in it – eventually – if you gain wisdom over it. You can even breathe yourself to sleep if you know what you're doing! Again the internet might unlock some sagely suggestions for you to follow if sleep is evasive.

If we lie perpetually awake, the troubled mind needs relief ... perhaps of locked or frozen emotions. Although it is true to say that a thorough examination of childhood experiences is not always necessary in overcoming anxiety, I have found that most clients are interested in their pasts and enjoy looking for clues in their upbringings that might have caused them present problems. Some therapists (particularly psychoanalysts, psychodynamicists, and transactional analysts) believe that the past is crucial in unlocking our anxieties, others (particularly cognitive behavioural therapists), place less emphasis on the past and use interventions that work in the here-and-now in order to effect a quick and effective remedy. Still others (psychiatrists) prescribe drugs. The psychotherapeutic jury is out on the efficacy of these treatments but there seems little doubt that talking therapies work. A cynic would say that CBT is only popular because it is short-term therapy and therefore cheaper than the others (and therefore favoured by the NHS and NICE). All forms of psychotherapy – from psychoanalysis to behavioural interventions – are successful to the extent to which they enhance change your life, and this can be as much to do with the relationship you enjoy (or not) with your therapist as with the model of therapy that you choose.

Whichever therapy you chose – if you chose any – it would be unusual if your childhood didn't crop up somewhere along the line. Some clients find this so very painful that they want to stick solely to CBT and this is their prerogative. All our experiences are stored up in our bodies. Painful childhoods form a kind of emotional scar tissue that often revisits us in later life and demands our attention. These demands may come in the form of a physical illness or a breakdown, but come they usually do. Whilst it is not always necessary to find childhood roots of what may have contributed towards our anxiety, it might be worth considering how you were brought up and whether you consider that any events that you might have experienced may have exacerbated your symptoms. This is one of the main tenets of Life Tree. It is also the reason why Britain appears to be so broken ... our pasts have ruined our futures.

Thoughts can be powerful if we believe or act on them all. Anxiety can throw thoughts into our minds that we have no intention of acting upon and never will. It is important to know that one cannot control one's thoughts; the mind has a free will. Anxious people can be very impressionable and give these thoughts more credence than they deserve. As I said earlier, much of life is about belief and these beliefs can emanate from single thoughts. Try not to become derailed by horrific thoughts especially if you recognise yourself to be fatigued or stressed. Thinking can have powerful effects on our bodies so even though thoughts can and will spring up, you have to be careful not to take them too seriously. In the not so distant past, doctors giving a patient 'six months to live' could have such a devastating effect in the patient that they actually died within that period. More robust patients decide not to believe their doctor's grim prediction and choose life instead.

If you're anxious and worried you could do worse than lighten up by watching Woody Allen's excellent film *Hannah and her Sisters*. It shows how anxiety can get out of hand if you catastrophize or fortune-tell your own fate. And it's very funny to see Woody at his hypochondriachal best. Additionally, comedy will probably make you feel better.

It is important to realise that a lot of anxiety and so called mental disorders have their roots in fear. Dorothy Rowe (2007) writes at great length about this in her weighty volume *Beyond Fear*. In my work with numerous clients, we scratch the surface of the presenting problem (which is never the underlying problem) and find that they are inundated with terror of some kind or other. Generally, the worse your upbringing, the worse will be your future life unless you repress it or, when it seeps out of repression, do something about it to make things better. Fear often lies at the root of anxiety; more often than not a fear of losing control, the inability to trust others, and a fear of annihilation. Clients may not be aware of this fear and a skilled counsellor can coax out these inner demons. Through anxiety, fear finds outward manifestations such as OCD, phobias and the like, but at the root of all the symptoms lies a pervasive fear of losing something. We must remember that into each life some rain must fall (Wadsworth Longfellow).

Exercise

The following box shows a list of events that might cause anxiety or panic attacks. You may like to draw your own list, based on this scale, to see if you have experienced any of these events leading up to your ill feeling. If you score high on the count, this may go some way to explaining your symptoms.

You might like to look at The Beck Anxiety Inventory (BAI), The Beck Depression Inventory (BDI), or The hospital anxiety and depression scale (HADS). All these 'tools' are commonly used in the treatment and improvement of mental health. An internet or library search should easily reveal these interesting questionnaires.

First of all, have a look at the list below and add your answers to your journal.
Taken from Baker (1995, p.84)

Society & Advertising

"All it takes for evil to triumph is for good people to do nothing" (Edmund Burke)

The trouble is … good people get their heads kicked in.

Advertisers usually create desires within us through their use of associations and anchors. They do this as it is the capitalist's desire to create demand; demand that would not have even existed if we were left alone. "Are you ashamed of your old phone?" asks one advert, thus anchoring guilt. Without a gadget or product we are made to feel worthless. If we had personal worth we wouldn't need a product to inflate ourselves ... this is what advertising is all about ... making us feel inadequate. Consumers buy avidly and often go into debt or grow fat as a parasitic industry thrives off their gullible weaknesses. Advertisers endeavour to hook our basic emotions (sexiness, fear, guilt, shame, anger, sadness, etc) and anchor it to a new product in the hope that we will spend freely. The consequences of this fabricated greed has wide reaching global implications such as the greenhouse effect and more personal ones such as anxiety and depression. However, all this greed and materialism is important for the Western world to flourish; it keeps the wheels of industry turning. We can maintain our anxiety and depression as long as we're spending. We are still functional and needed by society; we are consumers. We don't become any happier with all our purchases but it feels that way when we are actually spending.

The more loveless and craving a society, the more we buy. Everything man-made you see around you, you have been initially encouraged to have in some way … and then you're punished for having it. Like this: You see an advert for cakes; you buy a fat-making cake which is sugar laden and so tastes nice; then you feel guilty because you're already overweight. So you either go back to smoking, in the (false) belief that it controls your appetite, or you buy a diet drink or recipe thus fuelling the trade even more and costing you even more money. Additionally, in eating the cake you have triggered your body's insulin/glucose mechanism and you then want a second cake. This is just what manufacturers and their advertising agencies want to happen. They will write anything on the packet to make you believe that this is not the case, but the reality is that they want you to buy their unhealthy, carbohydrate/fat/sugar infested rubbish. Don't be fooled into thinking that they care about you – there is only money to care about in this society. America is the bastion of capitalism but, Oliver James suggests that the more like America a society becomes, the higher its rate of emotional distress (James, 2007).

More and more, I have noticed that we're living in an increasingly amoral society. This is fuelled by so many things discussed in *Broken Britain?* Amorality is a grand accusation and has to be controlled by the powers that be, so they become more punitive towards us. This is the reverse of love as we are punished in an Orwellian way for minor misdemeanours that have been increasingly criminalized during the past two decades. Parking attendants have never been so zealous, speeding fines so punishing, taxes so gruelling … all leading to increased alienation instead of social cohesion. Everyone who drives at 34mph in a 30mph zone will feel the wrath of the government just because someone once drove along that road at 65mph. In other words, everyone suffers for the actions of a rotten few who couldn't care less. Amorality means total lack of morals, nothingness, and a lack of care for consequences. In a narcissistic and materialistic capitalist society, amorality must be a result of years of lack of love and continual punishment (the introduction of weapon-scanners in schools, CCTV in the classroom, the smoking ban, political correctitude) … where does the nanny state end and when do we take responsibility for our own behaviour in the knowledge that this is our society and we are supposed to take care of it and ourselves.

Almost like a psychopath on the rampage, society seems to be out of control, seeking hedonistic goals and short-term gains. Advertising gurus are keenly aware of this and are totally in tune with the fact that Britons and Americans have veered out of control. The craze of wearing FCUK shirts offends some, but the ones who wear this garb are unconsciously buying into a rebellion that I think reflects the overall decline in moral values; they wouldn't admit or necessarily know this as it is unconsciously driven. The FCUK campaign was highly successful – a fact which tells its own story. The ones who wear this apparel are giving out the message: hey look at me, I'm a reprobate … and fuck you! It appears not to matter to wearers that it might infest a child's mind. Even when there's a 'clamp-down' to promote family values we later discover that ex-Prime Minister, John Major, (who championed such a cause) was having adulterous sex with Edwina Currie. The wonderful 'Suncream' song tells us that politicians will always be prone to philandering so perhaps we should expect adultery and flaws within us all. So, who is whiter than white and who can cast the first stone? Or is it a matter of degrees? Degrees of depravity or righteousness. The 'I might be dead tomorrow' attitude seems to prevail in 21st century Britain even though most people are alive tomorrow; perhaps this could explain the perpetual rise in sexually transmitted infections.

Sometimes the fast pace of modern life is just too much to bear, or at least it seems to be that way when we pound life's treadmill. It's as if many of us haven't caught up from our stone age past. "What is this life if, so full of care, we have no time to stand and stare" writes W. H. Davies. It's as if we all have to be busy, rushing here and there, to and fro. The Buddhists have a popular meditation called 'Just Sits' and the Quakers do a similar thing with their hour-long silences … both intended to give time away from business and hassle in order to reflect and process the hurly-burly of life. If only we could make a 'window' for these and 'diarize' them into our hectic schedules. Is all this rushing born out of fear? By this I mean fear of not having enough. Or perhaps it's fear of looking inside ourselves for fear of what we might find. Fear of not being able to afford designer labels and fear that we look poor in comparison to our peers. Fears can be myriad and I would suggest that society just compels and exacerbates these fears until we feel we have to escape … perhaps to Tibet or a small holding in France.

It is interesting to note, what the powers that be have decided to do about the abhorrent and rising crime rates. They make up crimes such as smoking bans and easy-target crimes such as driving whilst using a mobile phone (all of which are easily justified and spin-worthy) – so that they can criminalize a host of people who break the new laws in order to boost crime success rates and prove that crime is falling. In reality, 'real' crime and that which is hard to solve, is not falling as it's hard to detect. Perhaps it's not even being reported and we can't blame the police for that. By criminalizing marginal crime, it is possible to massage the figures so that the authorities can say they're doing their bit for law and order. Crime control seems to be an ersatz business.

But it's not only crime that is out of control. As well as the fragmentation of society, young people now have the burden of student debt as well. Marx would have had a field day with the concept of student loans. On the surface, designed to create responsibility and to pay for a commodity, underneath, this is a bourgeois ruse to take students and early workers into debt so that they are tied to the system they will eventually come to abhor. A system that will drain all their creativity, and, like a mortgage, by the time it's paid off (unless rich aunt pops off leaving an inheritance – as she would with the privileged), they will be grey, old, bitter, and ready to send their own kids to university to re-ignite the cycle of debt. Cynical or realistic? You decide.

Debt though is now an acceptable part of society. Carol Vorderman's loan adverts nicely anchor us into this acceptability: if she advertises loans, they must be okay because she's clever. It's strange how social norms become ingrained and accepted as givens and morays. For example, the dropping and leaving of litter in a theatre: a seemingly innocuous event where you observe even well-heeled middle class people leaving rubbish behind them as they leave *Phantom of the Opera*. This displays how social norms pervade the collective unconsciousness so that anti-social behaviour becomes normal. I wrote most of this book before the 2008 credit-crunch. We now see that initial American greed that encouraged people who couldn't afford it to get a mortgage, has risen and smacked us all in the face. Couple this with bonds and futures and you will see a complete façade, built largely on nothing but confidence and promises of future growth. When the thing collapses, as it just has, the poorest people will be the ones who suffer … as always. Those with the least to gain suffer the most!

The sociologist Emile Durkheim (1858-1917) argued that people comply with social pressures and follow what their peers are doing. This, Durkheim believed, has a functional effect upon people and the wider society in which they live. Society restricts us (laws and rules) and people are generally quite happy to acquiesce to these constraints. He went on to say that the actions of society are difficult to analyse because they are often invisible and, in my view, work unconsciously. However, when society imposes its will and causes us frustrations or a feeling of impotency, Durkheim called this anomie; a sense of drifting aimlessness and alienation. This I think describes the current yob culture in late capitalist countries. As a nation, we have no more 'jobs for life' and little security, a high divorce rate, a government that lies but pretends to be honest (well, it has to pretend or the whole ruse would be broken), fragmented families with steps- and halfs- all over the show; all leading to anomie. This anomie means that we are truly alone – as alone as when we were born. This is truer than ever as we see that we really have nothing to rely on in life – the credit crunch simply mirrors a chaotic world that has lost its confidence and is slowly polluting itself with pointless consumerism and toxic emissions.

Add to this the MP's expenses scandal and our so-called leaders with their snouts in the gravy train. I used to wonder why anyone would consider becoming an MP and in May 2009 I found out. It seems that a lot of our MPs have been lining their pockets and flipping their claims here and there in order to play their own self-created system. On BBC's *Question Time* (July 2009) I heard Julia Goldsworthy talking about an expensive rocking chair and how she claimed half of it on her expenses … then went on to say that for some time, she had been craving more transparency! Eh? It's the sheer hypocrisy that seems so appalling. It would seem that MPs can be as badly behaved as everyone else in society. Do they want transparency so they can't milk the system any more? Are we to believe that the same people who were taking advantage of lax rules actually wanted to be caught?

The author of *Yob Nation* (2007), Francis Gilbert, is someone who has taught in state schools and travelled throughout Britain interviewing a host of people involved with yobbishness: namely perpetrators, victims, and law enforcers. Gilbert makes some suggestions for change and how to repair our ruined country. It seems that there is no longer one bad apple that spoils the rest but a lot of bad apples and only a few decent ones left. Gilbert suggests that we must look at cultural attitudes, education, and the justice system if we are to improve our country. This is all very well but I think it goes much deeper and completely misses the real problem and the causes of social problems. Unlike Gilbert, I came from the gutter and he of course can't be responsible for being born privileged and attending what he calls a 'minor' public school; however, the vein of depravity that exists in society today (prostitution, drug abuse, binge drinking, amorality, incest, psychopathy, hedonism, etc) … is caused, in my view, by our upbringing and the influence of advertising. They also miss the point who believe that a lack of money creates scroatism. One only has to look at some lottery winners to see what happens to money in the 'wrong' hands. When some folk come into money they don't suddenly enrol onto a degree course and begin quipping Shakespearian puns. It's really all about love and how we were nurtured in our early months. In his epic *Nineteen eighty-four*, Orwell makes a beautiful comment about lotteries in the fictitious Oceania. And in our own non-fictitious Britain, for some, the lottery is their only hope of escape. Of course, Orwell wasn't referring to our own much-lauded lottery but you get the gist. Gambling, like any other addiction is a gap filler and a sad indictment of any society whose members wish so much to escape from their drudgery by taking part in something that they have VERY little chance of winning … something like 14,000,000 to 1. Ironically, many of the 'good' causes the British *National Lottery* funds are things like ballet, which the proles have no interest in and will never ever see. And if they do see it, they might raucously shout, "He's behind you … that black swan!" I can almost hear the middle class reader accusing

217

me of inverted snobbery as I write the last line, but the middle class reader who says that has never lived in a working class environment so cannot really comment; or they can comment and rattle about a bit, but their comments will be without real life experience. For example, they may suggest that the underclass would enjoy the ballet if only they could afford it. I have never met anyone from the underclass who would enjoy a ballet whether they could afford it or not. In these words I am certainly not being elitist ... just honest. Those who doubt, should walk round now to their local sink estate and ask a few street youths what they would like to spend £200 on. Make a list of their answers and see where ballet features. Similarly, my own local hospice spent thousands of pounds on artwork for their prayer room. There was outrage amongst the masses because the masses want scanners and medication and the middle class (who control the means of production and purchases of art) prefer to spend money on art work. The masses secretly know that most art is bullshit. The hospice money had come from public donations, from a public who expected their cash to go towards cancer care, not expensive art work.

In *Yob Nation* there is an account of Gilbert's stroll through the streets of Ayia Napa. He is met with the spectacle of young parents dragging their children through streets lined with drunkards as disco music pumps out. What kind of motherhood (or childhood) is this? He recounts how the children appeared to be in agony on their holidays. Fifteen years on and the children will be doing much the same thing. I haven't yet seen this spectacle in Blackpool – at least at night-time. Is this what motherhood is about? We often hear of neglect like this when paedophile or abduction cases reach the news. In the presence of chaotic and inadequate care – where the child's needs always come second – we learn that parents are 'shocked' to find that someone in the family was abusing their child: an uncle or a brother or a step-father. Are these shocked people too trusting or just plain stupid? Perhaps it's a combination of both. An Eminem song talks about 'little Eric' who falls off a hotel balcony because his parents weren't watching him; the phrase ends, "apparently, you ain't parents". I think that says it all. We delude ourselves when we choose to trust everyone in society.

Children's author Jacqueline Wilson makes much of these *sorts* of people in her many books and her acclaimed *Tracy Beaker* BBC programmes ... people who have children – often by mistake – and don't do that much about their care; sort of rough diamonds. At least Wilson can see the diamond shining. Wilson often writes about the sort of people that spawned fake abductee Shannon Matthews. Again, I found it hard to see any evidence of a diamond in this quagmire of corruption, greed, amorality, depravity and paedophilia. They even approached the Madeleine McCann fund to extort money from it!

Whilst we should live in a trustworthy society, we don't, so face it. If you have children, you have to watch over them. A parent's fury is doubled when a paedophile snatches their child: Firstly, they are consciously angry that paedophiles exist and how bad and unfair the world is, and secondly, they will be unconsciously angry with themselves for not being vigilant. They will fulminate and rage against everyone instead of looking at where the fault lies. Family paedophiles often show clues to their proclivities; the longing looks, perhaps inappropriate comments, other weird sexual requests, odd cuddles, etc, and you would have to be a dullard to miss these hints. If you are a woman who has a suspicion about her partner, address it immediately. It might mean the end of your relationship but you could be saving your own child's life. If you chose to remain in that relationship will you be able to live with yourself in later years when the child disowns you? My counselling rooms are full of older teens who have been let down by their parents. If nobody protects them, they break or become drug addicts or go mad.

Because being middle class has now become something to be ashamed of, and there is a quest for laddishness and a pride in being bad, this has taken hold across society. Nowadays, all males pretend to love football where once it was the reserve of the working class. The love and religion that is now football coincides nicely with this continual binge drinking culture that has swamped us. The Government obviously make more revenue from allowing the rise of binge drinking than they do from curbing it; if this were not the case, they would try to ban alcohol as they have with cigarettes. We are now a nation without a cause, meandering from one imported product to the next, hoping that the new design adds some dimension to our lives. Parents and governments have failed and we have failed ourselves. Britain is broken because we no longer know who we are or what we believe. We have little religion so we have to believe in computers or football or war.

Failed government initiatives are omnipresent and a list of failures appears later in *Broken Britain?* Not least of these failures was the Iraq war, about which reams have been written. It seems weird that we topple Sadam Hussain but leave Robert Mugabee in place (at the time of writing). I wonder why that can be? Could it be to do with oil and Western greed? Few would deny that Sadam was a despot but there are so many despots so why not pop them all off? Obviously, many parts of the Middle East are an untapped market and they sit on oil. The Western aim is to convince the Islamist to a more consumeristic thinking, just as it was the communist doctrine to see communism thrive throughout the world. Now it seems to be the Western ideology – led by American neo-cons – to sell its produce to anyone who can be seduced into buying it. Unfortunately, the Taliban and such like unwittingly play into the hands of the West as they make it easy for the West to villainize them and therefore go to war. Our own Government won't negotiate because they call it terrorism and anti-democratic, whilst the terrorists know that they can't get anywhere through the democratic vote, so loaded is mainstream society against their wishes. What choice do they have?

Immorality and the media

Immorality and how the media feed it – but does the media incite immorality or does the immoral society feed the media? Perhaps it goes both ways. I could cite numerous examples of sexual laxity taken from the British tabloid press. It's always written as a bit of a tease ... such-a-body wants S&M with so-and-so; someone else sells their lurid story about being spit-roasted by various sportsmen; another announces that most women are bisexual these days and that she loves sex with girls and men ... sometimes at the same time. This is typical tabloid news and perhaps this reflects normal British life. If nobody's eyebrows are raised by such stories, then it must be me and a few others who hold old-fashioned views.

It is usually the rich and famous who are keen to reveal their sexual forays and some people obviously want to know or the papers and magazines wouldn't sell as they do. In many ways this is how morality has declined, whereby anyone even slightly famous can talk about their sexual preferences and appetites. Obviously, sluts and trollops have always been around, but now they're *out* and even admired. Perhaps we envy them. The problem with the red top tabloids is that they often take the moral high ground with *The Sun says* this and *The Star says* that, but then they objectify women by showing a soft porn photograph on page three. It's this deep hypocrisy again that is so nauseating: like the sanctimoniously grinning MP pretending to be honest whilst she legally syphons the tax purse: The tabloid blanking out the f**k in fuck and then showing a pornographic photograph on page three. This is stupendous hypocrisy from the Government and the media. It is well known in liberal circles the harm this sort of pornography does and the message it portrays. Is it normal that a woman buys this paper and reads it near her children? Those papers I mention are good in one way in that they speak in a normal language but I simply cannot understand why *page three* exists or why any female would choose to appear there. I can almost hear the defences and they're always similar to those given by lap-dancers and other mild-form-prostitutes: We're not exploited because the men are giving us the money and they can't touch us.

So why is it immoral? Well, in my view it is immoral because it portrays women in the wrong light, as something to be stared at; it promotes pornography which is also exploitative, and ask yourself this: would those porn models be doing this job if they could do something else that paid as well? I don't think so. Having said this, I can totally understand why a man would buy such a paper – because it is titillating and always nice to see a healthy young woman undressed! That said, I would be in favour of a total ban because of societal implications. The same goes for the 'lads' mags'. Permitting these soft porn publications infects our collective unconscious as a society and makes us morally poorer as a result. I must state here, I am not against porn per se, but I am against it being shown in a national newspaper masquerading as a 'news' paper. This sort of thing then becomes part of mainstream culture and inculcates readers into a sense of normality about women being seen in this light. It also begs the question: where do you draw the line? Is it permissible to show a penis on page five? Why not have a pop-up erection on page seven? If not, why not? Then why show breasts with erect nipples? Why is this permissible? Who decrees what is and is not permissible? I recently witnessed a modern father reading a lads' mag whilst sitting beside his seven-year-old son. The son learns unconsciously that women are to be stared at and that they are objects. I understand that most women who use their bodies in this way do it for the money and I don't really blame them for anything in particular. I make the important point that a society that allows pornography into the mainstream and off the top shelf, is a society that is not promoting equality … despite what it says.

But surely the display of a female body is what the public want (men anyway) and so the papers guilty of perpetuating this are only meeting demand. Well, this might be partially true but most people, if they tried it, would want more cocaine. Should society meet that demand as well? When we allow the viewing of a semi-naked woman in a national newspaper we are declaring that this is acceptable, just as it is acceptable to spin the truth through advertising. We are accepting a form of brainwashing which infects our minds. (I hear the old argument about women being topless on a beach and that that is just like page three. Well it is not. A topless woman on holiday is not being paid so you don't have to be a professor of ethics at Cambridge to demolish that argument. If I approach the sunbathing nude and offer her Euros to show me her breasts, then if she complies, she becomes a sex worker and I become a 'john'.) Like advertising, we should not forget the power of the media and how pornography is all around us.

If *they* want us to buy something (whether it's a manufactured product or a new government idea), all they have to do is assemble a few psychologists and ad-men and, by their powers of manipulation, we will soon be grabbing it in handfuls. Consider the success of mobile phones. The ruling class control our behaviours – and the collective unconscious's stream of ideas – through the media which is fed by advertisers and governments. If we are given pornography we will happily consume it. Again, these words are not a rant against porn, but I believe that porn is having a negative effect on young people who are easily influenced and happy to buy into ideas which they take as being normal.

Psychologist and social commentator Oliver James, makes some brilliant points in his book *Affluenza* (2007). James seems to have absorbed the totality of the advertising world, and, finding it hard to digest, has spat out its detritus onto the pages of his several works. In a series of 'vaccines' against what he calls affluenza, James presents us with some solutions that might defend us against the rampant capitalism that infects our current society.

To keep our current society 'alive' in the way it exists, we have to keep spending on the latest gizmo or gadget, and we also have to accept uncomfortable notions such as pornography, crime, drugs, and general dissatisfaction. It is only when we are made to feel that our lot is inadequate will we spend on things we don't need. Who really needs a coffee-to-go? How thirsty can we possibly be? In the seventies, nobody ran around with a cardboard cup of coffee in their hands. Have thirsts increased or can it be simply down to brilliant marketing that we feel the need to buy a coffee to walk around with just in case we are seen as being inadequate without one. One could actually take a flask around and be thought of as peculiar ... like me. But a flask would destroy the illusion; the illusion of being a thirsty New-York lawyer who has just dropped off his kids at kindergarten before making a ball-breaking deal on Wall Street and scoffing a muffin in his hectic schedule. It's a hard life and then there's the cost.

There is a high level of dissatisfaction which currently manifests itself in depression and anxiety – see the current rates of people taking antidepressants such as citilopram, fluoxetine, prozac, seroxat; or even tranquillizers. (Diazepam being one of the most prescribed drugs of mind relaxation.) I don't think chemical imbalances in the brain have anything to do with the fact that anti-depressant usage is at an all time high. Even if there is an imbalance, this will probably be caused by stress which will be related to the society in which you live. Many of my clients have been offered antidepressants and drug selling is a big business in the Western world. We are offered a mind numbing, mood altering chemical to help us cope with living here. The best remedy for anxiety, depression, and stress is a new life. I know that's not possible for all of us who have to work, but it's something to aspire to. Your happiness would probably come from your freedom. But governments don't want us to be that free. Free souls do not make for a stable economy. This explains why student loans are good for the government (apart from relieving them of having to pay for your education). Student loans tie the student to future employment and a life of drudgery. It might be a disguised drudgery if you have star awards and appraisals, and use phrases like "going forward", but you will still be dancing to the tune of the corporate prison warder. Governments and employers must try at all costs to retain control.

So we buy things that keep the economy buzzing ... someone has to spend; and if you are lucky enough to be able to spend at the expense of the tax payer and have a *John Lewis list*, so much the better. In recent years, our spending has rocketed both as individuals and as a nation. We can see how the 'live now' mentality can lead to serious debt problems. We live now to ameliorate our sense of inadequacy caused by advertising and living here in broken Britain. In other words, we are made to suffer for living itself! Then we try to repair our hurts by spending on an item and then suffer more when the bill arrives. We don't really need a coffee to run around with so that our peers think we're successful, nor do we need a touch phone. Individually we need love and collectively we need a fairer society but I really don't believe that the latter will ever be thus.

Returning to pornography, there is also the influence such images have on teenage girls who are bombarded from every angle by the need to look a certain way. Eating disorders abound as the fashion industry insist on using wafer-thin freaks to whom we are all meant to aspire. James (2007) advises us to ditch all women's magazines due to their malign influence. You are not supposed to feel prettier after reading them ... you are supposed to feel inadequate so you will spend on the products you have viewed. You will also be observing the lives of the rich and famous ... lives that most of us will never enjoy.

Although society pretends otherwise, we really cannot have it all. Through the media we are given to believe that everything is possible. There was a phrase bandied about a few years ago: cash rich and time poor. This phrase in itself was a form of brainwashing as most people are never cash rich. After the recession we are now cash poor and time poor, even though most of us do not want to face up to it. Although we hope that everything is possible and buy this-and-that to make it so, in actual fact not many things are possible and most of us achieve nothing of the American dream. Many women today have full-time jobs, three children, do housework and cooking and try to satisfy their husbands. No wonder antidepressants are so popular.

Oxford Professor of Philosophy A.C.Grayling (2002) gives us a beautifully measured statement about all this: "There are those, however, who not only defend but extol the free-market order and the consumerism which it fuels. Sociological orthodoxy says that consumerism is oppression; skilful marketing people have manipulated us, says this orthodoxy, into a state of passive victimhood endlessly and aimlessly consuming ever-increasing amounts at the behest of an advertising industry which creates false desires in us by making us believe that to purchase an object is to purchase happiness. Studies of consumerism and what it involves ... make disturbing reading, because they suggest that the mechanisms of persuasion and coercion underlying capitalism are fundamentally malign. The orthodoxy tells us that marketing executives turn us into anxious yet docile creatures falsely made to believe that the way to find paradise is to buy stuff. A chorus of distinguished commentators … and the philosophers of the Frankfurt school, all condemn the waste, folly, false consciousness and victimhood of consumerist society, which they describe as a conspiracy to force us to labour so that we can purchase the crumbs of pleasure that the system lets fall from the tables of those whose unnecessary products we buy. And in the meantime we are engulfed in waste and pollution as we sit in the blue flicker of television advertisements, eating our unhealthy microwaved TV dinners. The orthodoxy suggests that if only advertisers would leave people alone, they would all begin reading Wittgenstein and listening to Mahler. The fact is, they would not." (p.147)

Exercise

Are you wasting your time in living the dream? Are you annoyed that almost every penny you earn seems to disappear?

You need to compile an inventory regarding your needs and wants: make two lists of each. Slowly go through each list and decide what you *really* need and not what you just want.

Add to the list the things that you have bought because of advertising or things promoted as must-have objects or foods.

Consider any purchases made because of your friends' influences.

Are you 'you' – or just a consumer?

Part 5 – What you can do to make things better

There exists no more difficult art than living. For other arts and sciences, numerous teachers are to be found everywhere. Even young people believe that they have acquired these in such a way, that they can teach them to others: throughout the whole of life, one must continue to learn to live and, what will amaze you even more, throughout life one must learn to die. Seneca

First of all, you have to start living in the now! Sure, look back on wonderful times, if you have any, and plan for the future, but try to live each day with enthusiasm and in the knowledge that you can change things for yourself, and make things better. I don't think anybody wants to lie on their death bed harbouring regrets...

Ron writes:

"I just wish I'd courted Marie when I had the chance. I was young at the time and she had it all ... looks, figure, beauty, intellect. We were both about twenty. At that time, I thought there'd be a hundred Maries. But there weren't. I've thought about her all my life, dreamt about her and wondered what she ever got up to. I was shy at the time and I now ache to have grasped her with both arms and told her how I felt. It's fifty years later now and I can still smell her scent. She was wearing a wrap-around summer dress and her face was the most carefree glow of youth I have ever known. I got to thirty and that time was already gone. At forty I cried. At fifty, I knew I would never know another Marie. As the sun now sets on my life I so really wish I'd have told her how in love we were and how we were meant to be together. We both knew it and felt it at the time, but I never did anything about it and it's too late now."

As W. S. Gilbert once said: "Love unrequited robs me of my rest."

Regrets. Apart from Edith Piaf, we all have them. Should have done this, should have done that. If you can't undo wrongs or revisit old flames like Ron might have done, then live today and embrace the moment. This doesn't mean becoming irresponsible or doing harm to others. It simply means acknowledging your gut instincts and following them through. Otherwise you might live to regret it. W.B.Yeats reflects Ron's existential angst in his poem *Politics*...

> *How can I, that girl standing there,*
> *My attention fix*
> *On Roman or on Russian*
> *Or on Spanish politics?*
> *Yet here's a travelled man that knows*
> *What he talks about,*
> *And there's a politician*
> *That has both read and thought,*
> *And maybe what they say is true*
> *Of war and war's alarms,*
> *But O that I were young again*
> *And held her in my arms.*

I wonder if Limbit Opik had read this poem when he ditched everything and followed his heart with the *Cheeky Girl*? Who can blame him? If this is so, at least Limbit won't lie in bed as an old man wishing he had followed his heart.

Non rien de rien. Non je ne regrette rien.

Apart from regret, much stress can be caused by change, or not so much the change as our reaction to that change. You will know by now that it is our reaction that matters and not change in itself. This is a most important distinction. Life itself is one long span of change: birth, school, adolescence, work, marriage(s), having children, your parents dying, your own death. All these things can cause stress – depending on how you look at them. Embracing change forms part of your flexibility as a person and gives you the opportunity to grow and become more rounded. Throughout your life you will make small and large choices that will have an impact on you. Whether it's choosing a pepperoni pizza or a marriage partner, each choice will have an effect and make changes within you. You might elect to have four pizzas and grow fat; this will be a result of your decisions. Often, change is about dealing with the unexpected which can unsettle even the most resilient amongst us. How we cope with the changes will be a defining moment for us. By looking at how you cope, you will have the chance to review your decisions and perhaps make different choices next time. We all know people who would have done things differently if they had their lives to live again, not least so Ron in the above story.

Perhaps you like others to make changes for you – your partner might make your decisions and you may passively go along with them? Change can threaten your security and ask you to leave your comfort zone. This will cause some anxiety for you but you will be better for it for having risen to the challenge and embraced change. As well as anxiety there will be uncertainty as you try to predict outcomes; your norms and values may be challenged. However, if you meet these opportunities for growth that are caused by change, you will be more fulfilled and stronger at having experienced and overcome the crisis. This is within your power and lies within all of us.

Highs & Lows

If you can accept the fact that your happiness does not depend on a chocolate bar you might then want to look at how you can be happier. To strive for happiness in itself is not really a worthy goal because happiness is hard to define. It is nebulous. If you want to feel happy you have to do something towards that goal as happiness in itself is a bi-product of doing something else. Unless you are an experienced Buddhist, it's hard to gain inner calm and contentment so you might like to examine what you could do in order to attain some level of happiness. But know that this happiness will be fleeting.

Sometimes happiness can be achieved with the removal of pain, so you'll be happy that you're not in pain any more. Or the situation might be less severe than this and you might be happy to have a warm bath after a gruelling day. So these feelings of happiness can come as a relief. Of course, joyous news will also lift your spirits, like winning the lottery or hearing that some dreaded hospital results are normal and you're not about to die.

Happiness is an off-shoot that won't last; the best you can hope for is some kind of middle ground. Holidays are only nice because they lie in apposition to the daily grind and so provide a welcome break: if you were on holiday all year, you would cease to think of it as a holiday. This could explain why some ex-pats, living in the sun, crave rain and fish 'n' chips: to remind them of how lucky they are to be away from the UK. Like happiness itself, the activity which creates happiness within us cannot last or our happiness would not be sustainable. In this way, happiness is dichotomous and relative and directly proportional to the misery of everyday life. Consider bi-polar disorder (formerly known as manic depression before pc re-branding) where sufferers are delirious and creative for a period of time and then chronically depressed another time. This is dreadful for those afflicted with it so the best you can hope for – assuming that you have normal brain chemistry – is an even mood. This means that some events will make you happy and some will make you blue, and, hopefully, neither mood will last too long. However you achieve this happy state (suggestions below), know that chemical substances and buying products will never give you anything more than a fleeting thrill and may indeed cause more problems for you in the long run. Whilst you may be enjoying a fleeting moment of happiness, know that it won't last forever! However, you might feel grim all the time. As well as things cited in Life Tree, this melancholy may be caused by faulty thinking. I will now briefly examine the most popular psychotherapy ... CBT, short for Cognitive Behavioural Therapy.

Cognitive Behavioural Therapy (CBT) in a nutshell

CBT involves changing the way we think about things and experiencing life in the here and now. CBT is not about dwelling too much on past traumas (that we can't change) but rather, looking forward to the future and making things better for yourself here on in.

The following techniques are a brief summary of the CBT model.

Homework diary – if you are feeling a negative emotion, try to record when you feel this way and write it down in a diary. Scale it from numbers one to ten (1 = okay/not bad at all, 10 = dreadful). Try to see when these bad feelings occur and in what situation and try to draw a conclusion to see if there are any triggers that cause you to feel bad at certain times. As an extension of this, you may also want to write about past traumas and how they make you feel now, again using the same scaling. These are called thought records.

Adaptability – try to push out your boundaries so you can experience more of life. Instead of lamenting, "I never do this or that", try it for once and see how you feel (not harmful stuff though). Go somewhere you've never been, do something you've never done – you might like it. Trying new things in this way will also increase your flexibility and make yourself into a more interesting person. If trying new things fills you with dread, try to go with it in the knowledge that it won't kill you; you may feel bad for a while, even quite anxious, but this will never hurt you. In confronting these anxiety-provoking situations, you will be re-teaching your brain that you are an achiever rather than a fearful, quivering wreck. And you will become proud of yourself.

Develop friendships – sharing your woes and good times with others makes life more rewarding and valuable. You may have chosen to cut yourself off from others and this is rarely healthy. So try to develop a network of friends, but not for networking purposes. Those without friends usually fear being hurt but you'll just have to take this risk if you want an enchanted life. I have often thought that the proliferation of talking therapies is a modern replacement of what used to happen in extended families. Two hundred years ago, perhaps a wise old crone would listen non-judgementally to you and offer advice; this is largely what happens today in psychotherapy … although one is encouraged to listen to oneself and advice can be sparse. I know there's more to it than that but it comes from the same place. Importantly, you should also get rid of useless people who judge you negatively or put you down.

If you have to pay for a counsellor, get one who is a member of the British Association for Counsellors and Psychotherapists (www.bacp.co.uk) as they have to leap through many hurdles in order to become accredited. At the time of writing, anyone can set up as a counsellor and since counselling attracts a lot of weirdoes and mystics, you will want one who won't lead you up the garden path to dance with the fairies (or perhaps you might!). Similarly, NHS counsellors are likely to be highly vetted (although the NHS recruitment process for counsellors is so laborious it results in long waiting lists … not because there are no counsellors, but because the NHS is an inefficient bureaucratic leviathan. After your wait, you may be astonished to learn that funding has been reallocated leading to redefined service or that counselling has been restructured in some way following a new incentive/directive. There will probably be a-lot of acronyms involved). So, get a friend or a counsellor … friends are cheaper and counsellors won't stay with you forever! (see my website www.worryguru.com for counselling bodies and links).

Get educated – go to college and re-educate yourself. If you are already clever, get another degree or learn a new language. This will bring new things to your life, away from stress, addictions and harmful influences. It will also keep your brain active which might serve you well in later life and stave off dementia (the jury's out). It will also make you more interesting to others. Do you want to lie on your deathbed having only ever watched television? If you are convinced that you couldn't live without your favourite soap well, I'm sorry but that's very sad. Try a week away from it and enrol onto a course somewhere. You will see that there are many adult learners present and once you've got over the nervousness of getting through the door, the rest will be easy. Colleges aren't like school and you are not a child anymore, so get over it and go for it. Don't assume what it's going to be like until you get there; don't rely on stereotypes or other peoples' horror stories.

Catastrophizing and Fortune Telling – try not to make your problems worse than they really are by trying to predict worst outcomes. Sure, bad things happen, but not all the time and not just to you. There are those who look on the bleak side of everything. Try some positive self-talk and watch your life turn around. Expect the worst, get the worst … this need not be the case. Don't prophesy or fortune-tell your own damnation and doom. Usually these traits are thought habits you might have slipped into, perhaps formed from how you were raised or in conjunction with your current partner. Try changing a bit and see what happens. To make these changes, you will need to challenge your own negative thought patterns (automatic negative thoughts or 'ANTS'), first by asking yourself: what's the worst that could happen? Then: what's the best that could happen? Then: what's likely to happen? You will discover that the worst thing doesn't usually happen. Remember that most of the things we worry about don't actually happen. Those with a tendency to catastrophize also have a tendency to globalize: this is to apply all bad assumptions to every event that occurs. It is important to remember that just because one thing has gone wrong, not everything will.

Try not to control events over which you have no power; it is the sure way to frustration. People will do what they want with their lives despite what you say to them. Acceptance is the key to a calmer life. Acceptance in the spirit of the serenity prayer: to change what you can change and accept what you can't etc… In the 1st century A.D., the Greek philosopher Epictetus said that it is not events but our interpretation of them that causes us to be upset. Most of the time we can and do chose our reactions to circumstances. Armed with this knowledge, we do not always have to flare up if someone enrages us. Perhaps it is time to act differently.

Freud spoke much about the pleasure principle and pleasure versus pain and how we try to avoid the latter. Quite often, pain (emotional and physical) and our assumptions about it are more derailing than the pain itself due to our tendency to catastrophize. Like a hot hand towel in a Chinese restaurant, crises can quickly go cold if we don't get too upset.

You may worry about dying as the fear of death can be so near as we get older. Sadly, it's the one thing we can be certain of. Try not to let this fear prevent you from living. I appreciate that the reaper's bony finger is always in our peripheral vision, and the deaths of significant others can serve to remind us of our own mortality. But don't despair; you might live until you're 107. You can do many things to enhance your longevity but much of it is about chance and your beliefs. Whilst you don't have to have your mind on death 24/7 – and who would want to? – we learn from the seventy-five year old Yalom (2008) that facing death can dispel grimness (p.197). Death is part of life, albeit at the end. You have to find a balance between living in the now and not doing things that are too risky and may kill you. You alone will know and make this choice. They say that procrastination is the thief of time. It can also lead to a lifetime of regrets. Perhaps it is time to unleash your dream even if this means developing long-term goals. Don't let the reaper catch you before you've done what you have to do or said what you have to say.

There are lots of wonderful things written about death that you can read from the great philosophers; try Schopenhauer, Nietzsche, and Seneca. But also try living too. Don't read so much that you forget to pursue your paramour. Since you are not dead when you read *Broken Britain?* you will have some choices to make, here in the now. Rejoice! You are alive! If you are assailed with anxiety and fear, living in the now can be scary, but try to push yourself ... panicky feelings won't kill you, so go with them and live your life in spite of them. This means live ... and live now.

If you feel compelled to worry, set aside a time for yourself which you can call 'worry time', say 7pm till 8pm every night, when you will go through any concerns you may be harbouring. Until your worry time, distract yourself and worry later.

With concerns that need attention, try to prioritize and rationalize your time and the effort you give. It's okay to be upset or angry and when those emotions have passed, try to work out a plan of action so you can make things better.

Rationalizing can help you cope with stress or a drama. Not panicking and trying to calm yourself down will help. This can be done quite simply by breathing techniques which can be found earlier in this book.

Importantly, the thing to remember about CBT is that many books on the subject really complicate the essence of it. I hope that the above steps serve to simplify it and make it doable for you. Therapy might help you get better, but it doesn't make you better ... you do. If you would like more information about CBT, *Mind over Mood* (Greenberger & Padesky, 1995) is the CBT workbook of choice. Also see www.babcp.com for CBT information.

When finding your cures, don't wait for the best doctor or a wonder drug to the exclusion of everything else. This means that you may have to compromise, and, for most of us, that's what life is all about. You may want the eminent and distinguished psychiatrist Raj Persaud to become your counsellor, but I guess he will be expensive and very busy. You might want Kelly Brook to be your girlfriend, but she might be engaged. Since life is about compromises, do the best you can, and avoid the wretched people who serve to drag you down. NHS counsellors are highly trained and CRB vetted and will probably do a good job for you. You might be on a waiting list for a long time. Tony Blair, Gordon Brown, then NICE, then Lord Layard, then the NHS are committed to CBT and talking therapies in mental health treatment. In 2006, a report published by Lord Layard of the London School of Economics (Centre for Economic Performance's Mental Health Policy Group, 2006) called for the recruitment of a further 10,000 cognitive behavioural therapists for the United Kingdom so that the National Institute of Health and Clinical Excellence's suggestions might be met in providing CBT for a range of mental health problems. These are just words and I doubt that these suggestions will ever come to pass. It sounds good for the electorate and it *appears* that something might be done ... but is it? The new acronym for all this is IAPT (Increasing access to psychological therapies) but an acronym never reduced a queue.

The recruitment of counsellors is so arduous that very little ever gets done. Or rather, a lot of talk happens, a lot of paperwork takes place, managers and administrators have endless meetings, new offices are built to accommodate the new directive ... but the end task is almost never accomplished. The NHS is so utterly smothered in management and business-speak, that waiting lists for such therapies grow and grow. This is NOT because there is a shortage of counsellors ... there is no shortage. Britain abounds with counselling diplomates and graduates all over the place who can't find work. The CBT brigade have over-intellectualized a simple concept in order to give themselves prestige, but even so, therapists are in proliferation. There is *simply* a complete inability within the NHS to recruit anyone quickly, so the situation is rather like this: we know that talking therapies work and have a better sustained recovery/relapse rate than antidepressants; we then ask our NHS managers to recruit some and this takes months or even years. Conspiracy theorists would argue that they don't really want to recruit anyone in actual fact, but they are heard to be trying to recruit. It's all a bit like Orwell's *1984*. The reality of recruitment is very different. Conversely, private providers have a different policy. When they want a counsellor for one of their clients, they look on BACP's website and find a counsellor in the area of their client. This can be done in a few days! Private companies often know that BACP counsellors have already jumped over hurdles to become accredited members of their professional body, so they cleverly source a counsellor from there. It's as simple as that. Why can't the NHS do this if they really want to recruit counsellors – as they say they do?

Anyway, if you're not entitled to BUPA healthcare, you might want to look at www.bacp.co.uk to find a counsellor in your area ... prices usually appear on this website. I don't mention this just because I am an accredited member of BACP, but because there are a lot of quack counsellors around and many treatments that will do you no good whatsoever. If your purse confines you to the NHS, ask your GP to send you to a community psychiatric nurse as they usually have training in CBT and will be likely to help you. This is the compromise you might have to make and don't let the word 'psychiatric' put you off as it's just a word. This is not a rant against the NHS; just an observation on how it's run. It's probably too big for anything to happen properly or quickly, but I'm sure it's run by well-meaning people. If any of us could see the bigger picture of the NHS, we would see a million people shuffling a lot of paper around and sending reports and emails hither and thither. In this process, the patient often gets lost. Read any policy document or mission statement to see what I mean.

To read a beautiful, tragic, and factual account of red-tape at its worst, see Michael Bilton's *Wicked beyond belief* (2006) which is an account of how the Yorkshire Ripper case was handled (or mishandled) by West Yorkshire police. Their wholesale inability to see the bigger picture and concentrate only on paperwork (with a system which was deeply flawed) cost several lives and led to institutionalised incompetence on a grand scale. It cost a lot and achieved nothing. In the end, the Yorkshire Ripper was caught by good chance. Similarly, a mental health problem can be cured by the passage of time as a hopeful patient waits on a bureaucratically induced NHS queue.

As you're waiting, you might try these ...

De-stressors

After a lot of searching and personal quests and reading and studying, I can heartily recommend Buddhism as the ultimate de-stressor; it's as simple as that. This does not mean donning an orange robe and chanting in the street. It would be too difficult to explain Buddhism here although the concept is extremely simple. Buddha was not a God and Buddhism is not the one right way that often leads to wars and intolerance. It is a state of being and a series of meditations that, if done properly, will lead to relaxation. It is a way of viewing life in a different way which means being awake and beholding consciousness and living in the present. Those who master Buddhism rarely look back, but don't try to force it. Buddhism is not about the worship of invisible notions; it is about embracing life whilst knowing its transience. The Buddha himself was not a God so you don't need to buy a lot of accoutrements to follow his teachings. You just have to be. Be aware. Be awake. Meditate. *Broken Britain?* does not seek to convert people to a certain religion and so I merely suggest Buddhism as a way of finding peace ... even enlightenment if you're lucky and don't try hard. If you don't fancy it fine. If you don't fancy it because others will think you're bonkers, that's too bad and perhaps it's time you examined your relationships. If you don't do Buddhism, try the following anyway ...

Exercise – a brisk walk will do if you cannot face anything else, although swimming is very useful too.

Breathing techniques – 7/11 technique – described earlier in this book.

Music – something relaxing like Debussy, Mozart, panpipes (and see my website www.worryguru.com too).

Yoga or Tai Chi

Socialising – with the *right* people.

Challenging your negative thoughts and irrational beliefs.

Guided imagery and visualisations.

Have a nice hot(ish) bath and melt into it. Try some aromatherapy oils with it.

Express yourself – this is probably the hardest thing to do if you're a bit of a flake. Try though. You'll feel better for having spoken. Why be a doormat?

Don't forget, you can despair with society and politicians and celebrities, yet you can still eat healthily, have a great garden and a job you enjoy and a loving family. All these answers lie within oneself.

The Gap

"There is something within me that can't be filled. I've tried shopping, eating, drugs, sex, but it just goes on and on and nothing seems to fill it up." (client 2008)

Tom writes:

"She craved a Mercedes sports car thinking it would make her life complete. She wore copious amounts of tasteless gold from a catalogue shop thinking that the bling would cast light upon her empty soul. She was King Midas's gimp who worshipped at the altar of translucent materialism. She was my first love, more of a prude than a lover, riddled with eating disorders and low self-esteem. She was a bit of a slut really; not in a sexual way but a tease. She would wear stockings without ever letting me near her goods. She eventually left me for a two-bit cabaret singer who had a gold plated microphone, a mullet, and a borrowed Rolls Royce. But she was my first love and it broke my heart. Twenty years later, it still hurts but the wound is not raw; there's scar tissue, some good hind-sighted memories, and a bit of anger. Perhaps this abandonment left a gap in my soul that left me searching, trying to recapture something that could never again be uncovered?

I remember one conversation…

T: You're such a materialist. (I said to Girlfriend [gf] as she drooled over a passing Mercedes sports car.)

Gf: But it's gorgeous and I bet you'd have one if you could afford it.

T: That's not the point (I replied, knowing my words fell on deaf ears).

Gf: It's just a great car and I'll have one one day.

I knew from that point that there would be a wedge between us as I never really aspired to tokens of success. She had been brought up very differently to me and the gulf was just beginning to show. Gf wanted everything and she wanted it now."

It transpired that Tom's girlfriend had been brought up with a vague sense of self, lost in society, aspiring to meaningless things and desires which manifested themselves in her eating disorder. The Mercedes sports car might have temporarily salved her trembling inner child and would have been an outward show that everything inside herself was okay … even though it wasn't. Tom could have got his head down and worked hard to buy his cravenous* girlfriend a Mercedes. She had a sister who had a boyfriend who did just that, gave her everything she wanted – until they split up because her black hole was too big. Tom could have been pious at his work, spending every hour there whilst his hungry girlfriend could have gone berserk with his gold card (if he'd had one). Tom made a calculation that since he wasn't getting what he wanted from his girl sexually, he would save himself the trouble of dancing to her tune. He probably saved a lot of money too in the long run because people like this are never satisfied. If they have an inner craving, this will never be fulfilled with purchases.

[*Cravenous is a compound word that I have made up, rather like the German language would enable me to do if I was writing in German. Cravenous is a cross between ravenous and craving.]

Often ignored for his abilities as a lyricist, George Michael makes some sagely comments in his song *Star People*, going on to remark about how even rich and famous people are never satisfied and that it's usually the same excuse; poor parenting. He's probably right. Although George aims his lyrics towards 'star' people, it could well apply to anyone in our society who has lost their soul … someone with a gap in their life … a hole in their spirit. This gap gives one the feeling that something is missing. This missing thing is manna for advertisers who try to 'help' us to fill it. You might possess all the trappings of wealth, and even cloddishly aspire to something you cannot afford, but when you have obtained the thing, you may find that your emotional life is just as barren. This is why the 'novelty wears off' very quickly after the purchase has been made. The lacuna cannot be filled arbitrarily by spending money; advertisers cleverly encourage us to believe that a purchase will satisfy us in some way but it invariably does not … and if it does, the satisfaction is only fleeting. This is why updates and upgrades and newer models are so important because they keep us spending. Yet our gaps never diminish. We know that advertisements are designed to make us feel inferior and lacking in something or other. We know that they promise to fulfil us if we buy something, and we also know that purchases never really deliver.

Some people embrace life – *carpe diem* and all that – and determine to whittle out all its possibilities, whetting their appetites at every turn. Others are passive bystanders who live their lives vicariously through others via the consumption of *Hello* and *OK* magazines. They watch cookery programmes but never cook, they watch Robbie Williams and Britney Spears whilst they sit on their interest-free leather sofas condemning them. They watch *Strictly Come Dancing* having never donned a felt-bottomed shoe.

These people are journeymen who are content to observe whilst a cornucopia of chances pass them by. It seems that the patina of real life is too rich for their bellies. They make excuses for not living … until they find it's too late. This is (sadly) particularly true of anxious people. The philosopher Seneca said that, "They lose the day in waiting for the night, and the night in fearing the dawn". You are not a film extra in your own life story … you have the main role. More recently, there is an internet vogue called *second life* where one can create an avatar and live another life online through your own creation. This is not living … it is gazing at a screen whilst life passes you by.

You don't have to watch *Big Brother* to have a life, you simply have to live your own. Over recent years it has become increasingly easy to live one's life through television and the internet. But this is not reality. French philosopher Jean Baudrillard (2004) would refer to this state as *hyper-reality* where a sort of fake reality is superimposed over the actual reality of life. Baudrillard called this non-reality a simulacra and it would apply to comedic irony and regurgitated music already cited in *Broken Britain?*

If you are one who lives life through the cyber world, you may find yourself becoming a kind of television extra as real life passes you by. Lots of people fall into the category of extras; perhaps they enjoy the reflected glory of being around stars, having nothing original themselves to contribute. If, as Shakespeare said, "All the world's a stage and all the men and women merely players" (Jacques: *As you Like it*), do you want to be an extra in your own play? William Blake in *A Poison Tree* suggests we ought to express ourselves. Speaking of resentment he writes "... And I water'd it in fears, Night and morning with my tears; and I sunned it with my smiles, and with soft deceitful wiles." Blake's poem is relevant to expressing our inner feelings and mirrors the way we should express our dreams if we are to live a true and fulfilled life. This is about being true and virtuous to yourself, lest some kind of catastrophe occur. The same can be read in Tolstoy's masterpiece *The Death of Ivan Illich* as previously cited and what happens when thoughts and dreams are repressed and allowed to fester. In this respect, our gaps can be better filled if we look inwards, to what we really want rather than outwards with the hope that some external thing or person (object) can satisfy our needs. This is the message behind George Michael's lament.

A Poison Tree

I was angry with my friend;
I told my wrath, my wrath did end.
I was angry with my foe;
I told it not, my wrath did grow.
And I water'd it in fears,
Night and morning with my tears;
And I sunned it with smiles,
And with soft deceitful wiles.
And it grew both day and night,
Till it bore an apple bright;
And my foe beheld it shine,
And he knew that it was mine,
And into my garden stole
When the night had veil'd the pole.
In the morning glad I see
My foe outstretch'd beneath the tree.
(Blake, 1794)

Blake is not only for Goths or those obsessed with death; Poison Tree expresses a message that perhaps we would all be wise to follow. Many clients, and friends, have a beef with someone, and never say anything; sometimes they go into a sulk that can last for years, or they just withdraw themselves from a situation. This is all very well (if it is) at one level but deeper than that lies the fact that you have not represented yourself, not stood up for yourself but instead, lived on your knees. In doing this you repress your angst and if the issue you are repressing is of some importance, it may come back to haunt you in the form of a physical illness. If you are to avoid this, issues need to be addressed and resolved. The sublime *Fawlty Towers'* series showed an American very aggressively asserting himself about a Waldorf salad, much to Basil Fawlty's disdain and annoyance. Perhaps the Americans know how to express themselves: an American trait even. Even if you have a small issue about something, all the literature suggests that it is best dealt with there and then, rather than left to fester. I have found in my practice that this is always the case.

As mentioned, the latest internet craze (which might be old fashioned when this book comes out) is called *second life* where you can live a virtual, internet web life and create a new you (using an avatar), make virtual friends and be anything you want to be online, with only a few restrictions. You could have huge breasts or a gigantic penis: or both! This is all very well and I suppose can be very attractive to those who haven't got much going on in their real lives. It is time consuming – like all internet activities – but is more than just a waste of time or a bit of fun. I believe that *Second Life* gives people a chance to recreate themselves in a virtual existence (a simulacra) and, at last, be who they really want to be. This means that, instead of binge drinking to escape reality, they can indulge online and make a whole new persona for themselves (a hyper-reality). This is another way to fill the gap in a dull real life, but it's just a futile distraction. However, since it's safer than binge drinking in Oldham, the Government will probably favour it and it's good for the economy in that people have to buy computers and upgrades in order to play.

An old friend of mine used to 'play' snooker on his computer, happily totting up his score as he went along. To me, snooker involves a stick and some balls, not some simulation on a screen. Nowadays, we see people playing on their Wiis – doing things that are real but not real, if you know what I mean. Now there's a Wii that skims and slices your ping-pong ball – virtually of course as there's no ball. Why not go out to a leisure centre and hire a table-tennis table and play for real?

Whilst searching for things to fill one's gap, you might come to the conclusion that there is no meaning! Philosophers have toyed and extrapolated this idea for many centuries. Existential psychotherapy (particularly that of Rollo May and Irvin Yalom) addresses meaninglessness and nothingness, in the assumption that these concepts create existential angst. Western ideals and religion in general are simply gap fillers. Karl Marx described religion as being the opium of the people, implying that it deadened the senses and provided solace in hard times. Dickensian *Hard Times* still exist today in different clothes. Marx believed that religion was formulated by the ruling classes in order to gain control over their workers. This is quite depressing if you are an agnostic but I can accept the idea that the working classes needed to be controlled so that they could be productive. Tie this into the Protestant work ethic and bingo ... you have a subservient workforce who are obeying not only their employers' demands but also the will of God. Because religion has been and is continually used as a divisive force in the world, you can see how men may have manufactured it for their own ends, but it does not mean that God does not exist. I will leave this debate to the illuminating Richard Dawkins.

Curiously and often, religion seems to do more harm than good. In late November 2007, a teacher of English in Sudan hit the headlines for calling a teddy bear 'Mohammed', or allowing one of her charges to call it Mohammed. The sorry tale tells its own story of how far religious views and intolerance can be taken. I am not here to judge, but is it not amazing that the word of God or Allah, can inspire such dogma and venom within its followers that a teacher is vilified and threatened with severe punishments, even though her intentions were probably liberally minded and in the best interests of the children. What is wrong with that? If God exists, would he want someone to be lashed or beheaded or stoned? If he did, what sort of God is that?

Anyway, if there is no meaning, and we have gaps within our souls, it follows that there are no answers. The only answers you will get are the ones that you'll find for yourself and these will be more fulfilling anyway because, even if you're wrong, you'll think you're right. And how can there be an answer if there is no question? And there is no question because there is no meaning. The answer is not the number 42. There is no metaphysical answer. Perhaps we should all accept that we are chance occurrences in a meaningless world and that we are lucky enough to have been born, should make the most of it and enjoy consciousness. The only meaning you will find is the one you arrive at when you ask yourself certain questions such as:

Exercise:

---

1. What do I really want?
2. Am I making the most of my life?
3. Am I in the right place at this moment in time?
4. Am I happy?
5. Do I have enough money?
6. Would my avatar match my real life?

Record your answers in your journal and you will then know if you have a gap within yourself. You will also know if you are real or just pretending; whether you are living your life in a congruent way, true to yourself or whether you are merely going through a script and doing things for others or doing things you think you should be doing.

From a counselling perspective, I find that questions like these are best asked just before falling asleep and to be kept to yourself. The answer may come in the night, in the form of a dream or a rude awakening. If so, write it down in your journal.

If you don't ask these questions of yourself, you may procrastinate forever, in the hope that you will *find yourself* in a better situation. This would mean that you are a victim of circumstance, passive, and happy to let events and opportunities pass you by. In this way, you won't be cementing your gap on a voyage of self discovery … you'll be lying back and thinking what might have been. Common gap fillers include food, sex, consumer goods, religion, extreme sports, all previously examined and all good to bad in varying degrees.

In the case-study of Tom, we found that his estranged girlfriend was a rampant materialist, craving things to fill her gap and subsequently leaving a gap within Tom when she left him. She left him for someone she thought would provide more booty for her. Whether her new lover did this is immaterial; it's the aftermath that matters and the emotional detritus. Twenty years on, Tom can either chose to continue pining for his unrequited love, or fill the chasm in a more fruitful way. He might ask himself the questions listed above, or he can use a variety of solutions that are discussed within these pages.

German philosopher Schopenhauer (1788-1860) believed that the only way to become happy (or happier) was to remove oneself from the wheel of greed and capitalism. Schopenhauer advised the artistic life, sprinkled with reading and learning in order to become free. The arts and self-denial leads one to an enlightenment that materialism cannot satisfy. *Broken Britain?* is not suggesting that you adopt Stoicism or become a Luddite – these things wouldn't be possible if you want to be part of our current society and you'd be thought of as weird (if you cared).

Perhaps, as Freud may have suggested, we are all looking to reconnect with the mother or that moment just before birth. He described an oceanic state of being which I believe to be similar to some Buddhist awakenings. Obviously, we will never recapture the womb. Several male clients have mentioned that they feel most content and at peace when they *enter* their wives, just before the moment of ejaculation; some have even commented that as their penis enters a vagina, they feel as if they are going home and a sense of completeness. If we also consider the fascination with the female breast alongside this notion, we go far in explaining the root of reconnection and the reason why a frothy coffee just simply isn't good enough. Perhaps this (sex, not coffee) is the nearest we will ever get to the paradise of being an embryo again.

Having the freedom to choose who you are and be what you want to be can go some way to ameliorating your gap and making sense of a chaotic world. In many ways, you make your own sense of it all. A forerunner of the Existential movement, the philosopher Kierkegaard (1813-1855) believed that existence meant a hope for freedom and that you might elect to be who you want to be; this, he believed, led to fulfilment.

The Rain that falls – nourishment

The rain I am talking about here is a metaphor, like the whole Life Tree idea. This rain is based on the idea of what you put into your body and how it can help or hinder you. We have already looked at the influence of food and drinks in the addiction section and, cherry-picked from a host of other books. I have come up with a simple but effective diet and lifestyle suggestion sheet in the hope that you may glean wisdom, cut out the things that might be harming you, and live a better life. I toyed with the idea of making a selection of recipes at the back of the book but instead I condensed the following 'diet' into a series of suggestions that can stay with you for life … if you like.

I use the word diet in a general sense but it's not a diet as such. You won't have to become obsessed with it then give it up because it's unsustainable. This is why most diets fail; because they are weight-loss diets. This means that, if you follow them to the letter, you will lose weight and then you'll have to stop eventually or you would die. When you reach your target weight, friends start congratulating and envying your new shape. You buy new clothes. If you are a celebrity, you bring out a fitness video, so you can make a lot of money and share your secrets with the world. As you stop your diet (because it is a diet and you would die if you carried on with it), you then begin nibbling a bit of this and that and gain five pounds. The jeans are a bit tighter but you can tolerate it and you argue with yourself that you are more shapely now and you nibble a bit more cheese or pizza or whatever. Eventually, you regain the four stone you had initially lost, much to your chagrin. At least if you're not a celebrity your embarrassment won't be so great. After Christmas, you go on another fad diet, determined not to make the same mistakes as last time.

They say that diets make you fat because you are imprisoning yourself into a cycle of feasting and fasting; rather like long-term bulimia. On another level, diets may simply give you something to do. If you did not believe what was written on empty-promise labels, and cut out refined carbohydrates and sugar, you would lose weight. Your body would then find its own ideal weight and stabilize itself at that point.

Anthony's Karma Life Diet comprises suggestions rather than dictats so you can easily incorporate this into your existing life without feeling deprived in any way. Remember that the multi-billion pound diet industry thrives on your being unhappily overweight. Conspiracy theorists would argue that the diet industry wants you to be a yo-yo dieter so it can continue to peddle its wares. In fact, you don't have to be much of a conspiracist to see the point. If you were not a yo-yo binger/dieter then the diet industry would go broke overnight. Your unhappiness at your weight fuels their bulging coffers. So, you can either choose to be unhealthy and fat, or you can get off your chair, stop watching adverts that pollute your subconscious mind, make connections with other people, do some exercise and get a life.

If I haven't made it clear already I'll say it again. Refined carbohydrates and sugar cause weight gain unless you are an athlete or do physically demanding work. Cut back on carbs and the pounds will fall off; it's as simple as that. But I assume that you don't just want to be thin and unhealthy? So try the following plan and be healthy and thin in the bargain. In a way, it's no use just wanting to be thin … you need to adjust your mindset and make yourself want to be healthy. Eating refined carbohydrates will not aid you in this pursuit and I hope that you will be able to break the link between chocolate and love. Your happiness doesn't love chocolate … and even if it did, your fat arse doesn't love it. If you free yourself from the misinformation of advertising, or at least become aware of it, you can smugly avoid chocolate, crisps, and any product that proclaims its love for you. You might struggle a bit with cravings but these should evaporate within a month. And, when you're tempted to hit the biscuits after a row with your cousin, think again, do some deep breathing, go for a walk, meditate, relax, have a bath, read this book, phone a friend ... but not all at the same time.

If you want to thoroughly examine your moods and the concept of emotional eating, you couldn't do better than to read *Mood Cure* by Julia Ross (2003). Because moods are so subtle and work on an unconscious level, there are a plethora of exercises and suggestions in Ross's book. It's a journey you might consider taking.

Rest assured that your unconscious mind can take care of many situations that life will throw at you. Since Freud's day, the unconscious mind has become more and more ignored by medics as its influence cannot be measured. Psychologists have long known its effect on our behaviour and advertisers are keen to exploit this. But the unconscious mind is also a force for good, guiding us to seek good things for ourselves. You simply have to embrace it and trust the answer that comes to you. Trust yourself. Use your instincts for they are often right. Similarly, what needs to be done for your self, will and can be done.

Anthony's Karma Life Diet

> General advice
>
> **Protein** with <u>every</u> meal (a small fistful): fish (brain foods: salmon, mackerel) chicken, lean red meat, eggs.
>
> **Olive oil** (extra virgin) – cook in this and use it liberally elsewhere.
>
> **Tomatoes** – very good and have anti-cancer properties.
>
> **Broccoli** – excellent stuff, packed with goodness.
>
> **Aspartame** and other diet sweeteners – try to avoid them if you can.
>
> **White bread** – this is simply bad news so avoid it: try seedy, nutty stuff.
>
> **Fruit & Veg** – 5 a day – you've heard the advice, great roughage & fibre.
>
> Identify your trigger foods that may set you off on a binge: who can have 1 chocolate or 1 crisp?

Butter is okay (because it's real) but not in excess (better for you than adulterated margarines which will often contain transfats and hydrogenated oils).

Refined carbs: avoid them – sweets, cakes, chocolate, biscuits, ice cream.

Carbs – bread, pasta, rice – avoid white rice. Brown rice is delicious and retains its nutrients.

Alcohol – medics and others say that the odd glass of red wine is okay.

Drink water (mineral if you can) and fruit smoothies as suggested by Jason Vale (2004) in his books, fruit teas, camomile particularly good.

Sugar – avoid it if you can; this can be virtually impossible as it's in everything but try, because it's addictive.

Nibble – sunflower and pumpkin seeds, apples, bananas, and a few brazil nuts.

Smoking – you might have tried it when you were young and carried on. It is an unadvisable addiction. Get rid of it as soon as you can unless you enjoy standing outside public places in freezing cold, miserable Britain with other addicts? As you get rid of it, try not to replace one addiction with another.

Avoid all processed foods particularly margarine and all the derivative spreads thereof; they are highly engineered and adulterated. These foods are made up by scientists to hook your cravings and their labels purport good health – this is just to make money for the manufacturers. Keep with real food*, not nutri-this-that-and-the-other.

Breakfast – Cereal – gives you energy but avoid sugared ones (or frosted, or honey coated: honey in cereals is usually a euphemism for sugar). Shredded Wheat are cool and granola is okay in moderation.

Eggs and bacon are the best start you could have although this breakfast has recently become known as a heart attack on a plate; this is only true if you have fried bread with it. Lean bacon, two boiled eggs, tomatoes, and a slice of nutty brown bread with a bit of butter – it's all good.

Lunch – have something light to stave off your hunger but make sure there's protein with it; this will allay your cravings for sweet stuffs.

Dinner – have protein – try a fillet steak, broccoli, brown rice (not white).

Supper – don't have any if you want to lose weight, but if you must, have something like soup or something very light that won't lie on your stomach as you sleep. You might have heard the saying: Breakfast like a king, lunch like a prince, supper like a pauper. This is the case as a heavy meal at bedtime will encourage weight gain.

Lifewise: walk a lot if you can't stand the gym (the natural daylight will do you good). Women (and a few men) like dancing and that is good too. You may re-ignite your love-life this way and thus avoid the need to have a love laced chocolate bar. You'll be having the real thing. Love does not come in a brown bar of sugar and fat; it comes with a certain look into someone's eyes and kisses that make you want to lose yourself forever in your lover's arms.

Don't castigate yourself for not following the diet to the letter because it's not really a diet; just a few suggestions. If you adhere loosely to it, you will find that you feel better and become addiction free. Its simplicity is the key to its efficacy ... just like a PostIt note!

* real food means food that will go off and has not been manufactured or processed; food that looks much the same way as it did when it was grown or discovered.

Exercise

The main exercise in this section is for you to incorporate Anthony's karma life diet into your life. Additionally, bear these (underlined) maxims ...

An unexamined life is not worth living. (Socrates)

So, look into your life and see if you have any deadwood. If so, whether it's people or things, make a list in your journal and work on getting rid of them. Avoid negative people who serve to drag you down or get away from them if you can. If you feel inappropriately encumbered by religion, get rid of that too if you feel you can live without it. You must examine your life and find your own freedom. A lot of these things can be hidden in the unknown unknown part of yourself (see *The circle of truth*), so ask yourself the question(s) and see what answers arrive for you. Jung claimed that <u>we can only move forward when we look into the dark</u>.

Remember that it is not the event but rather your interpretation and your subsequent reaction to it that will cause you emotional angst if you <u>choose</u> to react in a negative way. Eating will not solve your emotional problems. For once, try changing your reaction and see what happens. Rational Emotive Behavioural Therapy (REBT) states three stages: (a) the activating event, (b) your belief about the event and how you should behave, and (c) the consequence of your belief (e.g. anger, sadness etc). Therefore, by changing your belief, you can experience a new range of consequences that will improve your life. This can be hard to do at first but you'll get used to it.

There is a self-help cliché: <u>If you keep doing the same thing, you'll keep getting the same results</u>. So think and act differently and see results unfold before your eyes. This often means thinking for a while before you act; in other words, becoming reflective.

In this way you will <u>not let your reaction to a problem be bigger than the problem itself</u>. This is very important. Ask yourself how anger will help and if it is appropriate. If anger or any other emotion is not right for you, then choose something else. There are other ways of dealing with things. Whilst you're at it, ask if drinking a bottle of wine will help either, or hitting the freezer for ice cream. If it doesn't help, do something else that will. List all the times when you've unwittingly hindered yourself by behaving inappropriately.

And if you disregard everything else in this box, remember that <u>most of the things we worry about don't actually happen</u>. This occurs at all levels. Remember the big commotion about the super-casinos and whether Blackpool or Manchester should be *awarded* these dens (in order that their areas may redeveloped – bring in gambling!). Lots of people worried about the consequences and then nothing happened when the Government pulled the plug in February 2008. Similarly, on a smaller level, if you have a mole, it's probably just a mole and not a sign that you've got three weeks to live. The sooner you get it checked out, the better for stress levels and treatment.

The sun that shines – the light

Lots of us feel grim when we confront the reality of living here in rainy Britain; perhaps this partly explains why so many of us leave for warmer climes ... Spain, Australia and the like. Seasonal affective disorder (SAD) is a mood condition whereby you feel grim when the weather is bad; some people suffer from it more than others and it is linked to the pineal gland in the brain. The more natural sunlight you get, the better because it cheers you up. There are some nice natural daylight lamps that you can buy but nothing would be as good as living in Los Angeles – apart from the smog and the high crime rate. Anyway, we need light and the nicer the weather, the more inclined you are to take a walk and exercise. As I write this section, it is late January 2008 and the weather is absolutely awful here in Northern Britain. It makes me feel depleted and longing for Spain.

But it's not only natural sunlight to which I refer; we need other kinds of light as well ... metaphorical light ... the light that spiritual healers like Shakti Gawain (1999, 2002) and Deepak Chopra (2006) write about in their books. This light refers to our connection with the universe and the unseen particles around us that can influence our moods and consequently our lives. If you are going to live a happy and connected life you need to get in touch with your essence and find out what you are here to do ... your purpose or *dharma*. When you're doing what you feel you should be doing with your life, you will be living in the light. Life Tree hopes to help you further towards that light.

Some might interpret *Broken Britain?* as having a bleak outlook but that's not the point; any inherent grimness just reflects my view of the reality in which we live. But this is only *my* reality. You can only sort your own life out.

If we're going to save the planet (and I'm not holding my breath!) it would be very sensible to ban air travel, newspapers, motor vehicles, junk mail, television and all other forms of globally damaging carbon footsteppers. We would watch industry grind to a halt and, indeed, who would have the power or right to stop newly developing nations building power plants every week? Is it just me or does anyone else find it a trifle ironic when we are encouraged to go easy on plastic bags whilst building extra flight terminals like 'the fifth' at Heathrow? Statisticians: how many plastic bags make the equivalent carbon footprint of all the flights that will leave Heathrow's new terminal in a year? If I save one bag a week, will that offset the damage?

Governments pay lip service to global warming whilst allowing fifth runways. In any capitalist nation most governments will be only interested in economics and making money ... they have to embrace business and, at the same time, try to convince us that they are doing everything they can about climate change. Governments will always spin statistics and try to make you believe a certain thing when in fact you *feel* another thing. There is little room for feeling in randomized control trials or quantitative data gathering surveys. Look at the achievements and machinations of our British Government over the last few years (in no particular order) ...

> 1. They invaded Iraq on the proviso of finding weapons of mass destruction that did not exist. The country has more anarchy than before the war and another Northern Ireland has been created. Countless lives have been lost in an ill-conceived war and all the tragedies that accompany it.
>
> 2. Suspicion is aroused by the mysterious deaths of Dr David Kelly and dissenter Robin Cook. Clare Short, who speaks sense, is sidelined. Perhaps they knew too much. It seems to me that Alistair Campbell led the sexed up war effort when he was at his most potent. Perhaps Blair and Bush believed there to be weapons... Who will ever know?

3. An attempt is made to introduce so-called super casinos when nobody asked for them or wanted them, knowing full well that they would cause an increase in problem gambling. That's so obvious isn't it?

4. The 24-hour licensing law is introduced in the face of the fact that we are a nation of aggressive binge drinkers. Where's the logic there?

5. A smoking ban is introduced causing pubs and social clubs to gradually go bankrupt. Smokers tend to be drinkers and vice-versa.

6. NHS cleaning is outsourced, leading to superbugs like MRSA and Clostridium difficile. Dirty hospitals happen because there is no cohesion in the NHS and bought-in cleaners simply don't seem that bothered about cleanliness. They don't feel part of the hospital system so why should they care?

7. Speed cameras and speed bumps proliferate like triffids. This is because we have grown into a naughty nation that the government thinks needs punishing rather than educating. A simple way to prevent speeding and road crimes would be to raise the driving age to twenty-five. The youths who speed up and down a road near my house are almost always eighteen years old; they have crashes and kill their passengers and pedestrians. Is that ageist?

8. Faith schools spring up everywhere in spite of the fact that religion causes most of the wars and disruptions all over the world. Look at every war and try to find one where religion isn't involved. It's a struggle. Additionally, in April 2008, suspiciously close to April Fools' Day, Tony Blair launches his Faith Foundation. Like, why?

9. Promote globally catastrophic policies like the opening of Terminal Five at Heathrow. If air travel doesn't cause global warming what does?

10. The Labour government promised a referendum on some sort of European directive – nobody really knows what it was about as the document is indecipherable. After winning another term in office, this promise was withdrawn as they have fiddled about with some of the wording and then decided that the British public shouldn't have a vote after all. The reason they have withdrawn the referendum is because they know that most people would vote against further involvement in Europe, just as the Irish did until they changed their minds after the credit crunch.

11. The MPs' expenses scandal. Known as the *John Lewis list*. Much has been written about this in the media. David Cameron was right in saying that the rules were wrong and they're now being revised. I suspect that many MPs will resign or be ousted by the time of the 2010 general election. Being an MP is not so lucrative any more.

12. The recession – based on abject greed and the sophisticated juggling of complicated financial instruments. To me, the banking crash that caused the global meltdown (and cost the jobs of many innocent workers) was the highest degree of capitalism, with those at the top bleeding the system: the highest greed and the most catastrophic consequences. However, people in the West largely believe in capitalism and what's the alternative? Fair wages? What would be fair? Shall we try communism for a while?

Then they wonder why voter apathy exists. In the light of all these crazy policies, who can blame anyone for not casting a vote. What's the point? I could go on and on with this list but I don't need to. The point is, governments cannot be relied upon to make sound decisions. This is very obvious. And I haven't even mentioned immigration. It's not a case of 'let them eat cake' but 'let them play with their Wiis!' But politicians have to be slippery don't they? How could they come on TV and tell the truth … that the planet is doomed. Personally, I take a relaxed view on all these matters because there's not much one can do about it all. Suppose that David Icke and people like him are correct in their assertions … so what? What can you actually do? Probably nothing.

All this flimflam creates a ripe breeding ground for right-wing groups like the BNP. Anyone looking with an open mind at the BNP manifesto would be hard pushed to find elements that do not fit in line with the views of the majority of the white working- and under-class British population. If the BNP cleaned up their act and their perceived associations with the National Front, and removed the bits about repatriation, they would find that their party becomes more and more attractive to the electorate. Where will the main parties be then? This means that the main parties will have to embrace more stringent policies if they are to better reflect the wishes of their populace. Look what happened in Nazi Germany. There is great discontent within the white under- and working-class population. The liberal, mealy-mouthed political classes never seem to understand this growing anger.

The USA? As always, big business controls the means of production and, through advertising, our collective unconsciousness and our thoughts. Marx was right all along … I wish he was here to witness the captains of industry and politicians paying lip service to environmental issues and the pending global disaster that we all face. As Sting said in his songs: "If I ever lose my faith in you", "There is no political solution"… well there is, but no-one will take the aforementioned steps to save our earth. I don't blame them really. We're simply at the end of Western industrialisation and that's that. China and India will take up where we leave the stage. Perhaps the only hope is for green jobs and housing?

In criticizing any government one has to be aware of this: it is impossible to please any population all the time or even any of the time. Government, like life, is a balancing act and often needs only tiny adjustments in order to alter things. I don't even blame the MPs for milking the system but rather take the view that it is human nature to behave the way they did … they are very unpopular people that not many of the electorate even vote for, so they probably feel a bit better if they're buying themselves things at John Lewis's wonderful store. Democratic governments must balance freedom of choice and restriction in their laws and it's no wonder many of them make unpopular decisions. Bleat as we may, government is an almost impossible job and I cannot see why anyone would want to do it, especially as MPs have now been found out to be chancers. No government can ever be perfect and, like life, nothing will ever be perfect. All governments make mistakes and this must be accepted in some way if you continue to live in their particular country. In Britain, a change from Labour to Conservative will not make much difference ... that's just the way things are.

But there is no need to take a hundred paracetamols and hit the vodka! Individually, we can therefore only strive to make our egress from this planet a reasonably comfortable one and fill our gaps in a harmless and fruitful way. We must live, and laugh, and love, whilst expressing ourselves assertively, avoiding sugar and hydrogenated foods, and trying not to buy things because you've seen them advertised in the hope that you will look like Posh Spice. You won't. Neither will I. All you can hope for is to try to make a better life for yourself and the people you care about and know that in giving to others you also give to yourself.

My aim is simply to shed light on a doomed society that faces the brink of oblivion at the end-game of the industrial revolution. *Broken Britain?* is a book for individuals who might help themselves through reading my humble Life Tree message. In essence, you can only help yourself and a few others – if you're lucky. You might be an influential politician but your popularity will inevitably wane, and you will then only have yourself to deal with. We come into this life with nothing and we leave with nothing. You see, the thing is, people will do anything for money and to protect their share dividends. This is sadly ironic because if they ever stepped back and saw the bigger picture, they would see that they are part of the fracture. This will not happen will it?

As the news constantly unfolds, it has been hard to finish this book because of polarizing views about trivial things. It seems that the media want to iron out every issue that comes up, not content to leave things alone. Some things need no debate for they are not important. Life Tree, in a way, is about freedom and I hope you find yours. We are only here for a short time so why get bogged down in the futility of detail?

Desiderata

"You might find some comfort in this *Desiderata* which means 'something desired as essential...'

Go placidly amid the noise and haste, and remember
What peace there may be in silence.

As far as possible, without surrender, be on good terms with all persons.

Speak your truth quietly and clearly; and listen to the dull and ignorant;

They too have their story.

Avoid loud and aggressive persons; they are vexations to the spirit.

If you compare yourself with others, you may become vain or bitter,

for always there will be greater and lesser persons than yourself.

Enjoy your achievements as well as your plans.

Keep interested in your career, however humble;

It is a real possession in the changing fortunes of time.

Exercise caution in your business affairs, for the world is full of trickery.

But let not this blind you to what virtue there is;

Many persons strive for high ideals and everywhere life is full of heroism.

Be yourself. Especially do not feign affection.

Neither be cynical about love; for in the face of all aridity and disenchantment, it is as perennial as the grass.

Take kindly to the counsel of years, gracefully surrendering the things of youth.

You are a child of the universe, no less than the trees and the stars and you have a right to be here.

And whether or not it is clear to you, no doubt the universe is unfolding as it should.

> Therefore, be at peace with God, whatever you conceive Him to be.
>
> And whatever your labours and aspirations, in the noisy confusion of life, keep peace with your soul.
>
> With all its sham, drudgery and broken dreams, it is still a beautiful world.
>
> Be cheerful. Strive to be happy."
>
> *Max Ehrmann, 1927. Copyright Robert L. Bell*

Stick this on your fridge together with a copy of Anthony's Karma Life Diet plan.

"We are such stuff as dreams are made on, and our little life is rounded with a sleep." (The Tempest, Shakespeare)

Exercise

> *Broken Britain?* is not a book of advice and you don't have to take any of it on board and Life Tree is about aspiration; after all, who among us is perfect?
>
> So …
>
> Go. Live.

Selected Reading List & reference points

Amis, M (2008). The Second Plane. London: Jonathan Cape.

Appignanesi, R. & Garratt, C. (2007). Introducing post-modernism. Cambridge: Icon.

Atkins, R. (2003). Dr Atkins new diet revolution. London: Vermillion.

Baker, R. (1995). Understanding panic attacks and overcoming fear. Oxford: Lion.

Baudrillard, J. (2004). Simulacra and simulation. Michigan: Michigan press.

Berne, E. (1967). Games people play. London: Penguin.

Berry-Dee, C., Morris, S. (2006). Born Killers. London: John

Blake, W. (1996). William Blake. London: Orion.

Bilton, M. (2006). Wicked beyond belief. London: Harper Collins.

Bowlby, J. (2005). A secure base. Oxon: Routledge.

Branden, N. (1995). The six pillars of self-esteem. New York: Bantam.

Brown, D. (2006). Tricks of the Mind. London: Transworld.

Carnegie, D. (1998). How to win friends and influence people. London: Vermillion.

Casey, N. (2002). The nicotine trick. London: Metro.

Chopra, D. (2006). The seven spiritual laws of success. London: Transworld.

Chow, C. & Chow, J. (2003). Hypoglycemia for dummies. New York: Wiley.

Cialdini, R. (2007). The psychology influence of persuasion. New York: Harper Collins.

Cleese, J. & Skynner, R. (1990). Families and how to survive them. London: Mandarin.

Cowell, S. (2004). I don't mean to be rude, but… . London: Ebury Press.

Cozolino, L. (2002). The neuroscience of psychotherapy. London: Norton.

Danowski, D. & Lazaro, P. (2000). Why can't I stop eating? Minnesota: Hazelden.

Dawkins, R. (2006). The God delusion. London: Bantam.

De Botton, A. (2005). Status Anxiety. London: Penguin.

Dement, W. (2001). The promise of sleep. London: Pan.
Diagnostic and statistical manual of mental disorders (DSM-IV-TR). New Delhi: Jaypee.
Dryden, W. & Gordon, J. (1993). Beating the comfort trap. London: Sheldon.
Felitti et al (1998). 'Relationship of child abuse and household dysfunction to many of the leading causes of death in adults', the Adverse Childhood Experiences Study. American Journal of Preventive Medicine
Forward, S. (2002). Toxic Parents. New York: Bantam.
Fox, K. (2004). Watching the English. London: Hodder and Stoughton.
Freud, S (1974). New introductory lectures in psychoanalysis. (New York, 1974, p. 113).
Fromm, E. (2006). The sane society. Oxon: Routledge.
Fromm, E. (2007). Fear of freedom. Oxon: Routledge.
Gawain, S. (1999). Living in the light. Middlesex: Eden Grove.
Gawain, S. (2002). Creative visualization. California: Nataraj.
Gilbert, F. (2007). Yob nation. London: Portrait.
Grayling, A.C. (2002). The meaning of things. London: Phoenix.
Greenberger, D. & Padesky, C. (1995). Mind over mood. New York: Guilford Press.
Griffin, J. & Tyrrell, I. (2004). Human Givens – A new approach to emotional health and clear thinking. Sussex: HG Publishing.
Hammond, C. (2006). Emotional Rollercoaster. London: Harper Perennial.
Hill, N. (1966). Think and grow rich. New York: Wiltshire.
James, O. (2007). Affluenza. London: Arrow.
Janogly, L. (2000). Stop Bingeing. London: Elliot Right Way books.
Janogly, L. (2004). Only fat people skip breakfast. London: Thorsons.
John-Roger, McWilliams, P. (2001a). You can't afford the luxury of a negative thought. London: Thorsons.
John-Roger, McWilliams, P. (2001b). Do it! London: Thorsons.
Katona, K. (2006). Too much, too young. London: Ebury.
Kendrick, M. (2007). The great cholesterol con. London: John Blake.

Key, W.B. (1989). The age of manipulation. Maryland, Madison.

Kiyosaki, R. (2002). Rich Dad, Poor Dad. London: Time Warner.

Lasch, C. (1991). The culture of narcissism. New York: Norton.

Leader, D. & Corfield, D. (2007). Why do people get ill? London: Hamish Hamilton.

Lefever, R. (2004). Break free from addiction. London: Carlton.

Lowen, A. (1997). Narcissism – denial of the true self. New York: Touchstone.

Marshall, P. (1998). Unlocking your potential. Oxford: How to books.

Mason, P. & Kreger, R. (1998). Stop walking on eggshells. California: New Harbinger.

Martin, C. (2007). Perfect Girls, Starving Daughters. London: Piatkus.

Orwell, G (1949). Nineteen eighty-four. London: Penguin.

Packard, V. (1991). The hidden persuaders. London: Penguin.

Papadopoulos, L. (2005). Mirror mirror. London: Hodder Headline.

Pease, A. & Pease, B. (2003). Why men lie and women cry. London: Orion.

Peele, S., Brodsky, A., Arnold, M. (1992) The truth about addiction and recovery. New York: Fireside.

Persaud, R. (2001). Staying Sane. London: Bantam.

Poissant, C. (1994). How to think like a millionaire. London: Thorsons.

Ray, M. (2004). From here to longevity. Seattle: Shining Star.

Read, N. (2006). Sick and tired. London: Phoenix.

Riley, G. (2003). How to stop smoking and stay stopped for good. London: Vermillion.

Riley, G. (2005). Eating less – say goodbye to overeating. London: Vermillion.

Robinson, D. & Groves, J. (2007). Philosophy – A graphic guide to the history of thinking. Cambridge: Icon Books.

Ross, J. (2003). Mood Cure. London: Thorsons.

Rowe, D. (1992). Wanting Everything. London: HarperCollins.

Rowe, D. (2007). Beyond Fear. London: Harper Perennial.

Rutter, M. (1979) 'Maternal deprivation, 1972-1978: new findings, new concepts, new approaches', Child development, 50: 283-305; reprinted in Maternal Deprivation Reassessed (2nd edition), Harmondsworth: Penguin, 1981.

Saunders, P. (1990) Social Class and Stratification. London: Routledge.

Saunders, J. & Ross, H. (2002) Hypoglycemia – the classic healthcare book. New York: Kensington.

Schlosser, E. & Wilson, C. (2006). Chew on this. London: Penguin.

Selye, H. (1956) The stress of life. New York. McGraw-Hill

Sheldon, S. (1973). The naked face. London: Pan.

Sheldon, S. (2005). The other side of me. London: HarperCollins.

Siegel, B. (1999). Love, medicine and miracles. London: Random House.

Sting. (2003). Broken Music. London: Simon & Schuster.

Tolstoy, L. (2004). The death of Ivan Ilyich and other stories. London: Wordsworth editions.

Tolle, Eckhart. (2005). The power of now. London: Hodder & Stoughton.

Trickett, S. (1992). Coping successfully with panic attacks. London: Sheldon.

Vale, J. (2004). Chocolate Busters. London: Thorsons.

Waterman, N. (2004). Sugar addicts' diet. London: Thorsons.

Weekes, C. (2000). Essential help for your nerves. London: Thorsons.

Weil, A. & Rosen, W. (2004). From chocolate to morphine. New York: Houghton Mifflin.

Yalom, I. (1991). Love's Executioner. London: Penguin.

Yalom, I. (1999). Momma and the meaning of life. London: Piatkus.

Yalom, I. (2008). Staring at the sun: overcoming the dread of death. London: Piatkus.

Yudkin, J. (1988). Pure, white and deadly. London: Penguin.

Afterword

When I began writing this book I was myopic as to the demands of style and content. I had been more-or-less trained to write in an academic style having been involved with universities half my life.

The book you now hold contains almost no quotes or references yet this was not initially the case. In the first draft almost every page contained around ten references, all carefully researched and pruned in order to substantiate my theories. Such is the academic way. You state something and then corroborate the hypothesis with relevant evidence, quotes, and references. It became apparent only after writing that if I or my publisher was to obtain permission for all the quotes in my first draft, it would take nine years and greatly delayed publication – even if permissions were granted. It is my hope that (eventually) the original book will come to fruition, complete with references.

In the meantime, I hope the reader will have gained some enjoyment from my humble writing even without the relevant data that would have made them more compelling and credible. Hopefully, an academic version of this book will be released with its references intact as I initially intended. Therefore, if some of *Broken Britain?* doesn't make sense or seems too anecdotal, it will make more sense if the 'uncut' version ever sees the light of day or receives funding. Like many things, this is in the lap of the gods.

If you would like to know more about Anthony King or are interested in arranging counselling or psychotherapy with the author, please go to www.worryguru.com